The Spirit of H.H.Richardson on the Midland Prairies

Regional Transformations of an Architectural Style

The Spirit of H. H. Richardson on the Midland Prairies

Regional Transformations of an Architectural Style

Edited by Paul Clifford Larson
with Susan M. Brown

University Art Museum, University of Minnesota, Minneapolis
Iowa State University Press, Ames

Library of Congress Cataloging-in-Publication Data

The Spirit of H.H. Richardson on the midland prairies.

(Great plains environmental design series)
Bibliography: p.
Includes index.
1. Richardson, H.H. (Henry Hobson), 1838-1886—Exhibitions.
2. Richardson, H.H. (Henry Hobson), 1838-1886—Criticism and interpretation.
3. Romanesque revival (Architecture)—Middle West—Exhibitions. 4. Architecture,
Victorian—Middle West—Exhibitions.
I. Larson, Paul Clifford. II. Series.
NA737.R5A4 1988 720′.92′4 87—31091
ISBN 0—8138—0017—X

©University of Minnesota

Published by the Iowa State University Press, Ames, Iowa 50010

First edition, 1988

Great Plains Environmental Design Series

This publication and the exhibition which it accompanies were supported in part
by grants from the National Endowment for the Humanities, a Federal agency,
and the National Endowment for the Arts, a Federal agency.

(Cover photographs, left to right:) Detail of Ellis County Courthouse, Waxahachie, Texas, by J. Riely Gordon, 1894-96

Detail of commercial block, Windom, Minnesota, architect unknown, 1895

Detail of United States Post Office, Sioux Falls, South Dakota, by the Office of the Supervising Architect of the Treasury, 1892-95, 1911

J.B. Lynch House, Chicago, Illinois, architect unknown, 1892

(Cover background:) Ortonville granite similar to the stone used for the Minneapolis City Hall and Hennepin County Courthouse

(Inside cover and wrap:) Interior wall covering of the Church of the Epiphany, Chicago, Illinois, by Burling and Whitehouse, 1885

Series Editor's Introduction

Herbert Gottfried

There are a number of ways to define a region. A complete definition should include geological and ecological history and the history of human culture. In this book, we concentrate on culture, but not without reference to the physical qualities and environmental assets of the region. While we are not reconstructing a historical geography, we are documenting a significant force in the architecture of the last decades of the nineteenth century. The force is the architecture of Henry Hobson Richardson, and the overall effect of his presence is to give us our first modern public architecture.

The essays in *The Spirit of H.H. Richardson on the Midland Prairies* recreate the context in which Richardson's work was built, and they interpret the designs of regional architects and builders who extracted elements, patterns of composition, and forms from the master. Although Richardson's work is found to be generally appropriate to the land and the time period, the region's towns and cities use Richardson in different ways, their motives varying according to their aesthetic and political needs. In Chicago and St. Louis both Richardson's architecture and that of his followers respond to the emerging urban character of these quite different cities. In Texas, Richardson is employed to introduce a modern style that is vigorous enough to be useful as a state and regional symbol.

The forces that determined prairie cities—such as systems of transportation and commerce—are examined in detail. Lastly, we look at the land and its resources and their role in urbanization, in settlement patterns, and in the overall appearance of towns across the grasslands.

What we offer, then, in this our first volume in the Great Plains Environmental Design Series, is a logic about the interdependence of the regions within the broad geographical area we hope to define. In this case the logic is grounded in the powerful forms of a great American architect whose work was found most apt to represent our principal social organizations of family, community, and state. ✖

We have broken loose from the old bondage and are entering upon developments of style which seem to be actuated by our own local conditions… by far the best work in the West is done by the few structures that have risen like an exhalation from its own spirit.
Henry van Brunt, Kansas City, 1889

It is a crazy, lusty carnival which is held in the West by American architecture.
Die Staats Zeitung, Chicago, 1886

Table of Contents

8

▶1 View of prairie land in
central South Dakota

Foreword

Lyndel King

The University Art Museum's history includes a commitment to architectural exhibitions. In 1976, when we were still called the University Gallery, we presented the first ever exhibition documenting our state's architectural heritage and published, with the University of Minnesota Press and the Minnesota Society of Architects, *A Guide to the Architecture of Minnesota*. The *Bicentennial Exhibition of Minnesota Art and Architecture* and the *Guide* prompted a lot of Minnesotans to think about their environment in a new way. There is nothing like having a bank on your main street, or a house in your neighborhood that you have passed a thousand times without noticing, appear as a giant photo blow-up in an exhibit or as an illustration in a book to make one take notice. This sort of recognition prompts people to look at their main streets and neighborhoods anew and to become more appreciative of good architecture and more critical of bad.

We know that our efforts have assisted in historic preservation because I have seen the *Guide* cited in justifications for buildings nominated to the State Architectural Review Board for inclusion on the National Register of Historic Sites. We know that it has increased an awareness of architecture because of the phone calls we continue to get, more than ten years later, from people who remember seeing this building or that one in our exhibition and want to know how to get more information about it. In 1979 the Minnesota Society American Institute of Architects honored the University Art Museum's contribution to "bringing an awareness of art and architecture to a broad audience through the publication of the book *A Guide to the Architecture of Minnesota*. This book presents an enlightening and invaluable guide to the history of our architecture from the earliest dates to the present—something no previous publication has accomplished."

Since that landmark exhibition and publication, there have been several exhibitions that focused on more specific times or styles in Minnesota architecture. The University Art Museum presented *Cass Gilbert, Minnesota Master Architect*, an exhibition that featured Gilbert's designs for the University of Minnesota east bank campus mall and the state capitol as well as several houses, churches, stores, banks, railway depots, and other public buildings in Minnesota. We also exhibited drawings, furniture, photographs, and plans for houses by William Purcell and George Elmslie, who influenced Minnesota neighborhoods and towns with their gracious prairie style houses, banks, churches, and public buildings. We published a small *Annotated Checklist of Purcell and Elmslie Buildings in Minnesota* for that exhibition. We worked with University art librarian, Herbert Scherer, and Alan Lathrop, curator of the University's Northwest Architectural Archives, to present the art deco movie theaters of Minnesota architect Jack Liebenberg in an exhibition called *Marquee on Main Street*. All these exhibitions toured through the Museum's statewide traveling exhibitions program.

Another important regional architectural exhibition was the *Prairie School in Minnesota, Iowa and Wisconsin* which was co-curated by Paul Larson and Philip Larson for the Minnesota Museum of Art in St.

Paul in 1982. Given our history of involvement with architectural exhibitions, we were pleased when Paul Larson came to the University Art Museum with a proposal for another exhibition, this one featuring regional architects who were influenced by Henry Hobson Richardson, the nineteenth-century Boston architect who was the first American architect to give his name to a style — the Richardsonian Romanesque.

While Richardson never built anything in Minnesota, the towns and cities of the state enjoyed economic and building booms just around the time of his death (1886), when his influence was greatest. In talking with Paul Larson about his ideas, it became apparent that not only Minnesota but the entire prairie region had been particularly susceptible to Richardson's spell and that it would be appropriate to enlarge the boundaries of the project to include the area from Chicago west to the high plains of the Rocky Mountain range and from Minnesota all the way south to Texas.

Turn-of-the-century architects, buoyed by the high spirits of the developing prairie towns, took up the materials at hand—local granites, sandstones, and limestones—to make their banks, churches, city halls, county courthouses, post offices, schools, and houses for the newly wealthy merchants. They combined these with the squat round arches, massive silhouettes, bold use of color and texture, and decorative acanthus leaf patterns typical of H.H. Richardson's Allegheny County Courthouse and Jail in Pittsburgh or his Trinity Church in Boston. These architects created not disspirited copies of an earlier style, but something all their own—something in keeping with Richardson's spirit of using the architectural vocabulary of the past to create a distinctly American style. It was this spirit that Paul Larson proposed to investigate in an exhibition and book, and we were eager to be a part of this effort. With this collaboration of scholar and Museum, *The Spirit of H.H. Richardson on the Midland Prairies* was born.

With Paul Larson, whom we brought in as curator for the project, the Museum applied for and received a grant for initial research and photography from the National Endowment for the Humanities. The implementation phase of the project is supported by both the National Endowment for the Arts and the National Endowment for the Humanities. The University's Office of Research Administration and the Vice President for Academic Affairs were generous by cooperating fully with the Museum in special requests to the federal agencies. We are grateful also for the assistance of Herbert Gottfried and Richard Kinney at the Iowa State University Press who co-published this book with us.

Neither exhibition nor book would have been possible without the generous assistance and expertise of preservation officers, architectural historians, archivists, architects, and knowledgeable building owners throughout the plains region. The following individuals were particularly helpful in supplying information about the architects and buildings in their respective states:

Minnesota: John Baule, Hennepin County Historical Society; John Borchert of the Department of Geography, University of Minnesota, Minneapolis; Dorothy Burke, formerly of the Minneapolis History Collection, Minneapolis Public Library; John Decker, Stearns County Historical Society; Alan Lathrop, curator of the Northwest Architectural Archives in St. Paul; Eileen Michels of the College of St. Thomas; the entire research library staff of the Minnesota Historical Society.

North Dakota: Ronald L. Ramsey of Plains Architecture, Fargo.

South Dakota: Minneapolis architect David Erpestad; Geoffrey Hunt, formerly of the Siouxland Heritage Museums; Dorothy Jenks, a local historian in Yankton; Carolyn Torma, South Dakota Historic Preservation Center.

Iowa: Ralph Christian, Iowa State Historical Department; Deborah Greisinger, Dubuque Historical Improvement Company; Edward Storm, FEH Architects, Sioux City.

Nebraska: Lynn Meyer, Omaha City Planning Department; David Murphy, Nebraska State Historical

Society; Bobbi Raeder, formerly of the Western Heritage Museum in Omaha.

Illinois: George Irwin, Gardner Museum of Architecture and Design in Quincy; Michael Jackson, architectural coordinator of the Illinois Department of Conservation; Timothy Samuselson, Chicago Landmarks Commission; Wim de Wit, Chicago Historical Society; John Zukowski and Susan Perry, The Art Institute of Chicago.

Missouri: Dave Boutros, Western Historical Manuscripts Collection of the University of Missouri at Kansas City; William Brunner and Ron Fuston of Brunner and Brunner, Architects and Engineers, St. Joseph; Pete Manville of Graphic Services, St. Joseph; Preston L. Moss of Kansas City; Sherry Piland, Landmarks Commission of Kansas City; Nancy Sandehn of Mo-Kan Regional Council, St. Joseph; Carolyn Hewes Toft and Mary M. Stiritz, Landmarks Association of St. Louis; Duane Sneddeker, Missouri State Historical Society; Norbury Wayman, local St. Louis historian.

Kansas: Kurt von Achen, architect, Eudora; Fr. Angelus Lingenfelder, Atchison County Historical Society; Martha Hagedorn, Kansas State Historical Society; Nora Pat Small and Richard Cawthon, formerly of the Kansas State Historical Society; Clara Vanderstaay, Leavenworth Public Library.

Oklahoma: Arn Henderson, University of Oklahoma at Norman; Bill Peavler, Oklahoma Historical Society.

Texas: Kenneth Breisch, formerly of the Texas Historical Commission; Bruce Jensen, Austin History Center; Lila Stillson, Architecture and Planning Library of the University of Texas at Austin.

In addition, we are grateful to the essayists for this book—Kenneth A. Breisch, John C. Hudson, Richard Longstreth, Judith A. Martin, and Thomas J. Schlereth—for the patience and adaptability that writing for an exhibition program demands. The book was also intended from the beginning to stand on its own legs quite apart from the exhibition, and we are pleased to think that the combined efforts of our curator and other essayists have truly achieved that objective.

The curator and I would like to acknowledge the fine work of the Art Museum staff and others who worked on this project. Susan Brown, associate director, supervised the preparation of the catalogue including the editing and design production, as well as her normal Museum coordination duties. As usual, Susan's tireless devotion was a primary source of energy for the project. Sheila Chin Morris and Craig Franke of Frink Chin Casey, Inc. did an excellent job designing this catalogue under the usual tight schedule and were a joy to work with besides. Paul Larson served as installation designer as well as curator. William Lampe, our technical director, worked with him on the installation procedures and supervised the installation and preparation required for the exhibit, which was implemented by preparators Ian Dudley, John Sonderegger, and Steven Williams. Ian Dudley especially provided the expertise needed for construction of unusual installations. Registrar Karen Lovaas and her assistant, Cindy Collins, sorted out and kept in order many loans for unusual materials—limestone blocks—iron gates—and other things not usually cared for by an art museum registrar. Karen also coordinated the conservation of many of the drawings in the show. Gwen Sutter, our student clerical assistant, deserves a special star for her good work in typing the manuscripts for the catalogue. Jane Healey, administrative and clerical assistant, and Melanie Marshall, administrative assistant and principal secretary, also handled many and diverse details and, quite amazingly, retained their good humor and calm demeanor. Lisa Hartwig worked with the curator on public relations and with special events assistant Karen Furia and Colles Baxter Larkin, vice-chair of the Colleagues of the University Art Museum, our community support group, in planning the special festivities that accompanied the opening of the exhibition. We are grateful for Colles and the many volunteers who worked with her on this event, which brought our exhibition to the attention of a broad public. Colleen Sheehy, assistant director for touring programs, and her assistant Ann Milbradt organized the tour of the exhibit to at least one location in every state represented. Museum curators Fiona Irving and Timothy Rigdon contributed their enthusiasm for the project and read some proof for the catalogue and, I'm sure, will do numerous other things for the project that were not yet even imagined when this catalogue went to press. Accounts supervisor Cori Ander kept the NEH and NEA accountants and the University business office happy with us, as well as organized the museum sales shop for the exhibition.

Finally I would like to acknowledge the fine work of Paul Larson. His design sensitivity, vision, and scholarship made this exhibition and catalogue sing. We all learned a great deal from him, and it is a privilege to help pass his knowledge on to the public who will see this exhibition and read this book. ✛

Curator's Introduction

Paul Clifford Larson

Fifty years after H.H. Richardson's death, a private art museum in New York City organized the first exhibition of his work and published the first modern exposition of his accomplishments. One hundred years after Richardson's death, a university art museum in Minneapolis is presenting the first exhibition devoted to the work of his followers and sponsoring the first scholarly effort to assess these "Richardsonians" as a collective force in American architectural history.

The shift in focus and location between the Museum of Modern Art's program in 1936 and that of the University of Minnesota Art Museum, initiated in 1985, reflects a dramatic transition in American attitudes toward the architectural heritage of the late nineteenth century. Henry-Russell Hitchcock's *The Architecture of H.H. Richardson and His Times* continues to be the only comprehensive modern study of the architect's life and work, but Hitchcock labored under the early modernist assumption that Richardson towered in lonely isolation above those who learned from him. The unwritten assumption—who would have challenged it in 1936?—was that Richardson, like Louis Sullivan, required a posthumous redemption from the disordered excesses of his generation. The instrument of redemption was the same in both cases: anointment as a precursor of modernism.

For Richardson and his followers, the cost of this rescue was excessive. Not only were some of the most characteristic and influential achievements of Richardson's maturity shunted aside as retrograde compromises of his real work, but Richardson's immediate cross-continental influence was dismissed as beneath analysis. The problem for modern critics was that Richardson exerted his primary force in nineteenth-century America, not as a protomodernist but as a late Victorian.

Before the vast amalgamation of buildings in-spired by Richardson's achievements could be viewed as more than a galloping architectural disorder, several stages had to be set. First, late Victorian building design as a whole required assessment on its own terms. Such a reassessment began to sweep the country following, and largely because of, the indiscriminate demolition of inner cities and older residential neighborhoods in the 1950s and 1960s. The bland architectural forms and materials that displaced older buildings made even the fussiest of Victorianisms seem inventive, alive, and filled with architectural interest. Characteristically, the emerging preservation movement was galvanized into local political action by the demolition of major landmarks. In two of the most notorious midwestern cases, those landmarks were continually identified by unsuccessful preservationists as "Richardsonian": Minneapolis's brownstone Northwestern Guaranty Loan Building (E. Townsend Mix, 1888-90; fig. 2) and Omaha's granite United States Courthouse and Post Office (The Office of the Supervising Architect of the Treasury, 1892-1906; fig. 3). The "Richardsonian" label functioned both to classify the building stylistically and to borrow a piece of Richardson's stature for local use.

Saving local buildings was only the first stage in bringing the long-despised work of "the Richardsonians" to light. The second stage required overcoming widespread ignorance of firms and individuals responsible for the remnants of nineteenth-century architectural fabric that have survived decay and re-development. Thanks to the program of national registration and the concomitant creation of state historic preservation offices, the steady emergence of local preservation agencies, and the increasing scholarly efforts of local historians, this ignorance is gradually becoming a thing of the past. American cities have begun to celebrate their own architects and their own distinctive architectural resources

▶ 2 E.Townsend Mix,
Northwestern Guaranty Loan
Building, Minneapolis,
Minnesota, 1888-1890
(demolished 1962), view
shortly after completion

◄ 3 **Office of the Supervising Architect of the Treasury, United States Courthouse and Post Office, Omaha, Nebraska, 1892-1906 (demolished 1966), main entry arcade**

quite apart from the established masters and monuments of the textbooks.

But a third and final stage of acceptance and comprehension of Richardson's influence is not so easily reached. Architectural historians continue to assess Richardsonian architecture as if it were the unwitting offspring of Richardson himself, rather than the result of a number of formative conditions of which Richardson's work was only one. This perspective places any building that shows Richardson's influence in the uncomfortable position of being dismissed as imitative if it looks too much like its prototypes and condemned as provincial if it wanders too far from Richardson's practice. The only way out of the dilemma is an assessment of each "Richardsonian" building on its own merits and within the context of its own period, place, and architectural values. The present exhibition and collection of essays stands at the threshhold of this final stage.

This book, like the exhibition project that inspired it, is about architecture that: 1) is usually identified as Richardsonian Romanesque, and 2) occurs on the midland prairies. Both concepts require some preliminary elucidation, and the second, since it confines discussion to an area geographically remote from most of Richardson's practice, requires some justification as well.

"Richardsonian" is a much-abused term. As understood here, it is confined to masonry buildings, to which Richardson's contributions to nineteenth-century architecture are most distinctive. In general practice, "Richardsonian" and its near-synonym "Richardsonian Romanesque" have come to denote a cluster of specific masonry design practices which characterized Richardson's mature work but were neither invented by him nor consistently used by him: walls of sized stone ("ashlar") with the exposed faces pitched outward by chiseling ("rock-faced"); segmental and low-sprung semicircular ("Syrian") arches; and a mix of French Romanesque and Byzantine motifs such as cushion capitals, foliate carving, and open upper story galleries ("loggias"). Useful as such a distillation from Richardson's work might be in initiating analysis, citing the individual features as marks of a "Richardsonian" building grossly inflates his role in late nineteenth-century architectural development. Rock-faced ashlar was in common use among Victorian Gothicists; segmental and low-sprung arches already had a number of specific applications, such as bridges and warehouse entries, in which engineering considerations outweighed architectural fashion in determining form; and early medieval decoration was a stock component of the society architect's vocabulary.

What Richardson *did* with the various elements of his masonry design vocabulary is what distinguished his work and marked out the path of the Richardsonians. His accomplishment was threefold: 1) exploitation of the expressive potential of the varied masonry design elements, 2) melding of these elements into a unified style, and 3) subordinating all of the material and stylistic details of the building to a monumental projection of volumes. These accomplishments marked out the path for the Richardsonians.

How to treat a stone wall expressively was both the easiest lesson to learn from Richardson and the most adaptable to local conditions, tastes, and masonry practice. Richardson's contemporary champions notwithstanding, he never created a blank wall in the modern sense. All of his masonry walls were alive with varied texture, linear articulation, and carefully scaled stone detailing. His ashlar was invariably random in size and generally laid up either uncoursed ("broken field") or coursed in staggered wide and narrow bands. Calling into play a second stone color permitted diaper patterns, the enhancement of windows and entries, and the introduction of emphatic belts uniting wall openings, articulating surfaces, or accentuating the horizontal.

None of these techniques was lost on architects or builders in the hundreds of towns to boast a monumental block or house in Richardson's style. As Richardson himself had experienced in viewing the Boston wharfs, the laying up of stone by skilled craftsmen had enormous expressive potential, often without the guiding hand of an architect. Much of the detailing of Richardsonian buildings, especially in quarry-rich areas, owed more to Richardson's exploration of the aesthetic possibilities of laid-up stone than to his specific design program. Roman-

esque effects often appear to be generated by the mason's shaping, sizing, and placement of stone alone, with minimal use of carving and certainly without recourse to ancient European precedents (figs. 4 and 5).

Regional architects were also quick to pick up on monumental volume as a stylistic element in itself. Rectangular blocks with little ornament other than the play of voids and solids across the surface project enormous power and a sense of timelessness, as if the building had been rooted to the spot for centuries. Richardson talked this way about his buildings, and his followers took up the theme (fig. 6).

As such simple usages demonstrate, looking for the real strength of Richardson's influence is not at all the same as looking for "correct" specimens of his style. Richardson's buildings provided a wealth of ideas for local architects and builders to utilize in much the same way as Richardson himself exploited the color schemes of Auvergne, the facades of Provence, the rectangular volumes of Florence, and the rich interlace patterns of Byzantine Ravenna.

The present study is limited to ten states: Minnesota, North and South Dakota, Iowa, Nebraska, Illinois, Missouri, Kansas, Oklahoma, and Texas. These are referred to throughout as "midland prairie states." The term "midwestern" has generally been avoided as it has come to denote quite a different cluster of states. Locating these ten states on prairie land is likely to offend geographers who know that prairies did not conveniently follow state boundaries and that Galveston in the South, St. Louis in the East, and Duluth in the North are well outside of the intercontinental grasslands. The term is meant simply as a shorthand device for des-

▶ 4 I.J. Galbreath, Yankton National Bank, Yankton, South Dakota, 1893, gable detail

▼ 5 Edward Hammatt, Edward Edinger House, Davenport, Iowa, 1890, corner detail

ignating a vertical column of states roughly occupying the grasslands in the middle of the American continent.

What ties the states together, and justifies their inclusion in this pioneering study of Richardson's westward influence, is a common pattern and schedule of socio-economic development particularly conducive to the rapid spread of Richardson's style. The population explosion of cities and towns across the prairies in the early 1880s coincided with Richardson's meteoric rise into the pantheon of American architects. As a result, great concentrations of Richardsonian buildings arose in all the major urban centers of the prairies as well as in many remote farming communities. This central column of states, then, the "midland prairie states," is an ideal starting point for the exploration of the dispersion of Richardson's style and ideas. Oklahoma and North Dakota developed later than their neighbors but were included in the original survey simply because they are within the area and would otherwise form islands of ignorance; they also have made quite distinct, though limited, contributions to Richardsonian architecture.

Three essays focus specifically on Chicago, Kansas, and Texas. These have been chosen with reason: each is a locus of a distinctive aspect of Richardsonian influence. Chicago merits special attention as the major carrier of Richardson's ideas to the West, both as a built city and as the seat of the Western Association of Architects and its organ, *The*

Inland Architect. Of all the states covered, Kansas and Texas came the closest to achieving a unified Richardsonian program—the former because of its uniform material base (a soft and pale limestone) and the power of a small coterie of architects, and the latter because of its dual fascination with Richardson and its own Hispanic heritage. The "quartzite triangle" at the intersection of South Dakota, Minnesota, and Iowa deserves similar attention from future scholars, though its buildings show less richness in variety and detail than those in either Kansas or Texas. With these few exceptions, variations in the use and abuse of Richardson's ideas generally failed to acquire strong regional character on the prairies and tended instead to reflect the training and tastes of individual architects and their clients.

This study ends with essays by an urban specialist and a geographer with special expertise in plains development. These two essays are intended to provide a developmental context for the proliferation of Richardsonian architecture of the midland prairies. Neither purports to explain the course of that specific phenomenon; instead, each offers a series of geographical backdrops for the architectural events of the Richardsonian era. Hopefully, this is the kind of connective and contextual study that will inform future analysis of a remarkable architectural movement. ✂

◄ 6 Office of the Supervising Architect of the Treasury, Pope Hall, Fort Leavenworth Prison, Fort Leavenworth, Kansas, c. 1892 (burned 1957)

H.H. Richardson Goes West:
The Rise and Fall of an Eastern Star

Paul Clifford Larson

Richardson did more than any man who ever lived in this country to found an architectural style. But subsequent events showed that he did not found a school. He only obtained a following.

The Inland Architect and News Record,
September 1893

The fleeting Richardsonian era in American architecture grew out of an extraordinary personal synthesis. The full synthesis belonged to H.H. Richardson alone, for without the force of his personality, the conflicting tendencies that Richardson's work held in tension split into widely divergent lines of influence and development. Some of Richardson's admirers pursued his archaeological interests and others his search for distinctively American form; some championed his picturesque compositional schemes and others his penchant for simplification; some enlarged on the exuberance of his detailing and others on his respect for primal volumes. As a result, the decade between Richardson's death in 1886 and the onslaught of Beaux-Arts classicism in the mid-1890s witnessed an increasing fragmentation of Richardson's impact even as his work was becoming better known and understood.

Nowhere was this process plainer than in the midland states, which were, relative to the East, slow to absorb but quick to alter the various strands of the "modern Romanesque" style to suit local tastes and needs. The midcontinental prairies became, in effect, a vast workshop for the dislocation, hybridization, and regionalization of all the various facets of Richardson's work. West of Chicago and St. Louis, Richardson's most revered projects could be copied with a slavishness, parodied with an audacity, and vernacularized with an ease that would have come hard for an eastern architect working in the shadow of Richardson's practice and under the eyes of his academically trained peers.

For purposes of analysis, Richardson's influence on the architecture of the plains states can be distilled into three distinct phases: quotation, imitation, and assimilation. In an ideal model of architectural dispersion these might represent successive stages of conformity to a given architectural program, as its prototypes are gradually understood and accepted and then are gradually discarded in favor of other prototypes. Unfortunately, the Richardsonian movement in America does not yield to so tidy an analysis. Properly speaking, it was not a movement at all but simply a growing accumulation of buildings designed under the spell of Richardson's ideas, familiar architectural devices, and famed projects. In some midwestern locales, particularly outstate areas remote from established architectural practices, the primitive quotation phase was never surpassed; whereas in others, especially the larger cities, Richardson's work was often assimilated into design programs as fully developed as Richardson's own without benefit of the preliminary stages of absorption and imitation.

Even within particular regions or locales, the dispersion and absorption of Richardson's influence failed to form a linear pattern of development. Iowa's score of Richardsonian small-town courthouses rarely lets go altogether of the classical revivals between which their period of design was sandwiched (fig. 8); yet Sioux City, far and away the leading site of Richardsonian influence in Iowa, instantly, pervasively, and tenaciously welded Richardson's masonry devices to the Queen Anne style (fig. 9).

▲ 8 T.D. Allen, Hardin County Courthouse, Eldora, Iowa, 1891-92, main tower

▲ 9 Architect unknown, Poorbaugh-Roche House, Sioux City, Iowa, 1891

Chicago's myriad row house Richardsonians cribbed and crazy-quilted the master's work until the death knell sounded by the World Columbian Exposition in 1893; while in the same city John Root had, by 1885, fully assimilated as much as he ever would of Richardson and went on to design in his own manner.

All of these caveats aside, the phases of quotation, imitation, and assimilation can function as useful tools for uncovering the various guises Richardson's spirit took on the midwestern prairies. They are phases not in the narrow sense of marking out a regionally consistent chronology, but in the broad sense of ordering the spread of Richardson's influence into increasingly sympathetic and intelligent ways of viewing his work.

Quotation

The first wave of Richardsonian influence to reach the middle states was little more than a ripple on the surface of existing architectual programs. Whether through blind reverence for his stature or because of imprecise knowledge of his actual buildings, the initial concrete indications that Richardson's spirit was wandering westwards were isolated building components or mannerisms, too diffuse and diluted to constitute a style.

Quotations of Richardson's masonry idiom began to appear in 1883 and 1884 in Minneapolis and Chicago.[1] In late 1883, E.E. Joralemon in the firm of F.B. Long and Company designed the first Minneapolis residence to borrow heavily from Richardson's vocabulary, the W.W. McNair House (1884-86, demolished; fig. 11). In the following year, Cobb and Frost brought the same combination of design elements into Chicago for the Ransom Cable House (1885-86; fig. 12).[2] Both houses are of rock-faced ashlar laid up in broken range over a slightly battered foundation; both have low-sprung,

semicircular arched porticos and pierced stone balustrades. In addition, the Cable House boasts a heavy encrustation of neo-Byzantine carving. Houses with similar pastiches of Richardsonian features began to appear in St. Louis and Kansas City in 1886.[3]

These early midwestern examples typify the way in which Richardson's distinctive detailing was often married to alien building forms. Though the manner of the carved work in the Cable design was Richardsonian enough, it was attached to a corbeled tourelle clearly at odds with the ground-to-sky volumes of Richardson's own work. Richardson's corner towers, however small their girth, sprang emphatically from the building foundations. Similarly, the pseudo-Romanesque porte-cochere of the McNair design was undeniably Richardsonian in flavor, yet it was also just the sort of tacked-on volume that Richardson's own work so clearly avoided. In the most extreme cases, which were quite common during this initial phase, antithetical projecting elements such as these became the dominant or even exclusive carriers of Richardson's ideas in the context of otherwise eclectic domestic designs. This state of affairs demonstrates how Richardson was regarded during this phase, not as a great form-giver, but as the source of high-style design elements that could easily be grafted onto existing late Victorian design programs.

The same limitation marked Richardson's early influence on the design of public buildings. Charles A. Dunham's Coddington County Courthouse in Watertown, South Dakota (1883-84, demolished) and Charles Maybury's Houston County Courthouse in Caledonia, Minnesota (1883-84; fig. 10) were the

▲ **10** **C.G. Maybury and Son, Houston County Courthouse, Caledonia, Minnesota, 1883-84, drawing by J.N. Maybury**

▼ **11** *(left)* **F.B. Long and Company (E.E. Joralemon, designer), W.W. McNair House, Minneapolis, Minnesota, 1884-86 (demolished, 1960s), drawing by F.W. Fitzpatrick**

▼ **12** *(right)* **Cobb and Frost, Ransom Cable House, Chicago, Illinois, 1885-86**

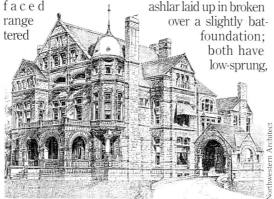

first public buildings in the midcontinent to borrow conspicuously from Richardson. Each carried a central frontal tower flanked by prominent gables, a common device for county courthouse design that Richardson would soon bring to a powerful climax in Pittsburgh. The influence of Richardson's earlier public buildings can be spotted in the masonry work, particularly the checkered gables, in the treatment of the window openings (arched above, transomed below), and in some of the tower detailing. But the main features of the buildings, including tower and gable placements, were typical of the pseudo-Gothic and Queen Anne courthouses that had become small-town prairie substitutes for the Second Empire public buildings still favored in larger midwestern cities.

Richardson's impact on commercial architecture is much more difficult to track than his influence on domestic and public building. Rock-faced walling, neo-Romanesque arcades, and emphatic belt courses appeared together in buildings in Chicago, Minneapolis, and Kansas City in 1884. Though all three design elements had appeared independently and

intermittently in commercial design for many years,[4] their appearance together in the early 1880s suggests a synthesis at least inspired by such Richardson projects as the Cheney Building (1875-76) in Hartford, Connecticut. Solon Beman's Pullman Building in Chicago (1883-84, demolished; fig. 92) was a famous example of this synthesis and one of the most widely admired buildings of its generation. Two stories of arcades quite similar to those of the Pullman Building also finished off L.S. Buffington's remodeling of the Boston Block in Minneapolis (on the boards by 1883 but not built until 1886, demolished; fig. 13). Further south, Levi Levering's Nelson Block in Kansas City (1884-85, demolished) was as ambitious a project as the Pullman Building, with an unabashedly eclectic design base. Its round-headed arcades were inserted into a tiered pile about which a Kansas Citian (perhaps Levering himself) could crow that there was a different style of architecture for nearly every story.[5]

Two of the most telling features of Richardson's mature work were conspicuous by their absence from all of the early borrowings from his designs—

▲13 *(left)* L.S. Buffington, Boston Block, Minneapolis, Minnesota, 1883, upper two stories, 1886 (demolished 1943), view shortly after completion

▲14 *(right)* Long and Kees, Masonic Temple, Minneapolis, Minnesota, 1887-89, from Long and Kees's office brochure

▲ 15 Long and Kees,
Minneapolis Public Library,
Minneapolis, Minnesota,
1888-89 (demolished 1959),
engraving by Ramsdell

▶ 16 Minneapolis Public
Library, entry detail, from
Long and Kees's office
brochure

residential, public, and commercial. One was his placement of gables so that they thrust up from the wall in a continuous, uninterrupted plane; the other was his connection of lintels, sills, or impost blocks into belt courses of contrasting material. These devices were obvious means of creating visual unity and a strong horizontal sense out of disparate surfaces and contours. But they were also difficult to subsume under historicizing stylistic categories. Their absence was yet another indication that imagery rather than form guided this primitive phase of Richardson's influence.

The critic Matthew Schuyler liked to dub particularly awkward misunderstandings of Richardson's principles "Western" in jocular reference to the emerging regional consciousness of leading architects in Chicago and Minneapolis.[6] But the problem was obviously much larger than "western" in scope, as Schuyler himself recognized. His field of reference was the nation as a whole, and his examples all eastern, when he lamented in 1891 that "in city houses the influence of Richardson…has consisted in fastening 'features' from his work upon buildings with inconsistent physiognomies."[7] It was all too easy for architects across the country to add Richardsonian devices to the already teetering High Victorian stock pile of pseudo-historical images. The lack of strong preexisting architectural contexts simply made such monstrosities stand out in the Midwest.

The ultimate silliness of turning Richardson's work into one more page in the Victorian copybook did not escape the attention of the increasingly assertive regional architectural press. Two of Minneapolis's most heralded buildings of the 1880s grew out of competitions begun in 1885. The first of these, Long and Kees's Masonic Temple (1887-89; fig. 14) was promptly castigated by a local architect as "a pitiful display of mongrel Romanesque" and "one mass of detail from top to bottom."[8] The second building, a public library by the same firm (1888-89, demolished; figs. 15 and 16) drew the same writer's ire that "the designer could not feel the importance of his work, and to be plain, hold himself down."[9]

Similar chagrin was expressed by a Chicago critic who lamented his city's recent invasion by a "crazy-quilt style" in which "variety, eccentricity, the bizarre, the unexpected, the startling, have prevailed in every direction.…All broad effects have been carefully struck out, and incessant, fatiguing,

St. Louis Through a Camera, 1892

◄17 Shepley, Rutan and Coolidge, J.R. Lionberger Warehouse (also known as Ely and Walker's Dry Goods Warehouse), St. Louis, Missouri, 1888 (burned 1897)

▲18 H.H. Richardson, Marshall Field Wholesale Store, Chicago, Illinois, 1885-87 (demolished 1930), view shortly after completion

◄19 Joseph Schwartz, Jewett Brothers Warehouse, Sioux Falls, South Dakota, 1899

vulgar details have taken their place."[10] The city suffered the further architectural disgrace of rows of "skin buildings," in which stone fronts rested on foundations of planks with ordinary brick laid on them below grade.[11]

Imitation

Such design and building practices would never have been countenanced by Richardson, yet they easily accommodated and even encouraged the quotation of his mannerisms. But the wind was changing. Even as these caustic reviews of local architecture were being written, a quantum leap was taking place in the level of architectural practice in the urban centers of the midland prairies. It

▶ **20 H.H. Richardson, Allegheny County Courthouse, Pittsburgh, Pennsylania, 1883-88, from an office drawing**

▼ **21 Palmer and Hall, Central High School, Duluth, Minnesota, 1891-92, detail of columns at entry**

▶ **22 Central High School**

layered wall design, from battered basement pierced by segmental-arched windows to a multistory arcade to multiple windows above the main arcade and finally to an abbreviated, sculpted cornice, inspired spin-offs in such far-flung sites as Minneapolis, Sioux Falls, Omaha, Kansas City, St. Louis, and Dallas. Shepley, Rutan and Coolidge's warehouse for J. R. Lionberger in St. Louis (1888, burned 1897; fig. 17) came the closest to matching the scale, materials, and spirit of the original. The cities of the prairie states returned again and again to the fundamental themes of Richardson's design. Even such faint echoes as Joseph Schwartz's Jewett Brothers Warehouse in Sioux Falls (1899; fig. 19) showed that the governing ideas of Richardson's design lost neither their compositional force nor their monumental aspect when rendered on a smaller scale in humbler materials.

The freedom with which the Marshall Field Wholesale Store scheme was adapted by plains architects revealed that they regarded the building as an inspiration rather than an icon. But the Allegheny County Courthouse (fig. 20) in Pittsburgh was another case altogether. Copies of it sprang up throughout the upper plains states, as if it were an ideal which the local architect dared not alter so much that his design did not instantly recall Rich-

brought with it a larger view of Richardson's achievement. Most architectural offices were still content to borrow, but they fastened onto large pieces of Richardson's work in a spirit ranging from bold imitation of his manner to wholesale reproduction of his mature achievements.

External Forces

A combination of external forces and internal developments contributed to the increasingly complex and integrated use of Richardson's idiom in the prairie states. The most obvious outside influence was the completion after his death of his most ambitious undertakings in the Midwest. Pittsburgh's Allegheny County Courthouse and Jail (1883-88) and Chicago's Marshall Field Wholesale Store (1885-87, demolished) gave architects in the middle states an increased opportunity to see Richardson's work firsthand. Prior to 1886, his major work had been confined to the East Coast and was accessible to the prairie states primarily through sporadic publication in trade and professional periodicals. Instrumental though these sources were to the dissemination of Richardson's ideas, they also fed the tendency to cannibalize rather than incorporate.

By the 1880s Chicago was already on the way to becoming a mecca for architects and builders from the Rocky Mountains to the eastern seaboard, and the Marshall Field Wholesale Store (figs. 18 and 65) became a major shrine of the pilgrimage. Its

◄ 23 Long and Kees,
Minneapolis City Hall and
Hennepin County Court-
house, Minneapolis,
Minnesota, 1888-1906, view
shortly after completion

ardson's masterpiece. Having one of these in its midst was a token of a city's cosmopolitan outlook and artistic achievement, however tiny and remote its population.

This iconizing attitude often had startling results. Minneapolis in particular succeeded in erecting a magnificent variation on the Allegheny County design that managed to walk the fine line between worshipful copy and individualistic achievement. The Minneapolis City Hall and Hennepin County Courthouse (1888-1906; figs. 23, 40 and 41) is espe-

cially instructive because copying Richardson appeared to be a requirement for winning the competition.[12] But Long and Kees revised their plans twice before execution,[13] the final result exaggerating further the independent monumental force of the corner pavilions and splitting the entry between opposite rather than adjoining sides. The contrast between the progressively sure handling of this design and the fussiness of their earlier Masonic Temple building shows how far this firm's grasp of Richardson had come in two short years.

▶ **24** *(left)* **H.H. Richardson, Trinity Church, Boston, Massachusetts, 1872-77, view shortly after completion**

▶ **25** *(right)* **Burling and Whitehouse, Trinity Church, Kansas City, Missouri, 1887 (demolished), view shortly after completion**

Schools as well as government buildings imitated the main features of the Allegheny County Courthouse: a high tower rising above the central entry, pronounced corner pavilions, dormers thrusting directly up from the wall face, continuous arcades, and elaborate stone carving in Romanesque or Byzantine fashion. Palmer and Hall's Central High School in Duluth, Minnesota (1891-92; figs. 21 and 22) continues to loom over the city with a grandeur that the civic buildings of the next generation never equaled. Oliver Smith's Winterset High School in central Iowa (1897, demolished) highlighted the architect's advertisement in the Des Moines City Directory for many years. Joseph Eckel's St. Joseph High School in western Missouri (1895, demolished) was the last great Richardsonian outburst of a firm which had lined the city's streets with "modern Romanesque" monuments.

However prevalent the imagery of Richardson's Pittsburgh and Chicago projects in the plains states, his major icon there continued to be his most widely heralded achievement in the East: the lantern of Trinity Church in Boston (fig. 24). That lantern became the centerpiece of suburban church designs from New York to Chicago to Kansas City. Pittsburgh alone contained three junior editions of Trinity.[14] Further west, Chicago boasted two, one of them rendered in brick;[15] and one Chicago firm, Burling and Whitehouse, produced a magnificent variation in Kansas City also called Trinity Church (1887, demolished; fig. 25). In a manner typical of

these regional variations on the Boston Trinity, the Kansas City design squared off the detailing of the lantern, emphasized its horizontal mass by introducing a broken clerestory and clustered colonettes, and brought its adjoining wings down to the scale of the suburban neighborhood.

In the process of being adapted to every conceivable architectural context, the Trinity tower underwent a truly astonishing series of transformations. In downtown Kansas City, it anchored the corner of a railway depot design that never quite got off the drawing board[16] and illuminated the interior of a short-lived produce market (fig. 26).[17] In suburban Omaha, a scoured-down sister of the church's great tower mightily embraced the standpipe of the city's pumping station (fig. 27). Curiously, all these adaptations of Trinity Church's lantern appear to have gone unnoticed by the well-traveled critic Matthew Schuyler, who commented in 1891 that "it is quite impracticable to reduce [the scale of Trinity Church] so as to make it available for a smaller and cheaper church. Otherwise we might see reproductions of it in miniature springing up all over the country, and this would be a result very much to be deplored."[18]

During Richardson's final years, a number of his apprentices struck out from his office to establish their own practices in the burgeoning young cities of the Midwest. Those whose work is known proved themselves masterful imitators of their mentor's style, without recourse to direct imitation of his buildings. Harry Jones, who moved to Minneapolis

Art Work of Kansas City, 1900

▲ 26 *(left)* Architect unknown, Kansas City Market, 1890s (demolished), view shortly after completion

▲ 27 *(right)* Mendelssohn, Fisher and Lawrie, Minnelusa Pumping Station, Omaha, Nebraska, 1888-89 (demolished), c. 1925 postcard view

▼ 28 Harry W. Jones, National Bank of Commerce, Minneapolis, Minnesota, 1888 (demolished 1960s), view in 1903

in late 1884, was probably the most able of these. Jones apprenticed with Richardson while studying at M.I.T. and later claimed some credit for the design of Richardson's Boston and Albany Railroad Station at Chestnut Hill, Massachusetts (1883, demolished).[19] Jones's National Bank of Commerce in downtown Minneapolis (1888, demolished; fig. 28), praised by Schuyler for its formal clarity and by our cantankerous Minneapolis critic for its sure handling of ornament,[20] helped launch the young architect on a long and illustrious career.[21]

Another, more obscure migrant from Richardson's office was Edward Cameron, who had come to Chicago in 1885 to superintend construction of Richardson's MacVeagh and Glessner Houses and the Marshall Field Wholesale Store.[22] On their completion after Richardson's death, Cameron returned to his hometown of St. Louis and by 1891 had formed a partnership with the rising architect Theodore Link.[23] Their dissociation in 1894 and Cameron's untimely death four years later have obscured Cameron's rightful recognition as co-architect of the Union Station in St. Louis (1892-94; fig. 55), one of the crowning achievements of the brief Richardsonian era in American architecture.

Several other architects who had close professional ties with Richardson and the eastern Richardsonians also went west in the early 1880s. Foremost among these was Henry van Brunt, a former student of Richard Hunt's and a founding member of the Boston Society of Architects. Van Brunt was also a personal friend of the president of the Union Pacific Railway and in 1884 sent his junior partner, Frank M. Howe, to Kansas City to establish a branch office nearer the heart of the railroad's operations.[24] The new location proved so promising that van Brunt himself followed in 1885 and soon was introducing the rock facings and Romanesque carving of Richardson's idiom to downtown Kansas City streets. Like many established eastern architects who worked in the West, van Brunt dragged Richardson's materials with him, insisting on Longmeadow brownstone from Connecticut for the fronts of his Bayard and Gibraltar blocks (1886 and 1888 respectively, both demolished).[25]

Henry Ives Cobb, who along with Solon Beman was instrumental in introducing a Richardsonian "look" to Chicago before Richardson himself arrived, immigrated in much the same way as did Cameron. Having arrived in the city in 1881 to superintend the building of the Union Club House for the New York firm of Peabody

Sweet photo

▲29 Cass Gilbert, William
Lightner House, St. Paul,
Minnesota, 1893

▸ 30 Edward Hammatt,
Edward Edinger House,
Davenport, Iowa, 1890

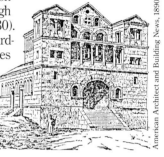

▲ 31 Architect unknown, the church at Tourmanin, Syria, sixth century (demolished, nineteenth century), from a de Vogüé drawing

◄ 32 Architect unknown, R.A. Smith Store and Apartments, Chicago, Illinois, 1886, detail of corner column

and Stearns, he stayed on to establish his own practice. First in partnership with Charles S. Frost and after 1888 as an independent, he quickly rose to the front rank of Chicago architects, leaving behind one of the purest monuments to Richardson's influence in the city, the Chicago Historical Society (1888-92; fig. 86). Cobb and Frost also introduced Richardsonian devices into towns scattered throughout the plains. Railway stations in Faribault and Owatonna, Minnesota (both 1888, both demolished) and Leavenworth, Kansas (1887-88)[26] and the Watkins National Bank in Lawrence, Kansas (1887-88) were a few of their farflung projects.

As the leading center of architectural education in the country, M.I.T was frequently the launching pad for Richardson-tinged midwestern practices. Cobb and a number of his Chicago peers were M.I.T graduates,[27] as was Harry Jones of Minne-

apolis. Jones's St. Paul equivalent was Cass Gilbert, another M.I.T. graduate, who arrived in 1884 with Richardson's medieval imagery in one pocket and McKim, Mead and White's Renaissance Revival in the other. Gilbert's penchant for fitting picturesque neo-medieval devices into classically ordered facades helped to give St. Paul's famous Summit Avenue its distinctive character (fig. 29).

Further south, Edward Hammatt went from M.I.T. to van Brunt and Howe's Boston office before setting up independent practice in Davenport, Iowa, in 1883.[28] From the first, his designs were pervaded with Richardson's sense of the relation between ornament and volumetric enclosure, though he took enormous liberties with color (figs. 5 and 30). Other connections between M.I.T. and the Richardsonian cast of many fledgling architectural practices in the prairie states will surely come to light as more is known about the work of lesser architectural offices.

Quite apart from the direct, personal impact of the eastern architectural establishment, Richardson's influence played off of an increasingly widespread interest in the same archaeological sources that inspired his imagination. Revoil's 1873 *Architecture romane du midi de la France* was a common holding of private architectural libraries,[29] and Edouard Connoyer's *L'Architecture romane* was abridged and translated in several consecutive issues of *The Inland Architect* beginning in March 1889.[30] De Vogüé's comprehensive and well-illustrated monograph on surviving late Roman architecture of the Mideast, the celebrated *Syrie centrale,* had been available since 1864, and frequent publication of its most famous image, the church at Tourmanin (fig. 31)[31] was a constant advertisement of the low-sprung Syrian arch and compact second-story loggia given new life by Richardson.

In addition, European travels of the sort undertaken in 1882 by Richardson himself brought architects such as Cass Gilbert in St. Paul, W.H. Dennis in Minneapolis, and J.L. Silsbee in Chicago into direct contact with the early medieval monuments that fired Richardson's imagination. Some of these travels, especially through Spain, were directly influenced by Richardson's work and the knowledge of its European sources;[32] but far broader stimuli were also at work. The English Society for the Preservation of Ancient Monuments did its best to whip the art-loving public into near-hysteria regarding the fate of the famed Byzantine interiors of San Marco, and many architects traveled to Venice or frantically copied pieces of its ornament from photographs in the conviction that they might be the last generation to enjoy the masterpiece before it "sank into the mud of the lagoons" or was irreversibly defaced by heavy-handed Italian restorers.[33] The great Byzantine monuments in Constantinople were also drawing unusual attention in the 1880s, leading to such technical achievements as the deciphering of the Emperor Justinian's monograms on the column capitals of many of his churches, starting with Santa Sophia.[34] This could well have been the inspiration for Richardson's use of his superimposed H-R monogram on capitals in the Allegheny County Courthouse and the Glessner House (see fig. 69).

As obscure and even lost to modern awareness as such ephemeral events tend to be, they helped to create a climate in which Richardson's archaeological passions could take hold. His phenomenal success is by itself hardly sufficient to account for such Frankensteinian anomalies as the full-scale transplant of a Byzantine capital into the corner of a humdrum commercial block in Chicago (fig. 32). The Byzantine craze was in the air; and its exploitation by a great architect needed only to supply a supportive context, not specific models, for its spread into lesser architectural offices.

Internal Developments

Probably more important than these external

forces in determining the precise character of Richardson's influence on the architectural practices of the plains were a number of internal developments connected to the maturation of the architectural profession in middle America. Chief among them were the emergence of a regional architectural press through the medium of trade journals and plan books, the formation of professional societies and sketch clubs, and the holding of widely publicized architectural competitions.

A midland architectural press sprang up almost overnight in the years immediately preceding Richardson's death. *The Inland Architect and Builder* and *The Northwestern Architect and Improvement Record* published their first numbers in 1883 in Chicago and Minneapolis, respectively. By 1886, they had been joined by St. Louis and Kansas City editions of *The Architect and Builder,* and Chicago was producing the competitive *Building Budget* and complementary *Sanitary Engineer.*

The influence of these journals in publicizing and illustrating architectural trends and advances can scarcely be overestimated. Robert McLean, the editor of *The Inland Architect* in its formative years, was from the beginning a staunch advocate of professionalism among his midwestern colleagues and a champion of their architecture. His magazine became the official organ of the Western Association of Architects upon its formation in 1884 and repeatedly published the views of John Root, Nathan Clifford Ricker, Irving Pond, and other leading progressives. The first thorough-going Richardsonian design to be published in *The Inland Architect* was a rendering of Patton and Fisher's Scoville Institute (1885, demolished) in Chicago in February 1885, at the very threshold of Richardson's western advance.[35]

The Northwestern Architect, under a succession of reorganizations and name changes, employed

▲ 33 C.A. Dunham, Brookings Public School, Brookings, South Dakota, 1887-88 (demolished)

▼ 34 Chicago Architectural Sketch Club Competition for a 25-foot City Front, February 1885, drawings by W.B. Mundie, W.R. Ray, R.M. Turner, Richard Wood, and T.O. Fraenkel

Inland Architect

Northwestern Architect

Fred Kees and Charles Dunham as its editors during its first decade. The crucial role these men played in the introduction of Richardson's idiom into the upper plains states has already been noted. Dunham's tenure, from 1889 to 1893, is particularly significant, for he had already published pattern books composed almost entirely of Richardson-inspired designs. His *Modern Schoolhouse Design* came out the month before Richardson's death in 1886, and his *Church Building Designs for Country Village and Town* the year following.[36] Curiously, though Dunham's Burlington office was in the extreme southeastern corner of Iowa, most of his executed schoolhouse designs were in South Dakota, the largest being at Brookings (1887-88, demolished; fig. 33).[37] Similarly, his three courthouse designs most indebted to Richardson were all built in Minnesota.[38] Only his church designs consistently found homes in his own state.

The emergence of a regional architectural press went hand-in-hand with the formation of professional architectural societies in the plains states. The Chicago-based Western Association of Architects was formed in 1884 in a conscious attempt to decentralize the American Institute of Architects and inspired the formation in the same year of a Central Architectural Association in Des Moines. The theme was identical: "We cannot build enduring pyramids balanced on one point."[39] Similar societies and associations sprang up in Minnesota in 1884, Kansas City in 1885, and Texas in 1886.[40]

The Western Association of Architects became the chief organizational means for the assimilation and dissemination of eastern trends and an important forum for debate regarding the relevance of

these trends to regional building requirements and practices. Issues such as the appropriateness of European-inspired styles for American buildings or whether load-bearing masonry designs like Richardson's could fittingly be adapted to the new steel skeletal construction were frequent subjects of heated debate, in which even Richardson's admirers and imitators often sharply disagreed.[41]

Architectural sketch clubs played an equally important role in stimulating an open exchange of ideas. They offered informal design training to fledgling architects, as well. The Chicago Architectural Sketch Club (CASC), founded in 1885, was particularly important, for a great number of the leading young draftsmen of prominent Chicago firms were either members or in frequent attendance.[42] Fledgling architects such as William B. Mundie, Theodore Fraenkel, H.C. Trost, Oscar Enders, Harry Lawrie, and John Coxhead all enjoyed close association and a common enthusiasm for Richardsonian mannerisms in the early years of the sketch club. Mundie, Fraenkel, and Trost all remained in Chicago through the 1880s as leading draftsmen-designers for W.L.B. Jenney, Cobb and Frost, and Louis Sullivan, respectively, during the Richardsonian phase of each of these firm's practices. The other three helped to spread Richardson's influence elsewhere: Enders to St. Louis, Lawrie to Omaha, and Coxhead to St. Paul and Yankton, South Dakota.

CASC competitions and exhibitions had a Richardsonian flavor from the first. The initial com-

◄ 35 G.W. and F.D. Orff, proposal for a Minneapolis warehouse, 1887, office drawing by F.W. Fitzpatrick

▼ 36 H.C. Trost, Initiation Sketch for entry into Chicago Architectural Sketch Club, February 1889

Building Budget

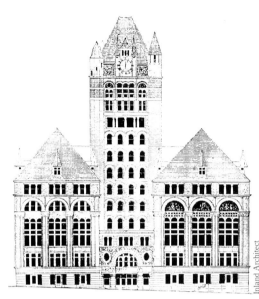

Inland Architect

Inland Architect

▲ 37 *(left)* Burnham and Root, accepted design for Kansas City Exchange, 1886 (demolished)

▲ 38 *(right)* Irving Pond, competitive design for Kansas City Exchange

▼ 39 *(left)* W.H. Dennis and Company, second place design for Minneapolis City Hall and Hennepin County Courthouse competition, 1888, from a watercolor by John Anderson

▼ 40 *(middle)* Long and Kees, first place design, free-lance drawing by D.A. Gregg

▼ 41 *(right)* Long and Kees, revised design, office drawing by A.C. Chamberlin

petition, for a row house, produced a line-up of designs consistently Richardsonian in detail, though not in composition (fig. 34). Other competitions for architectural details such as hearths and gates were equally saturated with Richardsonian devices. Trost's initiation sketch of a fireplace contained fragmentary allusions to Sullivan's ornament but framed everything within a magnificent composition of Richardsonian arcs and arches (fig. 36).

In the mid-1880s a similar but less heralded sketch club formed in St. Paul, to be followed by a sister club in Minneapolis in 1890. Harvey Ellis, a recent émigré from Rochester, New York, was the dominant member of the St. Paul club, as he was to be of the St. Louis club he formed with Oscar Enders and others in 1896. The force of Ellis's talent and personality in introducing both a deeper view of Richardson's work and a more picturesque means of rendering it seems evident enough from

the radical evolution in the drawing techniques of Minneapolis draftsmen such as F.W. Fitzpatrick (fig. 35), E.E. Joralemon, and A.C. Chamberlin (fig. 41) between 1885 and 1887.

A third internal development spurring Richardson's influence on the architecture of the plains states was a series of major competitions. In 1885, Richardson himself had entered and won such a competition for the Cincinnati Chamber of Commerce Building. This was followed the next year by a call for designs for a new Kansas City Exchange Building.[43] Richardson, along with fellow easterners George B. Post and Peabody and Stearns (who had recently opened a western office in St. Louis), was invited to apply but declined because of rapidly failing health. An even larger competition for the Minneapolis City Hall and Hennepin County Courthouse was held in early 1888.[44]

Each of these competitions promised large

Northwestern Architect

American Architect and Building News

Northwestern Architect

42 Long and Kees, F.B.
Long House, Minneapolis,
Minnesota, 1894 from Long
and Kees's office brochure

premiums, was widely advertised, attracted scores of applications, and was dominated overwhelmingly by Richardsonian proposals. Peabody and Stearns actually submitted two such designs for the Kansas City Exchange, and fellow Bostonian John Faxon submitted another. James McLaughlin, the premier Richardsonian in Cincinnati, sent in a plan for a hulking, arcaded box, and Chicagoan W.W. Boyington, who generally managed to steer clear of Richardson's influence, submitted a scheme for a vast assembly of turrets and gables perched on a Romanesque pile.

The finest Chicago proposals for the Kansas City Exchange were perhaps the most revealing, for they brought two of the city's strongest-minded and most "western"-oriented architects the closest they ever came to imitation of Richardson. The winning design by Burnham and Root, which was built as planned (1887-88, demolished; fig 37), clearly expressed Root's aggressive rectilinearity, but it was dressed up with an uncharacteristic gargantuan central tower. In a similar deference to the apparently

▲ 43 W.L.B. Jenney (W.B.
Mundie, probable designer),
Thomas Wright House,
Chicago, Illinois, 1889,
corner detail

▶ 44 Thomas Wright House

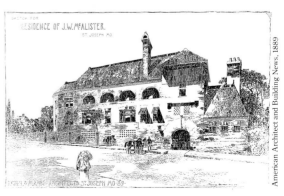

◀ 45 Frank, Bailey and Farmer (attributed), Longfellow School, Kearney, Nebraska, 1890 (demolished)

▼ 46 *(left)* Eckel and Mann (Harvey Ellis, designer), German-American Bank, St. Joseph, Missouri, 1889, side entry column detail

▼ 47 *(top right)* Joseph Pennell, Sketch of a Sienese farmhouse, 1885

▼ 48 *(bottom right)* Harvey Ellis, design for Eckel and Mann of a house for James McAlister, St. Joseph, Missouri, 1889 (unbuilt)

Robert W. Lull photo

American Architect and Building News, 1885

American Architect and Building News, 1889

unwritten Richardsonian bias of the competition, S. S. Beman's chief draftsman, Irving Pond, independently submitted a proposal that clearly anticipated the northern Italian flavor of his later work, but it also crowded strong corner pavilions against a central tower in a manner unmistakably allied to Richardson's Allegheny County Courthouse then under construction (fig. 38)

An even higher pitch of Richardsonian enthusiasm was reached in the competition for the Minneapolis City Hall and Hennepin County Courthouse. Dozens of doctrinaire versions of the master's style were submitted. Of the premiated entries, two were as close to clones of the Allegheny County Courthouse as the site and planning requirements would allow (figs. 39-41), while one was an exact copy of the Victorian Glasgow (Scotland) City Hall. Another superbly drawn proposal attached a replica of the campanile of the Renaissance Palazzo Publico in Siena to an undistinguished commercial block base.[45] But these gestures toward the British models of the past and the Italian-based harbingers of the future had at this moment no chance against

▲ 49 Eckel and Mann
(Harvey Ellis, designer),
J.B. Moss House, St. Joseph,
Missouri, 1889

▶ 50 Alfred Giles and
Guindon, Edwin Terrell House
("Lambermont"), San
Antonio, Texas, 1894, view
shortly after completion

▼ 51 H.F. Roach, James
LaPrelle House, St. Louis,
Missouri, 1896, view shortly
after completion

▶ 52 (opposite) Proudfoot
and Bird, Garfield (now
Friends) University, Wichita,
Kansas, 1887-88, central
pavilion

the burly Americanism of Richardson's achievement. Glasgow and Siena lost; Pittsburgh won.

The perception of Richardson's civic architecture as models of American public building infused smaller competitions throughout the prairie states. The YMCA, City Library, Masonic Temple building, and North and South High Schools in Minneapolis; the New York Life Building and Macalester College in St. Paul; the city halls in Sioux City (Iowa), St. Louis, Kansas City, and Omaha; the Union Depot in St. Louis and Grand Central Station in Kansas City; the high schools in Arkansas City, Junction City, and Emporia, Kansas; and dozens of county buildings throughout Iowa, Nebraska, and Texas all sponsored competitions that elicited entries of Richardsonian design at levels ranging from studied adaptation to outright cannibalization. County commissioners in Denton, Texas, actually mandated that their new courthouse adopt the Richardsonian Style,[46] with the unhappy outcome that construction was delayed ten years and the building ultimately followed the Italianate inclinations of its architect anyway.

At its best, this second phase of Richardson's influence on the plains was distinguished more by the occasional sophistication of its imitations than by creativity. Its highest achievement was the creation of a scattering of buildings so imbued with Richardson's spirit as to read almost as minor products of his office. Long and Kees's F.B. Long House in Minneapolis (designed 1892, built 1894; fig. 42) and W.L.B. Jenney's Thomas Wright House (1889; figs. 43 and 44) in Chicago show a skill in placing entries and window openings, simplifying rooflines, and composing unbroken masonry surfaces that places them in a class with Richardson's domestic designs. The Longfellow School in Kearney, Nebraska (attributed to Frank, Bailey and Farmer, 1890, demolished; fig. 45) and L.S. Buffington's Pillsbury Hall at the University of Minnesota in Minneapolis (1888; fig. 171) come even closer to achieving Richardson's distinctive alliance of picturesqueness and simplicity. But these are rare and isolated exceptions, both as original achievements and as examples of the work of the firms that produced them.

Assimilation

The third and climactic phase of Richardsonian absorption went beyond borrowing and imitation to assimilation. It could take place only in architectural offices which generated strong design programs of their own. By the time of Richardson's death in 1886, several such offices had grown up in the major urban centers of the plains states. John Root in Chicago was the obvious leader and the only midwestern figure clearly to have dispensed with the primitive phases of Richardsonian absorption well before Richardson's Chicago projects were under way. Root's work and that of his many followers in industrial centers throughout the plains states represented a conscious modernization of Richardson.[47]

Before dealing with the Chicago School, however, a few words should be said about Root's less progressive-minded contemporaries. The powerful figures of Harvey Ellis in the North, Proudfoot and Bird in the central plains, and J. Riely Gordon in the South entered this final phase of Richardsonian influence without tearing free from the master's Victorian moorings, yet they each managed to evolve a romanticized Richardson as distinctive and imaginative as Root's rationalism.

The precise role of Harvey Ellis in the importation of Richardson's ideas into the Upper Midwest is difficult to assign and has probably been exaggerated because of his considerable artistic gifts.[48] His enormous facility at pictorializing Richardsonian themes in itself created a distinctive body of work. He wandered over the same European architectural terrain as had Richardson, but Ellis tended to pick out features that were as fantastic as they were architectonic. For example, Ellis followed Richardson in borrowing the heavy arch moldings and colonette clusterings of French Provençal churches but added such features as the grotesques beneath the column bases, their tongues protruding in agony from the weight they are carrying (fig. 46). Looking to Italy, Richardson gleaned ideas from the fenestration patterns and tower-and-block compositional schemes of Florentine palazzi, while Ellis stole great chunks off Italian country houses. One of Ellis's most astonishing archaeological fantasies was a proposal for the James McAlister House in St. Joseph, Missouri (Eckel and Mann, built to a different design also rendered by Ellis in 1889), which borrowed the tower and inverted the fenestration of a medieval Sienese farmhouse sketched by Joseph Pennell and

published in *American Architect* in 1885 (figs. 47 and 48).[49]

The executed Eckel and Mann project which came the closest to pure Ellisian fantasy also had the most complex archaeological sources. In 1889, Ellis sketched a residence for Josiah Beattie Moss (1889; fig. 49) after Moss had returned from Europe anxious to have his own château. The owner himself had insisted on a roof garden like one he had seen in a house overlooking the Bay of Naples, a brick pattern recalling the Doge's Palace in Venice, and a doorway penetrating the foundation in the manner of a country house he had seen in England.[50] It fell to Ellis to weave these demands into a unitary design which was ultimately bound together with Richardsonian devices; the less glamorous task of making the building work was quite possibly left to the steadier members of the office staff.[51]

The theme of the castle endured in the work of the pictorializing Richardsonians. Castellated country houses had been in vogue for several decades, but now they were occupying city lots. Two of San Antonio architect Alfred Giles's clients approached him fresh from European travels, clamoring for stone residences.[52] One of them, Edwin Terrell, explicitly insisted on a "castle," to which Giles adroitly appended Texas-style Richardsonian verandas (fig. 50). The rugged, fortified Rhineland Schloss popular in earlier years was giving way to an urbane, but hardly less theatrical, quasi-Richardsonian château combining a monumental round or faceted tower; a Syrian-arched entry, often with mammoth voussoirs; a second-story loggia;

and a machicolated porte-cochere (figs. 51 and 182).

Richardson could also be adapted to late Victorian practice without such pretentious associative contexts. Architects such as J. Riely Gordon in San Antonio and Proudfoot and Bird in Wichita assembled enormous piles of Richardsonian volumes and ornamentation. Proudfoot and Bird found in Richardson a solution for one of the major problems of late Victorian architecture: how to create unified elevator building designs without simply repeating the elements of each story from bottom to top. The commonest solution, for the Chicago School as well as for the neoclassicists, was to sandwich a sequence of identical stories between a raised foundation and

Kettle River Quarries, 1895

▲ **53 Ricker and White, Library (now Altgeld) Hall, University of Illinois, Urbana, 1896, from an advertisement for Kettle River Sandstone Company**

▶ **54 George A. Berlinghof, Nemaha County Courthouse, Auburn, Nebraska, 1898, corner pavilion**

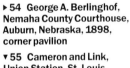

▼ **55 Cameron and Link, Union Station, St. Louis, Missouri, 1892-94**

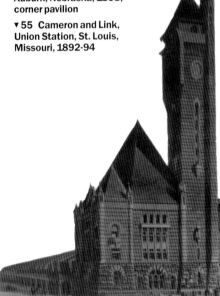

an elaborate cornice in a blown-up version of the classical base-shaft-capital formula. Proudfoot and Bird's solution was the far riskier one of composing each story anew, but retaining a vocabulary controlled enough to keep the assembly from fragmenting. In such designs as Garfield University in Wichita (1886-88; figs. 52 amd 113) and Wichita City Hall (1889-92; figs. 99, 114 and 115), they utilized Richardsonian devices both as a means of creating incremental upward transformations and as a discipline for tying the entire composition together. The soaring effects their programs achieved are exhilarating but utterly opposed to the quiet, earth-bound grandeur of Richardson's work.

The Chicago School wing of this final Richardsonian phase reacted against all of these additive Victorian compositional schemes. But it did not reject their Romanesque aspect. In fact the most obviously historical dimension of Richardson's work was often singled out by Chicagoans as particularly well-suited to modern aesthetic and functional requirements. In 1885, John Wellborn Root spelled out this point of view in a number of essays and lectures characterizing the Romanesque style as uniquely suited to modern development because it had never been "completed," i.e., had never produced a universally accepted model of building in

the manner of French Gothicism.[53] Professor Ricker, who headed the Midwest's first architectural department at the University of Illinois at Urbana, put the point more emphatically: the Romanesque style was an example of "arrested development" because the Gothic style had supplanted it for structural not aesthetic reasons. The "murdered" style's "probable course of further development" was thus an invaluable study for latter-day architects, particularly on account of its adaptability to modern requirements for public buildings and churches.[54] In the design of Library Hall on the Urbana campus, Ricker was given the opportunity to put his theory to use (fig. 53). This perspective on modern Romanesque design as the proper culmination of work left off seven centuries earlier was also echoed repeatedly by Henry van Brunt in Kansas City.[55] In 1891, Schuyler gave it a national airing via the *Architectural Review* when he declared that "the Romanesque may be commended as a point of departure for modern architects precisely because it has never reached its ultimate perfection, as Gothic did."[56]

However, all of this apparent unanimity regarding the suitability of the Romanesque style to modern buildings masked deeply divergent attitudes. Richardson himself admired the undisciplined vigor, the robust scaling, and even the crudeness of Romanesque building in the French provinces of Provence and Auvergne and in northern Spain. But these were not the qualities most appreciated by the architects and theoreticians who defended the modern use of Romanesque forms. The rough monumentality of Romanesque building was, in fact, increasingly regarded as its greatest liability to modern practice.[57] However, this apprehension did not deter vernacularizing architects outside of the major urban centers, especially in Kansas, Nebraska, and South Dakota. The magnificent play of void and solid across the lateral walls of Pope Hall at Fort Leavenworth Prison (c. 1892, demolished; fig. 6) and the powerful corner pavilions of George A. Berlinghof's Nemaha County Courthouse in Auburn, Nebraska (1898; fig. 54) point to the simple geometries of twentieth-century modernism as clearly as anything in the designs of Root or Louis Sullivan. But these were far too elemental and coarse for the Root-Ricker-van Brunt defense of Romanesque in modern practice.

As a theoretician, Ricker saw in the Romanesque style a means of solving a central problem of modern architecture: how to introduce ample light with-

◄ **56 Theodore Link, Second Presbyterian Church, St. Louis, Missouri, 1898-99**

out losing the sense of stability and quiet that only monumental forms can produce, thereby serving both the aesthetic and the practical needs of modern society. Link and Cameron in St. Louis apparently had the same vision for their Union Station (1892-94) when they selected "a free treatment of the Romanesque" on account of its "great dignity, together with a strong sense of solidity, [while] it lends itself at the same time most readily to the requirements of utility, especially in the manner of light"[58] (fig. 55). Significantly, the great clock tower, which so dominates the exterior of the finished work, was regarded as dispensible "without much injury to the general design." The modern Romanesque movement had come a long way from the self-conscious image-making of its beginnings.

St. Louis's Union Station fulfilled Ricker's central concerns by punctuating massive stone surfaces with clusters of enormous windows. Link's extraordinary concern with lighting the interior while sustaining the monumentality of the exterior reached its most extreme expression in the crossing tower of his Second Presbyterian Church (1898-99; fig.

56). This final midwestern tribute to Richardson's Trinity Church in Boston so enlarged the gable lights of the lantern that the tower lost its role as the anchor of the composition and hunched uncomfortably on the dense walling of the church beneath.

Brought to its logical conclusion, Ricker's thesis became a justification for de-Victorianizing Richardson by abstracting just those Romanesque elements that were best able to organize large surfaces and fulfill utilitarian requirements. Link never quite achieved this end, but Louis Sullivan did. In later years Sullivan was to profess repulsion for the "absence of logic and common-sense" in Richardson's work.[59] But at the time of the Marshall Field Wholesale Store construction, Sullivan plainly drew on Richardson's fenestration for the organization of his own Auditorium Building walls[60] (1886-89; figs. 57 and 79) and developed the scheme further in the Walker Warehouse (1888, demolished; fig. 81). "Logic" did away with the rock-faced surfaces, multiple belts, and cyclopean stone that gave Richardson's masterpiece so strong a pictorial character (Sullivan was later to describe it as "scene paint-

▲ 57 Adler and Sullivan, Auditorium Building, Chicago, Illinois, 1886-88, fenestration detail

▸ 58 W.B. Dunnell, Red Wing Training School for Boys, near Red Wing, Minnesota, 1889

◄ 59 *(left)* Burnham and Root, Insurance Exchange, Chicago, Illinois, 1884-85 (demolished 1912), view shortly after completion

◄ 60 *(right)* Burnham and Root, The Rookery, Chicago, Illinois, 1885-88, terra cotta and brick detail

ing")[61] in favor of an uninterrupted rhythm of linear arcades and a continuous multistory attic. All the Romanesque and Italianate overtones of the Marshall Field Wholesale Store were decisively pushed aside.

Schematizing Richardson became a favorite device of other midland architects as well. Large multi-pavilioned institutional buildings in particular demanded a means of organization which would unite a sequence of volumes into a single rhythmically articulated mass. Warner B. Dunnell, Minnesota's first though unofficial state architect,[62] devised a method of stretching out institutional facade designs which was at once Richardsonian in spirit, expressive of the building's diverse functions, and cost-effective. By staggering setbacks and varying window treatments, but uniting the entire mass over a sequence of arches, several distinct pavilions could be brought together into a united composition. This compositional device, first employed at the Red Wing Training School for Boys (1889; figs. 7 and 58), was simplified and extended into as many as nine pavilions for state mental hospitals at Fergus Falls and Rochester (both 1893-94, the former extant). A related rhythmic composition, in which arched porticos were placed before the setback pavilions, was used for Kansas state institutions by Seymour Davis during his tenure as state architect in the early 1890s (fig. 109).

Different as these various schematic treatments of Richardson's idiom were, each succeeded in adapt-

ing Richardson to modern demands by modularizing design elements drawn from his work. John Wellborn Root's method was different altogether. Though he also employed multistory, round-headed arcades, their proportions and arrangements clearly derived from a personal "constructive" method which did not require or utilize any design of Richardson's. Instead, he expanded on Richardsonian motifs to emphasize corner piers and entryways and to tie the diverse elements of his facades together.

For Root, the real usefulness of Romanesque and Byzantine architecture was its ornament, which effectively synthesized grace and power in a manner Root compared to a growing vine.[63] In opposition to the strict Richardsonians, Root argued that such ornament gained its vitality by adhering to a self-supporting structure, i.e., one in which the brick or terra-cotta that carried the decoration was veneered onto a steel frame. Only if Richardson's forms were "modified by [this] constructive type of building" could Richardson's kind of decoration be free enough of implied structural forces to achieve life. Root's favorite among his buildings of this type was Chicago's Insurance Exchange (1884-85, demolished; fig. 59). One of the most heralded buildings of his day and the best surviving testament to his theories concerning the Romanesque style is the Rookery (1885-88; figs. 60 and 84).

Root's openness to Richardson's influence was obviously bound to this larger view of the limitations of Romanesque architecture as a model for contemporary building designs. In Root's Romanesque idiom, the basement was of stone, the walls were of brick (by 1888 around a steel cage), the windows were broader than the piers, carved detailing was contracted into narrow string courses or splayed out on the corner piers, and the entries were raised semicircles set within emphatic squares. The foliate Byzantine ornament of Richardson's office was supplemented or replaced by low-relief interlaces of Celtic, Moorish, and Mogul design that were more suitable for terra-cotta production.

It was ultimately Root's idiom, and not Richardson's via Ricker or one of his stricter interpreters, that brought the "modern Romanesque" style into the commercial thoroughfare of the prairie cities. Minneapolis and St. Paul, Sioux Falls, Sioux City, Omaha, St. Louis, Kansas City, Topeka, and Dallas all erected major buildings in Root's manner. Omaha was at one time a showpiece of Richardsonianism a la Root, principally through the efforts of one firm, Isaac Hodgson and Son. Already successful as an architect in Indiana, Hodgson had gotten in on the beginning of the Minneapolis boom in 1882, then sent his son to Omaha to set up a branch office in 1886. Shortly thereafter, block after block of shipped-in brownstone or local limestone and brick began to combine the Romanesque/Moorish ornament, set-off geometrical entries, and pseudoclassical arcades of Root's Romanesque manner. The materials were frequently Richardsonian, but their organization was pure Root (fig. 61).

The output of the Supervising Architect of the Treasury between 1885 and 1895 perfectly encapsulated the rise and fall of Richardson as a force in the architecture of the midland prairies. "Uncle Sam's fearfully and wonderfully designed struc-

▼ 61 Isaac Hodgson, Jr., U.S. National Bank, Omaha, Nebraska, c. 1889 (demolished), view shortly after completion
From the Bostwick-Frohardt Collection owned by KMTV & on permanent loan to Western Heritage Museum—Omaha, Nebraska.

tures"[64] worked a steady progress from the Iowan Mifflin E. Bell's crude and hesitant borrowings[65] (fig. 140) to the Chicagoan Willoughby Edbrooke's mammoth compilations of cribbings from Richardsonian and European monuments to the Cincinnatian Willam Martin Aiken's urbane classicizing hybrids.[66] The notoriously slow construction schedule of many of the federal buildings erected during the Richardsonian era even permitted the consecutive recording on a single structure of the evolution of the "modern Romanesque" style. The United States Courthouse and Post Office in St. Paul (1892-1902; fig. 62) acquired an imitation of the Trinity Church lantern thrust 200 feet upward under Edbrooke's tenure, numerous interior references to famed Byzantine monuments under O'Rourke and Aiken,[67] and a Beaux-Arts Norman north tower under James Knox Taylor in 1898.

Taken as a whole, the evolution of public building designs in the 1890s marked the major path that the flight from the modern Romanesque took even more clearly than it marked the course of its public acceptance in the 1880s. H.-R. Hitchcock and Lewis Mumford, Richardson's first modern apologists, took great pains to separate themselves from the prevailing view that Richardson's work formed a bridge from High Victorianism to Beaux-Arts academicism.[68] Perhaps the modernist view of Richardson is correct so far as Richardson's own oeuvre is concerned. But in the hands of innumerable architects who planed down Richardson's walls, modularized his openings and bays, and stripped off his ornament—the staunch Richardsonian Cobb, the utilitarian eclectic Link, the virulent anticlassicist Sullivan, and the slick and slow architects of the Treasury Department among them—the Richardsonian era in the plains was melding insensibly into the new academicism.

It was fitting that the last preserves of reasonably holistic Richardsonian design were also among the last frontiers of vernacular practice untouched by academic training. William A. Wells's Oklahoma City Hall (1904; demolished) and J. C. Holland's several twentieth-century Richardsonian courthouses in Kansas (fig. 119) were located in the heart of prairie lands still served by architects more swayed by regional materials and practices than by the most recent winds of stylistic fashion. These were among the last areas in which unschooled architects dominated monumental building design and the last areas to relinquish Richardson's spirit. ✜

◄62 Office of the Supervising Architect of the Treasury, United States Courthouse and Post Office, St. Paul, Minnesota, 1892-1902

H.H. Richardson's Influence in Chicago's Midwest, 1872-1914

Thomas J. Schlereth

"The things I want to design," H.H. Richardson once said, "are a grain elevator and the interior of a great river steamboat."[1] Although the renowned New England architect never built either of these icons of midland America, his work had a significant influence on the midwestern built environment between the end of the Civil War and the outbreak of World War I.

Part of Richardson's impact on the architecture of the midland prairies came, as did so much else in America's Gilded Age, through its Chicago connection. Chicago served Richardson and the Midland as a center of architectural innovation and depot of style dissemination. The city's architects and architectural historians, then as now, recognized that in Chicago, Richardson's spirit underwent translation and travesty, transformation and triumph during the city's emergence as the region's major metropolis.

Several reasons demand that we consider Chicago as an essential case study in any analysis of the Richardsonian Romanesque in the Midwest. To begin, it was where the master made his architectural debut in the Midland with his American Merchants Union Express Company Building (fig. 64) on Chicago's West Monroe Street in 1872-73. While this commercial work has never been hailed as a Richardsonian masterpiece, two other Chicago commissions he designed—the Marshall Field Wholesale Store (1885-87) and the J.J. Glessner Residence (1885-87)—are, assuredly, among his outstanding achievements.

Finally, and most importantly for the theme of this volume, H.H. Richardson's own work had a vital and varied importance that expanded in two, concentric spheres of influence: one, which included Chicago and its suburban environs and which Thomas Tallmadge and Montgomery Schuyler identified as "the Romanesque Revival in Chicago";[2] and another, a regional orientation extending to wherever Chicago architects exported the "Richardsonian interlude" that Marcus Whiffen and Frederick Koeper see as "well represented throughout the Midwest in cities such as Minneapolis and St. Paul."[3]

This essay explores H.H. Richardson's architectural impact on Chicago's Midwest—the metropolis and the regional hinterland that Chicago architects built and influenced—on three levels: a) Richardson's own oeuvre in the city, 1872-1885; b) his impact on several practitioners in the first generation of Chicago's "School" of Architecture; and c) his influence on a specific Chicago architect, Solon Spencer Beman who transported the Richardsonian spirit (if not always its essence) to Chicago's midwestern rivals (Milwaukee, Omaha, St. Louis) as well as its smaller imitators (Grand Rapids, South Bend, LaCrosse).

Four specific Richardson projects—two commercial commissions (the American Merchants Union Express Building and the Marshall Field Wholesale Store) and two urban residences (the J.J. Glessner house and the Franklin MacVeagh house)—demonstrate his important contribution to Chicago's nineteenth-century built environment. Such Richardson designs Chicago architects could see firsthand in their city. The selected works of several such builders—here termed "The Chicago Richardsonians"—provide a collective case study of Richardson's influence in the city during his career and after his death. This group portrait of Louis Sullivan, John Root, Henry Ives Cobb, and S.S. Beman is drawn from a comparative study of both Chicago commercial work and various domestic projects.[4]

H.H. Richardson in Chicago

Although Richardson built more major commissions in Chicago than in any other midland prairie city, his work there was a numerically modest

H.-R. Hitchcock

◄ **63 Burnham and Root in their offices at the Rookery, 1888**

▲ **64 H.H. Richardson, American Merchants Union Express Company Building, Chicago, Illinois, 1872-73, rebuilt 1874-80 (burned 1930), unsigned office rendering**

▲ 65 H.H. Richardson,
Marshall Field Wholesale
Store, Chicago, Illinois
1885-87 (demolished 1930),
from an office rendering

achievement in a career of eighty-five completed projects and sixty-five unexecuted designs. His brief (1866-1886) architectural practice was even shorter in Chicago since three of his four projects in the city were commissioned in just over three months in the late spring of 1885.[5]

Richardson's Chicago corpus shares several characteristics. First, it is urban, the work of a city builder who recognized that post-Civil War America had developed special commercial/social zones that required distinct architectural forms. Second, it is stone work, cubic forms in rugged load-bearing masonry construction typical of Richardson's delight in natural materials and geometric symmetry. Third, the clients who brought Richardson to the Midwest had, like the architect, eastern connections. Either they were New England-bred like Marshall Field who first began storekeeping in Conway, Massachusetts, or, like J.J. Glessner (who had a summer home at Littleton, New Hampshire), they knew of Richardson through East Coast contacts.[6] Finally, Richardson's Chicago commissions, with the possible exception of his American Merchants Union

Express Company, were decisively executed in what has come to be termed Richardsonian Romanesque.

The American Merchants Building, commissioned in 1872, marked Richardson's entry on the Chicago architectural scene. A five-story building, executed in stone with occasional "Romanesque motifs" (in Marianna Van Rensselaer's opinion), the structure was topped by a mansard roof broken by dormers with pointed arches. Contemporaries such as Montgomery Schuyler, Peter B. Wight, and Thomas Tallmadge gave it passing grades.[7]

Richardson thought much better of his second commercial project in Chicago, the wholesale emporium (figs. 18 and 65) he designed for Marshall Field in 1885. Although he succumbed to Bright's disease when the building's stonework was barely visible above grade and never knew the structure beyond his working drawings, it was one of the two (the other being the Allegheny County Courthouse and Jail, 1883-88) he esteemed most important of his career.[8] Other observers, architects and critics, early and recent, concur in this self-estimate. Chicago architectural writers Dankmar Adler and R.C.

McLean were struck by the enormous stylistic advance made by Richardson since the American Merchants Building. The city's architectural journals, *Inland Architect* and *Western Architect,* accorded it universal acclaim. Eastern writers such as Edward Atkinson and Charles Dudley Warner similarly trumpeted its achievement nationwide, and its reputation has consistently risen in the hagiography of the "modern movement" with each new survey of American or world art and architecture.[9]

Inasmuch as the Marshall Field store has assumed a central position in the history of American architecture and, thanks to the careful research of James O'Gorman, is a documented topic in architectural historiography, here we need only summarize the structure's complicated design evolution and sources. The building's initial scheme was a complete rectangle with a central light court. This was changed to a broad U-shaped plan with a loading dock in the center of the U. The building rose seven stories above a basement with a total area of roughly 500,000 square feet. Each floor was divided into three rectangular sections by fire walls running north and south, separating the base of the U-shaped plan from the two sides. The otherwise open floors were supported by a regular grid of columns.

Rock-faced Missouri red granite was used for the exterior walls at the lower floor and cut East Longmeadow red sandstone for those above. Richardson, O'Gorman states, had also studied brick for the walls, but Field insisted on stone. The windows above the first floor were grouped under arches in a rhythm which doubled and then quadrupled at the higher floors. The masonry was laid up in even horizontal courses at the ground floor except for a narrow band at the window sills. A smooth-faced belt course formed the second floor window sills, and above that the masonry alternated in wide and narrow courses. A band of squared stones was introduced at the fourth floor arch spandrels, the whole topped by a cornice with a foliate motif and parapet cap.[10]

Frequently linked to the Florentine Renaissance palazzo of the fifteenth century, the Roman aqueduct at Segovia, and certain English stone warehouses and jails, critics have also suggested the Field Store's design precedents were more indigenous than imported, more Bostonian and New England than Italian or English. Montgomery Schuyler, for instance, noted the parallel to the granite commercial wharf structures that lined the Boston water-

front in mid-century, observing that Richardson had told him "that there was more character in the plain and solid warehouses that had been destroyed [in the Boston fire of 1872] than in the florid edifices by which they had been replaced." The arch-articulated facades of the mills in Lowell and Lawrence, Massachusetts and Manchester, New Hampshire are also cited as inspiration for the Field Store, as is Richardson's own earlier New England commercial work.[11]

When Richardson returned to Chicago in 1885 to do preliminary studies for preparing working drawings for the Field Wholesale house, he called on John Root in his private office in the Montauk Block in order to consult on the design of the proper building foundations, given the city's infamous soft soil. Donald Hoffmann argues that it is highly likely that Root showed his fellow architect what work he had on the boards, such as Root's McCormick Harvesting Machine Company Offices and Warehouse (fig. 66) of 1884-86, to be erected at a site (southwest corner of Jackson and Wacker) just two blocks west of the Field Store site. Hoffmann suggests it is also probable that Richardson took note of the general character of the city's wholesale and commercial district.[12] In so doing, he would have seen a stand (perhaps not up to his standards) of Romanesque facades that included Burnham and Root's Counselman (1883-84) and Insurance Exchange (1884-85) buildings (fig. 59). In fact, by 1885, Chicago contained a variety of buildings (particularly warehouses and commercial blocks) articulated by repetitive units and constructed of stone blocks piled up in either trabeated or arcuated facades.

Because of their own Romanesque tradition, Chicago architects found the Field Wholesale Store an impressive stone pile. The immense scale of the building—a blockbuster in the literal sense—seemed a grand and direct statement. Against the typical street front of Chicago in the mid-1880s, the structure appeared, in Louis Sullivan's estimate, to be "an oasis amidst a host of stage-struck wobbling mockeries." Others were less poetic. Adjectives such as "palatial," "Cyclopean," and "mammoth" were commonly used to describe the edifice of "that colossal man"—as Lewis Mumford called him—whose individual stones were unequaled in size anywhere else in the city. Chicago architects lauded Richardson's achievement because it looked its part. Only Marshall Field's name identified it, but the building spoke for itself. John Edelmann recognized this in calling it "a grim fortress of trade...a huge square

Inland Architect

▲ **66 Burnham and Root, McCormick Harvesting Machine Company Offices and Warehouse, Chicago, Illinois, 1884-86 (demolished), unsigned office drawing**

▶ 67 H.H. Richardson,
J.J. Glessner House, Chicago,
Illinois, 1885-87, 1891
drawing by Bertram G.
Goodhue

▼ 68 J.J. Glessner House,
ground floor plan

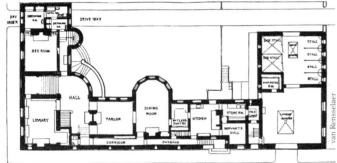

van Rensselaer

box with regular ranges of openings for light—
massive, simple, brutal, naive, the true expression
of its inward character." Sullivan similarly acknowledged it was a true "monument to trade, to the
organized commercial spirit, to the power and
progess of the age...."[13]

It is reasonable to assume that the thousands of
midwestern businessmen who frequented the Field
wholesale emporium for over four decades thought
so too. Richardson's building served the needs of
the small-town midwesterner on business in the
Midwest's Big Town. As O'Gorman notes, "it was a
matter-of-fact space, efficiently laid out to expedite
the buyer on a short schedule. He would travel to
Chicago by night train, debark in the morning at a
nearby station, meet the general salesman as he
entered the store, establish his credit, proceed from
department to department where he found wares
neatly but simply displayed, make his selections,

arrange for their shipment to his place of business,
and return to his hometown at the end of the day."[14]
Although we can never trace any direct connection
between what the typical midland burgher saw in
Richardson's masculine-oriented shelter and symbol of the Field company's wholesale branch, it is not
improbable that at least some travelers to Chicago
decided that the monumental properties of rough-
cut American stone might be an equally appropriate vocabulary in which to have their local architects
and builders express, if in more modest and perhaps less daring terms, their own aspirations for
civic, cultural, and commercial grandeur. Richardson's massive monument, however, did not survive
changing economic times as the Field company, its
wholesale operations dwindling, pulled the building
down in the 1930s, leaving his J.J. Glessner house
(figs. 67-70) as the only surviving example of his
architecture in Chicago.

The residence that Frederick Law Olmsted
claimed as "the most beautiful that has ever been
put on paper," George Pullman (who lived directly
across Prairie Avenue in a Second Empire mansion)
could not bear to look at, and Montgomery Schuyler
grumped "looked like a feudal fortress."[15] Richardson
anticipated the design would prompt controversy.
As he and Glessner surveyed the smoky corner lot
(the Michigan Central Railroad tracks were only a
block away) in the spring of 1885, Richardson asked
the farm implement manufacturer bluntly: "Have
you the courage to build the house without windows

on the front street?" Glessner said yes, and the next evening, after the last course of dinner, Richardson proposed, "If you won't ask me how I get into it, I will draw the plan for your house." He then proceeded to sketch out the basic L-shaped first floor plan (fig. 68) "almost exactly as it was finally decided upon."[16] To allow the house to turn its focus away from the street, the plan situated many of the principal rooms facing a quiet interior courtyard. In contrast to the severe, unrelieved street elevations of granite, Richardson introduced three modified turrets (fig. 70) that projected into the L-shaped courtyard environ.[17]

Contemporaries like Charles McKim and Nathan Ricker (head of the School of Architecture at the University of Illinois) and European moderns such as Mies van der Rohe and L. Moholy-Nagy (who made pilgrimages to the mecca immediately upon arrival in America) considered the Glessner house exterior to be Richardson's most successful.[18] Two stories high, with a full basement and attic, the residence was erected of heavily rusticated Wellesley granite topped by a red-tiled, steeply pitched gable roof. The Eighteenth Street elevation, particularly its arched entryway, was Richardson at his best. The stark power of the entryway's singular form may have inspired the similar simplicity of Burnham and Root's First Regiment Armory (1889-91) built only four blocks away.

Richardson, in one sense, imitated (but did not improve upon) himself in the Franklin MacVeagh residence (1885-87; fig. 71) on Lake Shore Drive and repeated the performance one time again in the J.R. Lionberger house in St. Louis, a scaled-down version of the MacVeagh manse. In the latter structure, many Richardsonian characteristics for the Romanesque residence were present: an asymmetrical plan, granite massing, and an arched entrance. Yet the MacVeagh commission never measured up to the Glessner project. Its walls were less rich in effect, its frequent plate-glass windows blank-looking distractions in the masonry facade, its height (three storys rather than two) equivocal, neither clearly horizontal nor clearly vertical. Nonetheless, in some respects, the MacVeagh house initially had wider influence in Chicago than the Gless-

▲ 69 J.J. Glessner House, capital detail

◄ 70 J.J. Glessner House, interior court

▶ 71 H.H. Richardson, Franklin MacVeagh House, Chicago, Illinois, 1885-87 (demolished 1922), view shortly after completion

▼ 72 Burling and White-house, H.N. Higinbotham House, Chicago, Illinois, 1890 (demolished), view shortly after completion

ner design. The rounded corner, compact tower, and second-story loggia were echoed in dozens of local designs, for example, in Treat and Foltz's James Bolton house (fig. 73), in Burling and Whitehouse's H.N. Higinbotham house (fig. 72), and in S.S. Beman's C.W. Brega residence.[19]

The Chicago Richardsonians

The Glessner and MacVeagh houses point up the complexity of the Richardsonian legacy to Chicago architects. The Brookline architect, like many of his midland admirers, saw in the Romanesque style an opportunity to bring quiet and order to an architectural era overwhelmed by historical and picturesque styles. Richardsonian Romanesque aspired to become an American aesthetic based upon elementary geometric masses. In the Glessner house, it almost succeeded; in the MacVeagh residence, it retreated. Even the Glessner achievement sent mixed signals. Paul Sprague has outlined at least two of the conflicting messages to be found in the Glessner "granite hut": the somber exterior street fronts contrasted with the picturesqueness of the interior gar-

den courtyard elevations and with the irregular variations and sequence of the interior plan. In Sprague's estimate, only his untimely death solved this dilemma for Richardson, the artistic challenge passing to those who drew inspiration from him.[20]

Thus the Chicago Richardsonians, particularly devotees like Sullivan and Root, were left at a visual crossroads. Like Richardson, they desired to drive forward to a new architectural aesthetic that they all yearned for and wrote so incessantly about, yet they also wanted to continue the picturesque manner that many of them had embraced for so long, often with excellent results.

Chicagoan architects rose to the Richardsonian challenge in various ways. Sullivan, for example, grappled with the geometric aesthetic—and the picturesque tradition—and went his own way, developing a highly singular idiom of his own. Root, also affected by the competing visual suggestions of the Richardsonian corpus in Chicago and elsewhere, likewise moved toward a personal adaptation of Richardson before he, too, died a young man of forty-two in 1891. Others, like Henry Ives Cobb, preferred to be careful translators of part of the Richardsonian spirit rather than to attempt its transformation. Finally, there were the followers, some sophisticated and sensitive like S.S. Beman and J.L. Silsbee, others merely imitative and prolific like Lawrence Hallberg and C.M. Palmer. The latter group, largely unknown now, were major contributors to the blocks and blocks of detached houses on ample lots on the city's south side and polychromatic stylistic mixes of the north and west side row house developments (figs. 75-77). While Richardson's own production in Chicago amounted to but a few commissions in the city's core, his followers produced progeny throughout its environs.

Of Sullivan's indebtedness, of course, we know much since the master was forever explaining himself. In *Kindergarten Chats,* he waxed lyrically over the Field Store in the fashion of sexing buildings typical of late nineteenth-century architectural criticism:

> Here is a man for you to look at. A man…that has active muscles, heart, lungs, viscera; a man that lives and breathes, that has red blood; a real man; a manly man; a virile force, broad, vigorous, energetic; spiritually an entire male….Four square and brown, it stands, in physical fact,…as the oration of one who knows well how to choose his words, who has somewhat to say and says it—and says it as the outpouring of a copious, direct, large and simple mind.[21]

Ever the poet, Sullivan's rhetorical flourishes could misstate basic facts since the Field Store was U-shaped and red originally. Yet the building's influ-

▼ **73 Treat and Foltz, James Bolton House, Chicago, Illinois, 1891, view shortly after completion**

▶ 74 Burnham and Root et al, V.C. Turner House and others on North Lake Shore Drive, Chicago, Illinois, c. 1887-90, c. 1910 postcard view

▼ 75 C.M. Palmer, Block of Residences for Potter Palmer on Astor and Bank, Chicago, Illinois, 1888-89, drawing by Frank Lively

▶ 76 (bottom right) C.M. Palmer, J.C. Bartlett Townhouse (part of block of Residences for Potter Palmer), Chicago, Illinois, 1888

▼ 77 (bottom left) L.G. Hallberg and C.M. Palmer, Row of Townhouses on State Street, Chicago, Illinois, 1888-94

ence on his own work, particularly the Auditorium Building, was direct and demonstrable. As has often been illustrated (figs. 79 and 80), Sullivan, after studying Richardson's project, consciously altered his original facade of the Auditorium with those of the Field Store in mind.[22]

Richardson's strong influence on Sullivan in the late 1880s shows not only in the Auditorium but also in other public work such as his Standard Club (1887-89) and in residences such as those designed for Ira Heath and Victor Falkenau (fig. 78). Hugh Morrison considered the Heath residence, built in 1889, the firm of Adler and Sullivan's best Chicago house scheme. "Here the extravagant depth of the voussoirs over doors and windows and the vibrant surface texture of random-coursed and quarry-face masonry endow the facade with much greater richness and force. Richardson himself could not have done better in a similar program."[23]

At least one other Sullivan project, the Walker Warehouse (also known as the Wholesale Store Building for Martin Ryerson; fig. 81), serves to demonstrate what the Chicago architect assimilated from the Boston mentor and what he developed on his own. Comparing Sullivan's Walker building with Richardson's Field Store, each is a seven-story warehouse occupying a full city block. In both, the massing is cubic, with only a slightly projecting cornice and a clean-cut silhouette; in both, ornamentation is virtually omitted, so that a plastic articulation of the larger forms produces the overall architectural effect. The difference between the two structures lies in the arrangement and treatment of these forms.

Hugh Morrison aptly argues that the Walker Warehouse goes beyond the Field Store in two essential respects:

> ...the greater freedom from historical or conventional forms, and the more precise statement of its elements of design in a firmly articulated whole. It is a sort of pure architecture, using the fundamental elements of the pier, the lintel, and the arch in an abstract composition, dissociated from the expression of specifically masonry effects.... The individual elements are both more clearly stated and more simply organized than in Richardson's building. The corner masses of the piers rise unbroken from pavement to cornice; the middle group of four stores is unchallenged by other and lesser groups. Every element is clean-cut, smooth, rectilinear, positive. In composition, the relationship of the two-story base to the main unit is happier than is the one-story base of the Field Building.[24]

John Wellborn Root, a brilliant designer whom Sullivan recognized as an "intuitive architectural

◀ **78 Adler and Sullivan, Victor Falkenau Flats, Chicago, Illinois, 1889 (demolished), drawing by Frank L(loyd) Wright**

Inland Architect

genius," can also be seen as a Chicago Richardsonian. Root and Richardson, often coupled as two American architectural Moseses who died before seeing the promised land of a truly indigenous American aesthetic, had much else in common. Both were Southerners, had trained abroad, and had eastern ties. Often each worked too hard, too fast, and at the end of a short career seemed bent on building everything at once. Both had women as their first biographers and both died in their forties.

Early in his career Root, as the chief designer in the firm of Burnham and Root, ventured into the commercial Romanesque, picking and choosing an element here, a detail there, to append to his commercial blocks. This was evident, for example, in the awkward Richardsonian entryway arch in the Counselman Building (1883-84) and the ponderous balconies (suggested by a less conspicuous detail of Richardson's R. and F. Cheney Building in Hartford, Connecticut) of the unpromising Rialto Building (1883-86). More complex relationships to Richardson's work occurred with projects like the Santa Fe Building (1883-84) in Topeka, Kansas (fig. 101), a structure Donald Hoffmann compares favorably with H.H. Richardson's later F.L. Ames Store of 1886-87, and the Insurance Exchange Building in Chicago (1884-85; fig. 59).[25]

Root quickly proved he could do sound translations of Richardson's Romanesque in various contexts. In the domestic line he produced the Edward E. Ayer home (1885-86) at the corner of State and

▲ 79 *(left)* Adler and Sullivan, Auditorium Building, Chicago, Illinois, 1886 scheme

▲ 80 *(right)* Auditorium Building, 1886-89, c. 1925 postcard view

▶ 81 Adler and Sullivan, Walker Warehouse (also known as M.A. Ryerson Wholesale Store), Chicago, Illinois, 1888-89 (demolished), unsigned 1889 drawing

Banks in Chicago, and the V.C. Turner residence at Schiller and Burton Place (1886-87; fig. 74), only a few blocks north of Richardson's MacVeagh house. The masonry of the Turner building was magnificent: entrances shadowed by cavernous arches and turrets set in place with a bold directness.

In commercial building, two other Chicago structures demonstrate Root's interest in the Romanesque: the already mentioned McCormick Harvesting Machine Company Offices and Warehouse and the Art Institute of Chicago (1885-87; fig. 83). The Art Institute, as much a rental property for clubs and artists' studios as an exhibition gallery, possessed perfect proportions for its small city lot. Its front elevation became a rugged fabric in Connecticut brownstone and Denver red sandstone. The only distractions were the portrait heads set in the gable and bizarre sculpture atop the peak (fig. 82). One critic chastised the latter element: the "selection of a torso to do the work as a finial," and perceptively noted that "the building might be mistaken as a club house." Within five years, in fact, it became the Chicago Club.[26]

Thomas Tallmadge thought the Burnham and Root firm the highwater mark of the western school of Romanesque Revival architecture in Chicago. Montgomery Schuyler thought so as well. Comparing the work of Richardson with that of Root, Schuyler characterized Root's use of the Romanesque in such Chicago buildings as the Insurance Exchange, the Rookery (fig. 84), and the Phoenix Building (fig. 138) as being lighter in expression than Richardson's monumental masonry.[27]

The Rookery along with Root's equally famous Monadnock Block (1889-92), a few blocks away on Wabash Avenue, remain as the lonely survivors of a cluster of multistory commercial structures (many of which were built by Burnham and Root) that formed the city's first LaSalle Street financial district. For almost a century, the Rookery's tenants have been brokerage houses, legal offices, and financial firms—commercial establishments whose businesses extended throughout the midland prairies. As with the Monadnock, the Rookery has been extensively studied; its dual construction methods, interior light court, and striking central lobby the subject of much architectural history. To contemporaries its style defied precise classification, various commentators calling it Moorish, Indian, and Indic as well as Romanesque. Yet the building also had Root's personal touch. Peter Brooks, Boston finan-

cier of the block, baffled by the elevation drawings, recognized the Rookery was something different, neither typically Richardsonian nor totally Romanesque.[28] In it, Root went beyond both in cutting his fancy free in a handsome, romantic interplay of solids and voids, stasis and kinesis, structure and space.

Root, like Richardson, also had his failures. To extend the Romanesque style to the commercial skyscraper, while an intriguing challenge, ultimately proved unsuccessful. For example, neither the Women's (W.C.T.U.) Temple Building (1890-92) nor the Masonic Temple (1890-92) was, despite their being the largest (fig. 85) of all Burnham and Root buildings, an achievement of merit. Root's project for the San Francisco Examiner Building also suggested the aesthetically problematic nature of marrying a steel frame with a masonry-bearing wall.

Inland Architect

▲ **82 Burnham and Root, The Art Institute, Chicago, Illinois, 1885-87 (demolished 1930), unsigned drawing of gable ornament**

▼ **83 The Art Institute shortly after completion**

Architectural Record

▸ 84 *(left)* Burnham and Root, The Rookery, Chicago, Illinois, 1885-88, shortly after completion

▸ 85 *(right)* Burnham and Root, The Masonic Temple, Chicago, Illinois, 1892 (demolished), c. 1920 postcard view

▾ 86 Henry Ives Cobb, Chicago Historical Society, Chicago, Illinois, 1887-92

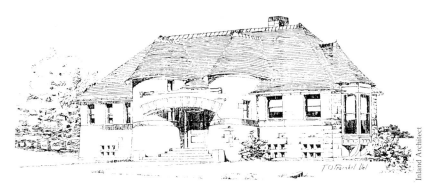

Inland Architect

Burnham and Root's presence on the West Coast indicates their geographical reach beyond Chicago. Typically, however, their sphere of operation did not extend beyond the midland prairies. Kansas City, for instance, particularly bears their impress. Between 1886 and Root's death five years later, several leading Romanesque models—the Midland Hotel (1886-88), Board of Trade (1886-88), American National Bank (1886-88)—were erected on this Missouri cityscape.

Henry Ives Cobb also contributed to the midland townscape, but his Chicago work is his best known. Born in Brookline, Massachusetts, he received more formal training than any of the other Chicago Richardsonians, first at Harvard, then at the Massachusetts Institute of Technology. He first worked in New England with the Boston firm of Peabody and Stearns, coming to Chicago in 1881 and forming a partnership with Charles S. Frost in 1882. The firm achieved early (1882) notoriety with their Gothic extravaganza for the Potter Palmers, a Near North side castle, the only element of which Richardson thought worthy was its mosaic floor. The firm dealt in all manner of revival styles, including the Romanesque wherein it achieved several stunning successes such as the Gymnasium (1890) and Durand Art Institute (1891) on the campus of Lake Forest College.

Although his design ability was less than Root's, Cobb's Chicago Historical Society (1888-92; fig. 86) came closer to the essence of Richardson than did Root's Art Institute. It was more emphatic in basic form and wall treatment; it adhered to a principle that other, less talented Chicagoan Richardsonians often forgot: the Romanesque worked best as a horizontal composition. Cobb and Frost had not completely mastered this in their early residential work such as the 1885-86 Ransom R. Cable house (fig. 12), but Frost certainly understood its importance

by the time of the Morgan Park and Wheaton public libraries in suburban Chicago (figs. 87 and 88).[29]

Other followers of Richardson in Chicago were less successful in adapting the Romanesque. Sometimes the quest for verticality was the problem, as in detached residences such as Treat and Foltz's Martin Ryerson House (fig. 89). On other occasions, the lot sizes and the demands of row house development—for example, S.S. Beman's own residence (fig. 90)—forced architects into unhappy collages. Typical of this resorting to swelling masses and fussy details to keep the eye alert and amazed were the blocks of polychromatic eclecticism that characterized many of Chicago's fashionable upper-middle-class west side and north side streets in the late 1880s. Here the work of Charles M. Palmer, Oliver Marble, and Lawrence G. Hallberg was more representative (stylistically and statistically) of the city's Romanesque than that of better known Chicago Richardsonians.

▲ 87 *(left)* C.S. Frost, Morgan Park Library, Chicago, Illinois, 1889, office drawing by T.O. Fraenkel

▲ 88 *(right)* Morgan Park Library, tower detail

▼ 89 Treat and Foltz, Martin A. Ryerson House, Chicago, Illinois, 1888, view shortly after completion

▶ 90 S.S. Beman, S.S.
Beman House, Chicago,
Illinois, 1892 (demolished)

MANUFACTURING TOWN OF PULLMAN · AND CAR WORKS · BELONGING TO PULLMAN'S PALACE CAR COMPANY.

Western Manufacturer, 1891

Although these vernacular architects frequently took every possible liberty with Richardson's models, although they failed to master his sense of massing or his reverence for a building's basic elements, they produced a busty and vivacious aesthetic, emblematic of Chicago bravado in the era when it became the most American of American cities. The robust and outgoing character, sometimes a block-long panoply of color, texture, and scale, of these streetscapes—solid yet boisterous, confident yet brassy—seemed appropriate to Chicago, a city fascinated with the gargantuan in an age prone to excess.[30] In Chicago in the 1890s, one could see the world's largest enclosure of space (i.e., the Manufacturers and Liberal Arts Building at the 1893 World's Fair) and the greatest reaching of height (i.e., Burnham and Root's 1892 Masonic Temple, then the tallest building in the world).

Solon Spencer Beman

In Chicago, one could also see Pullman (fig. 91), the world's largest industrial planned community, built (1879-92) by Solon Spencer Beman. Beman owed much to Richardson. His architectural scrapbooks contained photographs and descriptions of favorite Richardson buildings. Both men were client-centered builders, architects who designed building after building for the same owner, family, or firm.[31] Each fashioned monuments—Beman for George Pullman in Chicago's Graceland Cemetery, Richardson for Oakes and Oliver Ames in Sherman, Wyoming—memorializing the families so crucial as patrons in their professional lives. Each also de-

signed railroad car interiors and railroad stations, as well as all the other architectural symbols of the Gilded Age: men's clubs, apartments, and Civil War monuments.

Born in Brooklyn, S.S. Beman served his apprenticeship in the New York firm of Upjohn and Upjohn, who had first introduced (with the senior Upjohn's churches patterned after Lombard and Germanic prototypes) the Romanesque style into America in

▲ 91 View of Pullman, Chicago, Illinois, 1879-92

▼ 92 S.S. Beman, Pullman Building, Chicago, Illinois, 1883-84 (demolished 1956), drawing by Paul Lantrup

▶ **93 S.S. Beman,
The Omaha Bee Building,
Omaha, Nebraska, 1887-88
(demolished), early view
showing adjacent City Hall**

From the Bostwick-Frohardt Collection
owned by KMTV & on permanent loan
to Western Heritage Museum—Omaha,
Nebraska.

the 1840s. In the Upjohn office, Beman rose to be the project supervisor of the Connecticut State Capitol, a commission won in competition with Richardson. While practicing independently in New York, Beman, at age twenty-eight, came to the attention of George Pullman who enlisted him to design an entire industrial town—factory complex, civic buildings, and housing for over 10,000 workers on a site south of Chicago.

Young Beman's first architectural foray into downtown Chicago came with his Pullman Building, a ten-story office and apartment block (fig. 92) constructed opposite the Art Institute, at the corner of Michigan Avenue and Adams Street, in 1883-84. Marked features of Beman's Adams Street elevation included Marat turrets on the building's corners and a series of colonnades that flanked an elliptical granite entrance arch. From this grand portal, Beman constructed a sky-lit inner court extending inwards eighty feet. The inner court provided light and cross-ventilation to the upper stories, as well as bifurcated the building's elevation. The Pullman Building's open court, like the dramatic design of

the Arcade Building interior he had done in his Pullman town, was another example of a Beman forte: his ability to design interesting interior commercial spaces. This talent would manifest itself further in his Northwest Insurance Company Building in Milwaukee (1885, demolished) and in his stunning interior for the Grand Central Railroad Station in Chicago (1885-90, demolished).

The Pullman "hive," as locals dubbed the building, enjoyed critical success in an opulent age that welcomed, as Tallmadge aptly put it, "a mix of the Romanesque Revival seasoned with a bit of the Queen Anne" in its commercial palaces. *The Inland Architect* published a handsome line-drawing perspective of the building as its first venture into centerfold, sepia-toned print engraving. The editors were doubly proud when *Building News* (1884), a London architectural journal, reproduced the illustration and commented favorably on Chicago architecture as represented by Beman's work.[32]

George Pullman provided his architect with many contacts in Chicago's professional and commercial circles. For example, Pullman suggested

Beman's name to various midwestern associates in the railway industry including Robert Todd Lincoln, Joseph T. Torrence and C.W. Brega, all of whom hired Beman to design their houses. The Pullman connection also led to important commercial commissions throughout the Midland where he exported his commercial style and Chicago's architectural prestige. These projects included large blocks like the Omaha Bee (1887-88; fig. 93) and the Pioneer Press Building (1888-89; fig. 94) in St. Paul as well as smaller, main-street scale projects.[33]

Beman produced a number of domestic designs during the 1880s and 1890s—the most creative decades of his career. His spacious mansions could be found along Chicago's prestigious "society" streets. By the mid-1890s, Lake Shore Drive north of the Chicago River had several of Beman's Romanesque houses. The Jones-Torrence-McCormick mansion (1885), formerly at the corner of Bellevue Place and Lake Shore Drive, was typical of these structures. So was the H.M. Wood house (1888; fig. 95). The south side of Chicago, where Beman himself lived throughout his life (and the area of the city with which he most closely identified), came to contain a still wider array of his early Romanesque work.[34] In addition to his domestic work in the Romanesque, he adapted and combined other styles to suit a client's family needs, social aspirations, personal fancy, and economic status.[35] This is evident, for instance, in the château-style masterpiece (1890) that he erected for W.W. Kimball at 1801 Prairie Avenue. Standing eyeball-to-eyeball with Richardson's Glessner home across the street, the Kimball mansion (ironically, more so than any of his more numerous Romanesque designs) has become Beman's most famous extant domestic structure.

Simultaneously with the residences he erected for midland merchant princes and their subalterns, Beman built business blocks to house their downtown corporate headquarters. In addition to those already mentioned, he completed two Chicago office buildings/warehouses for the Studebaker firm—the 410-20 South Michigan Building (1885; fig. 96) and the 623 South Wabash Building (1895). Both are still landmarks of the city's late nineteenth-century commercial core.

The first comprised a carriage showroom (first two floors) and a light manufacturing and vehicle assembly plant (remaining floors). Beman reworked the entire building in 1896, converting it to a cultural center renamed the Fine Arts Building.[37] In renovating the structure built a decade earlier, Beman gave his creation a facelift and a thorough interior remodeling. The domes, the attic, and the original facade of the eighth floor were removed and were replaced with a three-story addition, creating a total of ten floors. The architect made the greatest changes, however, within the building's interior: a structure initially devoted to commerce was converted to an atelier of the arts. Thus, a visitor to Chicago in the 1890s could see samples (fig. 97) of three of the city's Richardsonians lined up, cheek-to-jowl, on a single block: Sullivan's Auditorium, Beman's Studebaker/Fine Arts, and Root's Art Institute/Chicago Club.

What Chicagoans and visiting midwesterners

▼ 94 S.S. Beman, Pioneer Press Building, St. Paul, Minnesota, 1888-89, unsigned drawing

Architectural Record

▶ 95 S.S. Beman, H.M. Wood
House, Chicago, Illinois,
1888 (demolished), view
shortly after completion

took away from this showcase of the Romanesque we will never know. Nor can we estimate precisely the impact upon the thousands who came from and journeyed to the midland prairies through S.S. Beman's Grand Central Station (fig. 98), a monumental edifice that Carl Condit called "the most original" of Beman's designs and yet "one of the least publicized of important Chicago buildings."[38]

Opened on December 8, 1890, the Chicago Grand Central could boast a number of superlatives. Its 247-foot Norman bell and clock tower became an instant Chicago landmark. Only its eastern forerunner, New York's Grand Central, then had a larger single-span balloon train shed. Beman's iron-and-glass engineering marvel is recognized by historians of American technology as one of the true wonders of the railroad age. As Carroll Meeks noted, comparing it to the Field Store, "Beman's towers and arches incorporate huge blocks, an innovation of the period. These were derived from H.H. Richardson's enormous quarry-faced stone or boulders used for textural contrast."[39] The complex was distinguished by a spacious well-appointed depot (complete with a waiting room seating 1,800 people), handling over 75 trains and 10,000 passengers daily, a deluxe hotel, and a carefully planned traffic concourse and taxi rotunda. Architectural historian Folke T. Kihlstedt concluded Beman's Grand Central "of all the nineteenth century American stations, came the closest to achieving a formal synthesis between the

◄ 96 S.S. Beman, Stude-
baker Building #1, Chicago,
Illinois, 1885, unsigned
office drawing

architecture and engineering worlds."[40]

It is fitting to conclude this brief review of H.H. Richardson's influence on Chicago with a railroad station since Richardson designed over a dozen such structures. It is also appropriate because Beman's Grand Central Station symbolized the complexity of Richardson's influence. In it one can see many of the things he and other Chicagoan architects admired about the Richardsonian corpus—its Olympian amplitude, its romantic energy, its established (and Establishment) presence; it also embodied certain other proclivities of the Chicago Richardsonians—the desire to emulate European precedents, the tendency to favor stone-clad and brick-clad over more expensive, load-bearing construction, and the shift away from massive stone surfaces by masonry builders who were also iron, glass, and (increasingly) steel men.

The more conservative among them (and their clients) took readily to the fortress, donjon-like quality of a Glessner house, seemingly secure against all outside agitators. Those of them searching for an appropriate form and architectonic means for modern commerce quickly recognized the potential of a Field Wholesale Store, an original achievement in urban coherence and city design. Individually their indebtedness was acknowledged and evident. Sulli-

van's sensitivity to composition and Root's fascination with elementary volumes were enhanced by the Richardsonian spirit. They saw in Richardson's accomplishments an aesthetic which they took in many directions in their own city and elsewhere in the Midwest.

Richardson did not, the claims of many twentieth-century critics and architects to the contrary, make them modernists. He himself was not (and some of his Chicago followers were not) *primarily* interested in technological innovations and absolute structural expression. Nor did he show any special concern for the new materials of glass and steel.[41] In fact, some of the directions in which Root, Sullivan, Treat and Foltz, Cobb, and Beman took certain of his ideas he might have objected to as much as the hackneyed imitations of his Romanesque promulgated by lesser lights elsewhere in Chicago and fin-de-siècle America.

Rather what the Chicago Richardsonians saw in his momentary, but monumental, contribution to their city's architecture were the beginnings of a style adaptable to American needs and, possibly, symbolic of America itself. As numerous contributors to the *Inland Architect,* the Chicago building fraternity's most serious forum in the late nineteenth century, continually attested, the Chicagoans saw Richardson (and themselves) as participants in a crucial transitional state of American architectural history.[42] Richardson's attention to basic shapes, surfaces, and textures as well as to the native qualities of stone, brick, and shingle seemed one fruitful direction in which to try to create a distinctive architecture appropriate to the environmental and cultural conditions of their time and the American place. ✖

▼ **98 S.S. Beman, Grand Central Station (originally Wisconsin Central Station), Chicago, Illinois, 1888-90, (demolished 1969), early rendering**

Richardsonian Architecture in Kansas

Richard Longstreth

Kansas is not well known for its Richardsonian work, or indeed for most of its buildings aside from generic images of grain elevators and plain wooden farm dwellings. The state is removed geographically, and some would argue culturally, from centers of architectural innovation. Kansas cities are not very large; this is a state of small towns (though every incorporated town is officially designated a "city") set amid vast expanses of agricultural land. Given these conditions, it is tempting for one not familiar with Richardsonian work there to postulate that it would be little more than an echo, one seldom expressed in a very sophisticated manner, and occurring, more likely than not, later than in places well recognized for their architectural achievements.

What is fundamentally wrong with this approach is not only that it places too much value on stereotypical assumptions, but that it posits Richardson's oeuvre as the one valid basis for architectural assessment, rather than examining the diffusion of the mode on its own terms. Influence contributes much to the stature of any architect, yet all too often most of the products are regarded in condescending terms. As a result, the reasons why an architect such as Richardson had a profound impact on design across the country and the richly varied nature of application and meaning at the local level are ignored. This approach further assumes a simplistic method of emulation to be the essential motivating force. In effect, one postulates that people in the heartland want to be up-to-date but lack much contact with the newest developments in a given field. Eventually they get wind of what has occurred elsewhere, perhaps only secondhand through the introduction of these developments to regional centers nearby. Without much awareness of the time that has elapsed since that tendency's inception, they adopt its trappings, cer-

tain that it is still quite the fashionable thing. This pattern does exist; however, it can take place anywhere—in cities as well as in outlying areas.

On the other hand, people in a remote region can absorb a tendency while it is still new, and they can use it for their own reasons. This is what occurred in Kansas, where Richardsonian design was rapidly and widely assimilated prior to 1890.[1] The process reflected not so much a desire to imitate Boston or any other one city as it did the drive to create a generalized image of metropolitan development. Locally, Richardsonian architecture became a hallmark of urban aspirations and material progress. Furthermore, it became a symbol of a maturing architectural profession in a young state. The persistence of the mode there was a testament to its success, but also indicative of shifts in objectives and mood that were occurring by the early twentieth century. Richardsonian architecture in Kansas hence provides a salient means to examine the complex, evolving nature of the place.

Richardson's influence in the state began early with work by nationally prominent architectural firms located far afield. In 1881 the Santa Fe and Union Pacific railroads commissioned Bostonian Henry van Brunt to design the public library in Topeka (fig. 100). Van Brunt had already gained a favorable reputation for his experience with this building type, and it is likely that the directors of both railroad companies, also headquartered in Boston, were involved in selecting him for the project. As realized, the library was among the most advanced in the nation, with a large stack area set adjacent to the reading room and a multipurpose auditorium above. The scheme also marked a turning point in van Brunt's designs, representing his initial experiment with the bold masses and simple forms he so admired in Richardson's building.[2]

Two years later the Santa Fe again embarked on

◄ 99 *(opposite)* **Proudfoot and Bird, Wichita City Hall, Wichita, Kansas, 1889-92**

▶ **100 Henry van Brunt,
Topeka Public Library,
Topeka, Kansas, 1881-83
(demolished 1961)**

▼ **101 Burnham and Root,
General Office of the
Atchison, Topeka & Santa Fe
Railroad, Topeka, Kansas
1883-84 (demolished
c. 1924)**

▶ **102 Van Brunt and Howe,
University of Kansas Library,
Lawrence, Kansas, 1893-94**

a significant building project, this time for its general offices located just down the street from the library (fig. 101). Once again, the company chose architects, Chicagoans Burnham and Root, who were closely identified with the building type. And, further paralleling the library commission, the Santa Fe offices constituted an early instance of Root's learning from Richardson, here giving a sense of order, unity, and strength to a large, blocky mass. At the time of their construction, both buildings were far more sophisticated in programmatic development and formal design attributes than anything else in the region. The client in each case retained some of the best specialized talent in the country, no doubt considering practitioners in the state and in adjacent Kansas City, Missouri, as ill-equipped for the task.[3]

The full impact of these two buildings on the local scene is difficult to assess fully; few subsequent works appear to have been directly derived from them.[4] Yet their presence, conspicuous through contrast, may well have fostered the setting of new standards in the area and induced a new sense of competitiveness among resident architects. Whatever the reasons, out-of-state practitioners seldom secured work in Kansas during the years of prolific building activity that followed. There were, of course, exceptions. Sometimes architects from elsewhere received commissions there because of established ties to a given business sphere or because they were known to cosmopolitan investors. Chicago's Cobb and Frost, for example, designed the Union Depot at Leavenworth (1886-88) and Watkins National Bank at Lawrence (1887-88). On occasion, too, outsiders were selected as the result of a competition, as was the case with H.C. Koch from Milwaukee for the Marshall County Courthouse at Marysville (1891-92), or Charles Sedgwick of Minneapolis for the high school at Arkansas City (1890-93).[5] However, these buildings are few in number and do not seem to have exerted a decisive influence on local patterns.

Among midwestern centers, Kansas City, Missouri, would be the most plausible candidate for cultural hegemony in the region. By the late 1880s, it was far larger than any place in Kansas and a fulcrum for much of its neighbor state's economic development.[6] Yet Kansas City had little direct impact on Kansas architecture. Practitioners in the metropolis eagerly sought work across the border, and throughout the late nineteenth century they comprised the largest contingent of architects listed in Kansas business directories. Among them, Henry van Brunt, who moved to Kansas City in 1887, secured commissions for Union Pacific depots in Junction City (c. 1890, demolished) and Lawrence (c. 1890) and, also at Lawrence, the University of Kansas Library (1893-94; figs. 102 and 103). But few colleagues enjoyed comparable, let alone greater, patronage in the state.[7] Kansans were determined to become self-sufficient in architecture as in a growing number of other realms.

From the early days of settlement, Kansas was marked by a strong sense of independence and pride. The once-common belief that the region comprised the "Great American Desert" was quickly supplanted by the image of an agricultural Eden once immigrants began to occupy the land in the 1850s. Promotional literature never failed to proclaim the state's abundance of rich soil, grazing land, and natural resources; the absence of forests to be cleared; the blessings of a moderate climate; or the resoluteness of the farming population. At the same time, town building was an equally intense pursuit, and the people attracted to these new towns tended to be aggressive and entrepreneurial. Competition between towns to dominate their precinct and, eventually, the region was as pronounced as it had been anywhere in the nation. Boosterism permeated this realm with each place trumpeting its ostensibly unequaled advantages and spectacular accomplishments.[8]

The actual situation, of course, could be very different. Many platted towns remained tiny enclaves or never materialized; many others grew only somewhat larger; none emerged as a true metropolis. Numerous Kansas residents no doubt viewed the prophesies enunciated by boosters with skepticism. Yet the very extent of promotional efforts and the very keen competition between communities could not help but engender a spirit of chauvinism. Given these circumstances, it is understandable that Kansans self-consciously sought to divest themselves of dependence upon interests elsewhere to the greatest extent possible. At a time when buildings ranked among the most valued emblems of material and cultural attainment, hiring an out-of-state architect to design an important work could well have been construed as an admission of weakness.

By the mid-1880s ample justification existed for an optimistic outlook. Following the tumultuous ter-

ritorial years, from 1854 to 1861, the decade following the Civil War was marked by economic instability, compounded by several severe droughts and insect plagues. After the mid-1870s, however, growth and prosperity predominated. Much of the state was now settled, farm production swelled, the population was rapidly increasing, and the percentage of urban inhabitants was mounting at an even faster rate. Building booms occurred in Topeka, Wichita, Kansas City (Kansas), and many other communities, with speculative activity reaching a height from 1886 to 1888. These places were seen as essential centers not only of processing and distribution, but also of manufacture. City leaders talked ever more of a time in the near future when Kansas would become a primary economic region in the United States—a major supplier of goods and among the country's most populous areas.[9]

This surge of urban expansion and buoyant predictions coincided with the time when Richardsonian buildings began to appear in number. This architecture was closely identified with cities and city building; it became a symbol of the transforming landscape, of prosperity, confidence, and the desire for a sophisticated metropolitan appearance. These buildings were also a conspicuous departure from the more elementary ones which had heretofore characterized much of the state's settlement and may now have been viewed as relics of the pioneer days. The greatest concentrations of Richardsonian architecture were in the state's two most important cities: Topeka and Wichita. While Kansas City, Kansas, had the largest population by 1890, it remained, at least perceptually, in the shadow of its Missouri namesake. Atchison and Leavenworth had long been leading centers; however, their position relative to others in the state markedly declined during the 1880s.[10] That decade saw Topeka rise to preeminence. Besides being the state capital, it became a major

▲ 103 University of Kansas, front gable

railroad, banking, retail, and distribution center. Manufacturing endeavors were launched, utilities installed at a feverish rate, and dozens of additions to the city platted. The range of these developments suggested a solid base for future greatness. The euphoric mood was epitomized by the words of one chronicler at the height of the boom:

> As the capital of the greatest State in the Union, she has attained a prominence not enjoyed by any other city, East or West, in politics, music, education, art, science, and the philosophy of progressive euchre. Topeka is at once a standard, a model and a marvel.... Once a village, now a metropolis...the center of a populous empire....the time is not far distant when Topeka will be the champion inland city on the map....no city in the whole country has exceeded her in rapidity of development or permanency of improvement.[11]

▲ 104 Quarried blocks of Cottonwood Falls limestone in stone yard, St. Mary's, Kansas

Wichita's rise seemed even more miraculous. Founded in 1870, the town contained almost 5,000 people ten years later, making it the sixth largest in the state. Spectacular growth occurred over the next decade. Population estimates ran as high as 48,000 in 1889 and, more realistically, were measured at about half that number in 1890 after the boom's end. Until then a tenacious citizenry had succeeded in creating extensive wholesale and retail trades, manufacturing plants, railroad lines, and educational institutions. Wichita became the undisputed center for southern and western portions of the state and for much of the territorial lands beyond.[12] In both Topeka and Wichita, the urban fabric was remade and extended severalfold before the boom's collapse. They were seen as modern cities, the most tangible evidence of the state's ascendant role and harbingers of an even more promising future.[13] As exemplars, Topeka and Wichita influenced the character of development in the small communities around them. The abundance of Richardsonian buildings in both centers no doubt stimulated the mode's swift acceptance throughout much of Kansas.

Several other factors probably contributed to the diffusion process. By the mid-1880s, Richardsonian design was becoming popular in the Midwest as well as in the East. To some observers, it was the basis of a new national style. Unlike High Victorian modes such as Queen Anne, Richardsonian design was readily adapted to numerous building types and to small, simple designs no less than to large, elaborate ones. Among architects, Richardson's premature death in 1886 may have added a sense of urgency to continuing his cause.[14] On the other hand, it is doubtful whether many Kansas clients knew of Richardson or his work. For them, Richardsonian design was in all likelihood seen as a striking new way to express modern conditions—there or anywhere else. Without the influx of new people and new capital to the state's communities, and without the optimistic, expansive mood that fueled the building boom, the mode's acceptance might well have occurred at a much slower pace.

Richardsonian architecture may have embodied a new era in Kansas, yet the mode was probably not perceived as a complete break from attributes already well established. Since the 1850s, the majority of the state's buildings had been designed in a simple, straightforward manner. Much of this work continued vernacular traditions of American neoclassicism. By the 1870s, Victorian modes began to have an impact, and into the next decade the most widely used mode for commercial and institutional buildings was Italianate. Here, too, elemental qualities remained prevalent. Highly ornate work was rare before the 1880s and, with few exceptions, confined to the handful of the state's aspiring cities.[15] Economic considerations no doubt played a role in restricting embellishment. Yet there is also evidence that many of the state's residents preferred simplicity in design, regarding this trait as more practical and appropriate to a diligent, hardworking society. When van Brunt's Topeka library design was unveiled, it engendered criticism, not because it was different, but because it was considered fussy. One account derided the scheme as "simply a grotesque pile of inharmonious colors and materials, designed after the ultra Queen Anne style and is as objectionable as well could be....It is a specimen of aesthetic taste...run into the ground."[16]

The agitated forms, panoply of motifs, and restless qualities endemic to so much High Victorian architecture may well have carried an aura of pretentiousness and affectation, and indeed been associated with aspects of East Coast culture that Kansans wished to avoid. In contrast, Richardsonian work at its best accommodated a taste for simplicity and forthright expression. The results could be picturesque without seeming impractical;

imposing without seeming ostentatious. Burnham and Root's Santa Fe offices were much admired in this regard. The exterior was depicted as a handsome and "fitting companion to the State Capitol" across the street.[17] Richardsonian architecture maintained respected values while offering a new sense of polish and sophistication. Such an outlook could only have been reinforced by the fact that the state's two most admired materials, stone and brick, were the very stuff of expression for this new mode.

Kansas was unusually well endowed with limestone. Deposits of more or less even quality and color (light buff) lay close to the surface throughout the eastern half of the state and were scattered in other sections as well (fig. 104). Contemporary accounts emphasized that the material could be easily cut, yet proved durable when exposed to the elements. These conditions enabled local limestone to be used extensively for building. By the 1870s, such work acquired symbolic overtones, representing the permanence and prosperity of settlement. One observer described Beloit as a "model young city built of this matchless material. Here are churches, hotels, stores, shops, school houses, banks, residences, and barns of stone from elegant flagging... to noble dimension blocks. It takes the finest finish, even to a brilliant polish.... They have built up Beloit

with unusual elegance and solidity." Limestone architecture was seen as a democratic phenomenon by its very extent. What was considered a luxury in numerous places, here was a material the common man could afford—"as if planned by the Great Architect to best serve the people of the whole state."[18] Unlike most High Victorian modes, Richardsonian

design seemed especially well suited to the broad, unornamented expanses of stonework that had become ubiquitous in the region. Local practices, in turn, had an effect on the interpretation of this new mode; work in Kansas tended to be less polychromatic and less encrusted with decoration than often was the case elsewhere.

The other salient material for Richardsonian buildings was, of course, brick. An abundant supply of shale clay led to a profusion of brick manufacturing concerns in Kansas during the post-Civil War years, and production steadily increased during the decades that followed.[19] Brick was not venerated like limestone but served as a respectable substitute. Furthermore, it could be much less expensive to use than dressed stone of any type. As a result brick was widely employed, often to good effect, for Richardsonian work in Kansas, giving planar crispness and subdued textural richness to the mode's simple forms.

Richardsonian design proved compatible with existing building practices in Kansas; however, it was not easily assimilated by established practitioners. With one exception, the leading designers in this mode were newcomers who settled in the state during the prosperous mid-1880s and who may have considered that work in this vein gave them a competitive edge. From a practical standpoint alone, these young men needed to be aggressive in pursuing their careers, for the local field had attracted many colleagues since the Civil War. Almost thirty architects are listed in an 1866 regional business directory. By the mid-1880s, their numbers were steadily increasing. Large communities supported several firms, and many smaller places had at least one. Thus for some time a substantial portion of the state's commercial, public, and religious buildings, as well as some of its large residences, were the products of individuals who called themselves architects.[20]

Few of the early arrivals were professionally trained. Most of them began in the building trades, and many continued to work in this capacity even after they assumed the more prestigious role of architect. Biographical details are scarce; however, published accounts are sufficient to suggest a general pattern in their careers. More often than not, these men were raised in rural areas in the East and Midwest. After acquiring trade skills, their lives tended to be itinerant. Some remained in Kansas for long periods; others stayed briefly. Most of

▼107 Haskell and Gunn, Douglas County Courthouse, Lawrence, Kansas, 1902-4, gable detail

▶108 Douglas County Courthouse

these people had little, if any, firsthand experience in major cities. The architecture they knew was that of towns and the countryside, supplemented by what must have been a limited number of plan books, builders' magazines, and manufacturers' catalogues. Richardsonian design belonged to a very different world, and it is unlikely that architect-builders in Kansas or anywhere else were inclined to work in this vein, at least until the realization of local examples made the vocabulary a familiar part of their own experience.

Members of the younger generation of Kansas architects who designed Richardsonian buildings differed from their elders in background and practice. Most of them had some professional training and had spent time in large cities. Once settled in Kansas, they worked exclusively as architects, distinguishing themselves from many of their predecessors and from a number of contemporaries as well. When the boom collapsed in the late 1880s, some of these men were able to maintain their practices; others left the state for ostensibly more fertile ground, but there were no reversions to the combined field of architect-builder. Richardsonian design was a hallmark of this maturing professionalism—the product of individuals who consciously pursued artistic no less than technical competence and who regarded themselves as belonging to an elite corps.

One figure was an exception to all of these general patterns: John G. Haskell, the elder statesman of Kansas architecture, who had been working there since the territorial period. Unlike most of his contemporaries, he enjoyed the benefits of higher education (Brown University) and professional training (with an unidentified Boston architect). In 1857, the death of his father, who had settled in Kansas with the rest of the family several years earlier, prompted Haskell's moving to Lawrence. After the Civil War, Haskell became architect of the capitol in Topeka. Subsequently he designed numerous other facilities for the state in addition to courthouses, schools, college buildings, churches, and commercial blocks.[22]

By the early 1880s, Haskell's practice was probably the largest and most prestigious in Kansas. He was also the first resident architect to draw from Richardsonian precedent. The Boswell Library at Topeka's Washburn University (1885-86) is a compact building and at the same time assertive in its display of Richardsonian elements, as if the designer wished to bury the past and demonstrate beyond any doubt that he could use this new vocabulary (fig. 105). A less erratic step, one more predictable given the architect's earlier work, is the concurrent design for Snow Hall at the University of Kansas (fig. 106). The building continues the region's plain style while incorporating a few chaste Richardsonian and other medievalizing details.[23] Buildings rendered in this simple manner marked Haskell's subsequent work during the next two decades. On occasion, however, a scheme such as the Douglas County Courthouse at Lawrence (1902-4; figs. 107 and 108) reflects more the spirit of massing and composition associated with the fully developed Richardsonian mode.

The extent to which Haskell himself was responsible for the designs of these projects remains unclear, but he may well have relied on the talents of younger assistants in at least some cases. The Boswell Library, for example, suggests the hand of Seymour Davis, who came to Topeka to join Haskell's office in 1883.[24] Details concerning Davis's background are meager. A Philadelphia native, he apparently learned carpentry there and attended the Pennsylvania Academy of Fine Arts in 1880.[25] After establishing an independent architectural prac-

▼ 109 Seymour Davis, Adair Building, Kansas State Insane Asylum, Osawatomie, Kansas, c. 1893-94 (demolished), early view

American Architect and Building News

◄ 110 *(opposite)* Seymour Davis, Library and Science (now Fairchild) Hall, Kansas State University, Manhattan, Kansas, 1893-94

▲ 111 *(top)* Seymour Davis, project for a Unitarian Church, c. 1891, drawing by Davis

▲ 112 *(right)* Seymour Davis, Crawford Building, Topeka, Kansas, 1887-88, early view

◄ 113 Proudfoot and Bird, Garfield (now Friends) University, Wichita, Kansas, 1886-88, early view

tice about 1886, Davis soon rose to the front ranks of the field during Topeka's boom years, securing commissions for new office buildings, several of the city's largest residences, and the Kansas Building at the 1893 World Columbian Exposition.

Youthful and ambitious, Davis picked up new ideas quickly. While his biggest debt was to Rich-ardson during these years, he was also inclined to experiment, creating, on occasion, work in a distinct personal idiom. During his 1893-95 tenure as State Architect, he designed the Library and Science (now Fairchild) Hall at Kansas State University (1893-94), which is an eloquent tribute to the master's work (fig. 110). At the same time, the Adair

▲ 114 Proudfoot and Bird, Wichita City Hall, Wichita, Kansas, 1889-92, elevation detail above entry

▶ 115 Wichita City Hall, 1906 view

◄116 J.C. Holland, Topeka
High School, Topeka,
Kansas, c. 1893-94 (demol-
ished c. 1931), early view

Building at the State Hospital in Osawatomie (c. 1893-94) suggests Davis's refusal to rely on formulas (fig. 109). The scheme employs an unusual arrangement, with a hierarchy of service spaces attached as if they were saddlebags onto a long box housing open wards, to create a bold exterior form that mitigates the uniformity often resulting from such a program.[26] An earlier unexecuted project for a Unitarian church (c. 1891) is among the architect's most unorthodox schemes, exhibiting a taste for clarity in expression and, at the same time, a love of exaggerated picturesqueness perhaps inspired by the drawings of Harvey Ellis, who was then working for Eckel and Mann in nearby St. Joseph, Missouri (fig. 111).[27]

Indeed, Davis was continually searching for new ways to resolve a scheme. Four Topeka office buildings, designed in 1887 and 1888, are all about the same size and draw from Richardsonian examples, yet each employs its own method of composing the facade. One of the most interesting solutions was developed for the Crawford Building (1887-88), where a balance is sought between composing the street elevations as piled layers and as a unified vertical block (fig. 112).[28] Davis ranks among the most creative architects to practice in Kansas during the nineteenth century, and for a while, there was a

steady demand for his services. However, he was either unwilling or unable to ride out the depression of the 1890s. After completing his term as State Architect, Davis returned to Philadelphia, where he remained for the rest of his life.

Two other young architects who made a conspicuous start in Kansas were Willis Proudfoot and George Washington Bird. Even less is known about their early lives than of Davis's. Proudfoot was born in Iowa and may have attended M.I.T. for one semester in 1884. He arrived in Wichita and established a practice during the early months of 1885. Proudfoot was soon joined by Bird, who came from Philadelphia. By the end of that year, the office had received numerous commissions, and, like Davis's, it rapidly gained a prominent reputation.[29] One of their early projects was for the newly formed Garfield (now Friends) University (1886-88), an immense pile, more elaborate than any other educational facility in the state at that time, located at Wichita's western fringe (fig. 113).[30] As is characteristic of much of the firm's work, the scheme employs a more-or-less Richardsonian vocabulary, while maintaining the High Victorian penchant for agitated vertical masses. The effect is restless and filled with energy—appropriate for an upstart institution—while enough was learned from Richardson to give the building coherence.

A more forceful integration of these qualities came with Proudfoot and Bird's competition-winning entry for the Wichita City Hall (1890-92; figs. 99, 114 and 115). Departing from regional patterns, the city commissioners were determined to erect a conspicuous landmark for the municipal government, and this design clearly rises to the occasion.[31] Height is matched by compactness. These factors, necessitated by an ambitious program and constrained site, are set in tension by an unrelenting sequence of corner turrets, a center section at once robust and fanciful, and an elongated tower. Bold forms are matched by large-scale details. Without being set apart in an open square, as were most midwestern courthouses, the building itself stands as a forceful civic presence amid what was then a dense mercantile landscape. But even before the City Hall was dedicated, its architects won the competition for a much larger counterpart in Salt Lake City. As with many other recent arrivals, Proudfoot and Bird left Kansas once the boom ended, never to return.[32]

The virtuoso performances of Davis, Proudfoot, and Bird were short-lived and largely concentrated in their respective cities. The offices of J.C. Holland and George Washburn, on the other hand, sustained long-lasting and wide-ranging practices

in the state. Both men remained faithful to Richardsonian precedent into the twentieth century and through their designs left a distinctive mark on the regional landscape. Holland was among the best-trained architects to establish a practice in Kansas before 1900. He spent three years apprenticed to a carpenter in his native Lima, Ohio, one year as a draftsman for a Toledo architect, another five as a contractor, two years at Northwestern Ohio University, and two more at Cornell's school of architecture. Holland moved to Topeka in 1885, entering a partnership with C.B. Hopkins. Four years later he established an independent office which was continued by his son after his death. Holland served as State Architect (1895-97) and architect to the Santa Fe Railroad (1897-98). He also designed numerous projects for the Wells Fargo Express Company.[33] Although starting on his own at the time of the boom's collapse, Holland developed a solid practice, making a specialty of public buildings, and it was in large part through this work that he became known statewide. An important early commission in this respect was the Topeka High School (c. 1893-94), considered a model facility of its type (fig. 116). The building also exhibits Holland's typically restrained and respectful use of the Richardsonian vocabulary, even though here picturesqueness supplants unity above the

▸117 J.C. Holland, Shawnee County Courthouse, Topeka, Kansas, 1893-94 (demolished 1965), early view

◄118 Holland and Squires, Osborne County Courthouse, Osborne, Kansas, 1907-8

▼119 Osborne County Courthouse, entry detail

◄120 J.C. Holland, Junction City High School, Junction City, Kansas, 1903-4

cornice line.

Even more influential for Kansas architecture was Holland's design for the nearby Shawnee County Courthouse (1893-94; fig. 117). This was one of the architect's most spirited works, unusual not only in its vigorous modeling of form but in its exuberant polychromy with striations of the ubiquitous native limestone set between red sandstone. Aside from the State Capitol and the Sedgwick County Courthouse in Wichita (1888-90), this was the costliest building yet erected for general public use in Kansas, and for some time it remained among the most lavish in design and appointments.[34] However, perhaps far more than Richardson's courthouse in Pittsburgh or the many others that emulated that building in other regions, the design set the standard among Kansans for the type. Again and again, Holland adapted the scheme to the more modest requirements and budgets of the eleven

other judicial facilities he designed across the state between 1898 and 1911 (figs. 118 and 119).[35] These projects may be less compelling, more straightforward exercises in what had by then become an idiom, but nevertheless they attuned that idiom well to their small-town settings. In this milieu, Holland was the consummate professional. He did not experiment. When designing courthouses and other public buildings such as the high school at Junction City (1903-4), he gave new focus, even monumentality, to a place while creating a dignified image that epitomized public decorum (fig. 120).

George Washburn also built much of his reputation on courthouses, designed during roughly the same period as those by Holland. He, too, developed a more-or-less standard pattern for many of these buildings. Yet Washburn's work adhered less

to Richardsonian models, relying more on popularized High Victorian conventions to which Richardsonian motifs were applied. The amalgam might be expected considering the architect's background. Washburn was at least ten years older than Davis, Proudfoot, Bird, or Holland. The son of a builder-architect, he spent much of his youth on a Missouri farm. He learned carpentry and other building trades in Quincy, Illinois, attending night classes in drawing at Bryant and Stratton's Commercial College. Apparently he also took a course in some of the practical aspects of architecture through the International Correspondence Schools. From 1878 to 1882, Washburn supervised the construction of out-of-state projects designed by Cross and Taylor, the oldest and most respected architectural firm in Kansas City, Missouri. Thereafter, he settled in Kansas—not in one of the upstart cities, but in the

considerably smaller town of Ottawa, where he remained in independent practice until retirement
some twenty-five years later.[36] All these circumstances suggest that Washburn's world was anchored
in provincial settings and his career in the tradition
of the highly skilled artisan who worked hard eventually to gain professional status.

Washburn could employ a fairly extensive reper-
toire of Richardsonian details. But even in such
cases, as with the First Baptist Church in Ottawa
(1886-87), the basic forms are general to the
period and the given building type (fig. 121). And, in
contrast to Holland, he never seems to have been
content to follow high-style patterns alone. Washburn
was at his best when mixing sources, developing a
personal manner which appears in part to have
been predicated on a preference for brick. Cost
was probably not a central factor. Washburn's courthouses tend to be as expensive as Holland's, sometimes more so.[37] The architect may have found it
easier to find good bricklayers than stonemasons;
or he may have been partial to the aesthetic qualities of brick, including the polychromatic effects
resulting from its use with limestone trim; or the
choice may simply have been a matter of habit,
based upon years of working with that material in
various High Victorian modes. Whatever the rea-

sons, Washburn nurtured a lively style, at first play-
ing Queen Anne elements against Richardsonian
ones, as with the Franklin County Courthouse at
Ottawa (1891-93; fig. 122). A decade later, the Richardsonian patterns remain clear, while many details
are now inspired by contemporary classical work,
as can be seen with the Butler County Courthouse
at El Dorado (1908-9; fig. 123). Throughout this
evolving sequence, Washburn consistently imbued
his work with a vivacious character rooted in High
Victorian design. The academic world, no less than
that of Richardson, was mined for embellishment,
but not for salient qualities of expression.

The careers of these five architects indicate patterns shared by their colleagues who also contributed to the widespread use of Richardsonian design in Kansas. A few members of the old guard,
such as Theodore Lescher, adopted the mode on
occasion. Newcomers such as Alfred Gould in Wichita came and went with the building boom of the
1880s. Others such as John Stanton of Topeka remained and became respected for their work in the
public sphere. Finally, practitioners such as Charles
W. Squires settled in smaller communities—in his
case, Emporia—where they designed in a manner
more closely related to that of the architect-builder.[38]
Richardsonian design in Kansas was never mono-

▲ 123 *(left)* George P. Wash-
burn and Son, Butler County
Courthouse, El Dorado,
Kansas, 1908-9

▲ 124 *(right)* Architect
unknown, American National
Bank Building, Arkansas
City, Kansas, 1886 (altered),
early view

▲125 *(left)* Dumont and Hayward, Zimmerly Building, Wichita, Kansas, 1887-88 (demolished 1956), early view

▲126 *(right)* J.C. Holland, Ness County Bank, Ness City, Kansas, 1888-90

lithic, nor was it ever dominated by a single figure or school. From the start, the work was developed in various ways by persons differing in background and style. Many of the buildings were concentrated in the state's major centers; however, examples abound in smaller places just as early and just as late. And, just as the diffusion process was multifaceted, so it affected both public and private sectors, manifesting itself in a spectrum of building types.

No more extensive use of Richardsonian design occurred than in the commercial sphere where it was employed for banks, retail establishments, office blocks, and hotels. Since these buildings were highly prized as markers of urban progress and the mode carried similar associations, it is not surprising to find examples early on in places where aspirations and the competitive spirit ran high. Before either Topeka or Wichita had Richardsonian commercial buildings, for example, the American National Bank (1886) was erected in Arkansas City (fig. 124). The town experienced a population increase of more than 800 percent during the 1880s and hopes for rivaling Wichita as a regional center seemed well founded.[39] The building itself was as imposing as any of its type yet realized in the state. Wichita soon assumed the lead, however, with construction of several four- and five-story office blocks that might well have been significant additions to cities several times its size (fig. 125).[40]

The drive among communities to outdo one another affected much smaller settlements as well. Ness City was one of many towns harboring new commercial projects that embodied the vision of local entrepreneurs—men who believed their home would someday become a place of import (figs. 126 and 127). The depression put an end to such ventures, and when the economic situation improved by the late 1890s, the architecture of cities and towns became more differentiated. Richardsonian design lost its currency for commercial work in the largest centers, where counterparts in Chicago, St. Louis, Kansas City, and other metropolises tended to set the example.[41] On the other hand, the mode enjoyed some resurgence in the more provincial atmosphere of the small town, where new buildings were often rendered in much the same vein as they had been more than a decade earlier.

Railroad companies enhanced the popularity of Richardsonian architecture in Kansas; however, they do not appear to have played a major role. By 1890, Atchison, Leavenworth, Topeka, and Wichita each had at least one such station. Atchison's Union Depot (fig. 128) and Wichita's Santa Fe Depot (both c. 1890) rank among the finest expositions of Richardsonian design in the state, recalling the elaborate libraries Richardson had designed in New England a decade earlier.[42] Yet these are isolated examples. For the great majority of their stations, railroad companies were loathe to invest more than a minimum expenditure. Enormous outlays were already being made to repay debts, construct trackage, con-

◄127 Ness County Bank,
corner columns

solidate lines, and develop new markets. Furthermore, a community's future prospects could fluctuate as much as the returns on crops and the other goods the railroads carried. A division office, such as that for the Rock Island in Herrington (1887, 1906; fig. 129), could receive greater funding, and the Union Pacific created model stations in Lawrence and Junction City (both c. 1890) just before the depression. Otherwise, facilities were of simple, standardized design, constructed of wood, and without high-style overtones until the 1910s.[43]

If the depot was seldom an accurate gauge of the railroad's importance to the region, the architecture of institutions was quite another matter. Buildings for universities, colleges, academies, and public schools in Kansas generally represented large investments—sometimes larger than the institution itself warranted. Work in this realm was of great consequence both in the initial diffusion of Richardsonian design and in the mode's longevity. Kansans had always placed a high value on education, at least in principle, and perhaps an even higher value on the status associated with having centers of learning in one's own community. Booster publications seldom failed to cite these facilities as significant assets of a place. Private colleges and universities were the most aggressive in procuring plans for imposing quarters during the boom years. Garfield University ranked first in this regard; however, it was only one of six designed for Wichita and nearby Newton in 1886-87 alone.[44] Over the next few years, Richardsonian piles were erected for other new institutions in Atchison, Salina, and Sterling as well as for established ones in Ottawa and Topeka.[45] Wichita also took the lead during the late

1880s in erecting public schools—most of them by Proudfoot and Bird (fig. 130)—which were widely emulated.[46] Prior to Holland's admired high school in Topeka, costly ones had been completed in Arkansas City, Lawrence, and Effingham—the latter to serve the rural populace of Atchison County.[47] Only after the mid-1890s did Richardsonian design become a basic staple of the state university at Lawrence and especially at the agricultural college at Manhattan.[48] Together with courthouses, these latter buildings comprise the most conspicuous corpus of Richardsonian architecture in Kansas today. Rather than representing the infusion of a new idea, they are testaments to the perpetuation of one well founded.

The persistence of Richardsonian design at the state level was fostered by the creation of the State Architect's office in 1891, a post then unique in the region. For the next two decades, the men who ran this office played either key or supporting roles in popularizing the mode. Haskell, Davis, Holland, and Lescher served two-year terms in that order, followed by Stanton, who remained from 1899 to 1909.[49] The position carried prestige and offered a welcome source of income during the depression years, but it also became an instrument by which to influence practices in design around the state.

There was, of course, no centralized authority determining the character of county courthouse design; however, county rivalries led to a desire to conform, thus yielding comparable results. Prior to the 1890s, elaborate courthouses in Kansas were the exception, and in a number of cases the necessary quarters were contained on the upper floors of commercial buildings.[50] With the start of economic recovery at the end of the 1890s came a wave of new courthouse construction, almost all of which was Richardsonian. In county after county commissioners planned for an impressive building that would be a centerpiece of the town and a long-term symbol of progress. Following what had become a common practice in the United States, these men often visited other

▼128 *(left)* Perkins and Adams, Union Depot, Atchison, Kansas, c. 1890 (demolished), early view with retouched tower and roof outline

▼129 *(right)* Architect unknown, Rock Island Depot, Herrington, Kansas, 1887, 1906

facilities in-state and beyond to determine the features, visual qualities, and even the architect they wanted. In the building campaigns that followed, counties sought not so much to upstage as to emulate one another. Singularity became less important than following a common standard. In all but a few cases these buildings were designed by either Holland or Washburn, both of whom proved adept at political maneuvering and at capitalizing on their respective records in public building design. County commissioners in at least one case went so far as to request a scheme from Holland that was "as near as practicable" to several others he had done, and they received a near replica.[51] Washburn's courthouses were more varied, but nonetheless adhered to a common formula.[52]

The underlying causes of this trend to perpetuate things is difficult to pinpoint. A central factor may well have been a growing conservatism in the state. After forty years of rapid growth, the population stabilized during the 1890s and increased only slightly over the next decade. Missouri, Minnesota, Wisconsin, Illinois, the Dakotas, Colorado, Oklahoma, and Texas all experienced higher population growth rates between 1900 and 1910. The rate of increase was sharper in Kansas's largest cities, but the gap between them and the metropolises of the central United States steadily widened, and the vast majority of population centers remained under 3,000.[53] The idea that Kansas would become a pivotal manufacturing and trade center for the nation must have seemed ever less realistic. Development in towns also may have become less motivated by the desire to become a city. The state was prosperous enough to build and build well; however, with the decrease in the influx of ambitious people to push for rapid change, building as one had built before occurred more often.

The growing conservative tone is reflected in the fact that Kansans did not embrace the academic movement with nearly the speed or the enthusiasm they had Richardsonian design. In the public and institutional sectors especially, the refined classicism that was becoming a hallmark elsewhere was slow to be accepted in Kansas. Richardsonian architecture may have been considered more appropriate to the place, more solid and stable, more suited to the continued use of favored rough-faced limestone—a mode less showy and less "Eastern." Not until the 1910s did academic design begin to make a conspicuous showing in the state,

and even then, much of the work was markedly plainer than was to be found in many other parts of the country.[54] And in many cases, too, after vestiges of picturesqueness fell from fashion, when a classicizing symmetry and sense of order prevailed, the effect remained elemental, rugged, and ever so faintly Richardsonian (fig. 131). New design can be welcomed when all things seem possible, less so when conditions stabilize or the future seems less certain. In Kansas the architecture had not changed so much as the mood of the populace. ✖

▲ 130 *(top)* Proudfoot and Bird, McCormick School, Wichita, Kansas, 1889-90

▲ 131 *(bottom)* Commercial buildings, Junction City, Kansas, early twentieth century

The Richardsonian Interlude in Texas: A Quest for Meaning and Order at the end of the Nineteenth Century

Kenneth A. Breisch

Although the influence of Henry Hobson Richardson's Romanesque Revival first appeared in Texas in the mid-1880s, it did not become widespread until the following decade and had already begun to wane by the end of the century.[1] Despite its short-lived career, however, it proved to be of major significance. Among its progeny, for example, can be numbered several of the state's best-known monuments: the Ellis County Courthouse in Waxahachie, the Driskill Hotel in Austin, the Bexar County Courthouse in San Antonio, and the Ashbel Smith Building ("Old Red") in Galveston. Its introduction into the state in the late 1880s represented an early attempt by the still-nascent Texas architectural profession to promote a self-consciously intellectualized and "modern" style, as well as a distinctly regional iconography, representative of the type of local bravado—or chauvinism—long associated with residents of the Lone Star State.

With the exception of the depression of the mid-1890s, the decade and a half that coincided with the popularity of the Richardsonian style in Texas generally comprises an era of prosperity and growth. The state's preeminence in the cattle trade and its expanding cotton production assured it a strong economic base, and the growth of the railroads during this period only helped to secure this foundation. Between 1880 and 1890, the value of manufactured goods produced annually rose more than four-and-a-half times, and the population nearly doubled, transforming Texas into the seventh most populous state in the Union by the turn of the century.[2]

This was also a period of political unrest and change. The strongly populist, antimonopoly platform of the People's Party, for example, helped to nurture a mood of reform in state as well as local politics. This culminated in the 1890s with the passage of strong antitrust and regulatory legislation by the Democratically controlled state government.[3] The populist movement also served to further reinforce and focus a traditional, regional independence and pride that had long been evident in the state.

A similar mood of reform can be perceived in the actions of the state's most prominent architects, who, following the lead of the Western Association of Architects in Chicago, met in Austin early in 1886 to form the Texas State Association of Architects.[4] A primary goal of this group was to solidify their status as professionals through self-promotion and legislatively enforced regulation. If they were to flourish as architects, argued James Wahrenberger at their meetings in 1889 and again the following year, they would have to set themselves apart from the contracting and building trades; nonprofessionals, who were "producing nine cases out of ten piles of brick and mortar, turrets and towers, without lines of grace and beauty—modern Queen Anne, Americanized Renaissance and other blackguardisms."[5] This separation could be accomplished by introducing a system for registering architects into the state and also, in order to display the architects' specialized skills as designers, by employing a new, "modern" style of building appropriate to an "age of steam cars and electricity."[6] To fill this demand for a new style, many members of the group, including architects such as Nicholas Clayton, Alfred Giles, James Riely Gordon, Eugene T. Heiner, and Jasper N. Preston, soon turned to Henry Hobson Richardson for inspiration.

The first major building in Texas boldly to exhibit any Richardsonian features was the Driskill Hotel by Jasper N. Preston and Son (1885-86; fig. 133). This hotel opened in Austin just nine months after the death of Richardson in December 1886. While

◄ **132** *(opposite)* **James Riely Gordon, Ellis County Courthouse, Waxahachie, Texas, 1894-96**

▲ **133 J.N. Preston and Son, Driskill Hotel, Austin, Texas, 1885-86, view shortly after completion**

Courtesy Amon Carter Museum, Fort Worth

Courtesy Amon Carter Museum, Fort Worth

▲134 *(left)* Nicholas J. Clayton, Ashbel Smith Building, University of Texas Medical School, Galveston, Texas, 1889

▲135 *(right)* Nicholas J. Clayton, Colonel Walter Gresham House, Galveston, Texas, 1888-92

▶136 James Riely Gordon, Clifford Building, San Antonio, Texas, 1890 (demolished), view shortly after completion

its massive round arches clearly owed a debt to the master's own work, its fussy, if somewhat amusing, ornament and proliferation of porches and gables tended to obscure their effect. Still, at the time it was hailed as being "without doubt the purest example of [the Romanesque style of architecture] to be found in this part of the country."[7] Its multiple

porches, moreover, were a result of the Prestons' attempt to adapt the building to Austin's hot southern climate. A further concession to this climate was the inclusion in the plan of a central courtyard and fountain (no longer extant), which were described in 1894 as being "quite similar to many Spanish places of the kind."[8] Despite the building's prominence the design of the Driskill does not seem to have been immediately influential, and the Prestons themselves moved their practice to California the year of the Driskill's completion.

Somewhat more Richardsonian in overall effect was Nicholas J. Clayton's Ashbel Smith Building for the University of Texas Medical School at Galveston (fig. 134), which was designed in 1889 following an investigation by the architect of medical colleges in Philadelphia, New York, and Boston. Clayton's use of the round arch, especially the massive character of the semicircular arcades that flank the entry porch, parallels contemporary eastern examples of the Richardsonian style.[9] In spite of the prominent Richardsonian arcades, however, the Ashbel Smith Building, with its proliferation of vertical elements and layering of polychromatic arches and decorative wall planes, exhibits a complexity and exuberance that likewise might be related to a High Victorian "Gothic" aesthetic. Although this may betray the influence of Richardson's own earlier designs for buildings such as the R. and F. Cheney Building (1875-76) in Hartford, Connecticut, or the Winn Memorial

Library (1876-79) in Woburn, Massachusetts, it also would seem to reflect Clayton's own strong predilection for Gothic, as opposed to Richardsonian, compositional motifs. This High Victorian bias is evident throughout the work produced by him between 1880 and 1900, including his "round-arched," but even less Richardsonian, designs for Sacred Heart Church in Galveston (1884-92) or a series of schools, which he erected in the same city around 1890.

A similar aesthetic is discernible in the other major Richardsonian work that Clayton erected in Galveston, the Colonel Walter Gresham House (1888-92; fig. 135). Here, in a manner reminiscent of both Richardson and several later designs of John Wellborn Root, Clayton mixes Medieval Romanesque and French Renaissance motifs. The overall form of the Gresham House and even its stony quality, in fact, may be related to Root's Edward E. Ayer House (1885-86), which was published in the *Inland Architect and News Record* in 1887.[10] The lavishness of the granite, limestone, and red sandstone masonry might be considered to be in the Richardsonian vein, but, again, the complexity of the building's surfaces and silhouette, in spite of their lithic quality and Richardsonian sense of volume, exude little of the feeling of repose that we normally associate with the later work of the master.

Not surprisingly, perhaps, the designs for several early Richardsonian commercial buildings in Texas also appear to owe as much to the Chicago School as they do to Richardson. In Dallas, for example, A.B. Bristol's Sanger Brothers Complex (c.1888), with its prominent central pavilion and bay windows, suggests contemporary office buildings in Chicago, especially those designed by Burnham and Root.[11] The early Richardsonian commercial buildings of the San Antonio architect James Riely Gordon, on the other hand, while still to some degree looking to the Windy City, are far more original, if somewhat more Victorian. Only very rarely did he borrow an overall compositional scheme directly from Richardson. This he did in his design for the Clifford Building of 1890 (fig. 136), which derived its arcade from Richardson's F. L. Ames Store (1886-87) in Boston.[12] Even here, however, Gordon added a belvedere to his composition. This element imparted a Spanish or Mediterranean character to the building, a quality that pervaded this San Antonio architect's later Richardsonian work.

During the first years of the 1890s Gordon

◀ 137 James Riely Gordon, Proposed Store for the Kampmann Estate, San Antonio, Texas, 1894, unsigned office drawing

▼ 138 Burnham and Root, The Phoenix Building, Chicago, Illinois, 1885-87 (demolished), drawing by H.D. Nichols

American Architect and Building News

▲139 *(left)* James Riely Gordon, Wright Building, San Antonio, Texas, 1890-91 (demolished), view shortly after completion

▲140 *(right)* Office of the Supervising Architect of the Treasury, United States Courthouse and Post Office, San Antonio, Texas, 1887-90 (demolished), early post-card view

broke ground on half a dozen other commercial structures, all of which are marked by a bold and inventive use of the Richardsonian arch. This motif first emerged most forcefully in his 1890 design for the Kennedy Building in San Antonio, where the ground floor opens into a single, yawning archway of a type noted by James Fergusson in 1891 as especially characteristic of "the later Richardsonian school."[13]

Similar archways dominate his renderings for a store for the Kampmann Estate, reproduced in the *American Architect and Building News* (fig. 137) in 1894, and his facade of Temple Emanu-El, a building erected in Dallas in 1898-99. These arches are reminiscent, in both their forms and rich use of ornament, of archways employed by John Wellborn Root on structures such as the Rookery (1885-88) or Phoenix Building (1885-87) in Chicago. The Phoenix Building (fig. 138), in particular, exhibits an arched entryway that invites comparison with that of the Kampmann block. In response, perhaps, to contemporary illustrations of Root's work, which tended to isolate the arch, Gordon uses it as the dominant thematic element in his designs, whereas the Chicago architect employed this motif as the ornamental focal point of a much larger composition.[14]

In Gordon's larger structures, such as his Wright (1890-91; fig. 139) and Alamo Fire Insurance Company (1890-92) buildings in San Antonio, he also turned to Chicago for inspiration, often articulating

his central bays with arcades, balconies, oriels, and gables in the manner of Root or William Le Baron Jenney. In response to San Antonio's climate, and perhaps following the lead of the Driskill Hotel in Austin, Gordon opened up many of his central bays as porches or loggias in order to better ventilate his buildings during the summer months.[15] Evolving designs appropriate for Texas's southwestern climate was a concern that continued to shape Gordon's adoption of Richardsonian motifs throughout the nineties.

The Panic of 1893, however, appears to have cut short any more immediate regional interpretations of Richardson's Romanesque style in the commercial arena. It was, rather, in the field of public architecture, which continued to be constructed throughout the depression years of the 1890s, that the most significant of these variations were to evolve. An important building in this realm, which signaled not only the introduction of Richardson's style into Texas but also its regionally oriented adaptation, was the San Antonio Courthouse and Post Office (1887-90, demolished; fig. 140). This was designed in late 1886 or early 1887 in the Office of the Supervising Architect of the Treasury in Washington under the direction of Mifflin E. Bell, and the bulk of its construction was superintended by James Riely Gordon. A rendering of this building along with a design for a new Galveston Custom House, which also exhibited some Richardsonian characteristics, was published in the *American Architect and Building News* in 1887.[16] Although labeled as "modified Moresque," the San Antonio building presented a much more direct example of Richardson's style than any other building erected in Texas during the 1880s. It also acted as an important catalyst for the ultimate acceptance of this fashion as an idiom appropriate for other public and governmental buildings in the state.

In response to San Antonio's summer heat, the second story of the Courthouse and Post Office's main facade, facing Alamo Plaza, incorporated a long, open Romanesque arcade. Although similar porches and loggias were incorporated into the main elevations of a number of other federal buildings erected in Texas during this period, none were nearly as Richardsonian in character. They all, however, seemed to reflect the general concern of the Supervising Architect's Office for evolving some type of regionally appropriate designs and associations for their structures. Bell himself was from the Midwest and, according to Montgomery Schuyler, believed that "Eastern conventionalities had had altogether too much sway in the previous conduct of the [Supervising Architect's] office...." In reaction to this, he stated, he intended "to embody 'Western ideas' in [his] public buildings."[17] This attitude not only introduced designs tailored to the Texas climate but also appears to have affected the office's choice of a Spanish and/or Moorish style for four of its late nineteenth-century Texas buildings: those at San Antonio (1887-90), Galveston (c.1886-92), Houston (1887-91), and El Paso (1888-92).[18] At San Antonio, in particular, the "modified Moresque" details included, in addition to the arcaded loggias, low-hipped roofs and a castellated and balconied tower, which—a la Richardson's Brattle Square Church in Boston (1869-73)—was originally intended to exhibit a carved frieze representing scenes from San Antonio history. This was supposed to have been supplied by Gordon but was never executed.

Significantly, even though Gordon would later

become the most proficient and successful practitioner of a regionally oriented Richardsonian style in Texas, it was the Moorish influence of structures such as the new Galveston and Houston Federal Buildings, and not the more Romanesque details of San Antonio's Courthouse and Post Office, that would have the most immediate impact on his work. In 1889, for example, he designed the Aransas County Courthouse in Rockport as a "Moresque" temple, reminiscent of the Houston Federal Building, replete with onion domes and horseshoe arches. Several of his residential commissions of this same year exhibited similar Hispano-Moorish motifs and polychromy. These included two large residences of 1889-90 in San Antonio for Mrs. W. E. Lowry

▲ 141 James Riely Gordon, Thaddeus M. Smith Residence, San Antonio, Texas, c. 1892-94 (demolished), unsigned office watercolor rendering

▼ 142 James Riely Gordon, Fayette County Courthouse, LaGrange, Texas, 1890-91, skyline of tower and gables

and W.B. Wright. More of a melding of Moresque motifs with a Richardsonian monumentality is evident in Gordon's slightly later designs for the Benjamin F. Yoakum (c.1890-91) and Thaddeus Smith (c.1892-94; fig. 141) houses, both of which were erected in San Antonio.[19]

Although it was being employed quite freely all across the country at this time, Gordon's choice of the "Moresque" style in both Aransas County and San Antonio probably related, at least in part, to Texas's own Spanish past. San Antonio, in particular, maintained a strong identification with this aspect of its heritage. During the 1880s, for example, many of the city's leading citizens were investing in the San Antonio and Aransas Pass Railroad, which was known at the "Mission Route" and was intended to connect San Antonio directly with Rockport on the Gulf of Mexico.[20]

More Richardsonian and compelling than the Aransas County Courthouse or his San Antonio residences was Gordon's design for the Fayette County Courthouse in LaGrange of 1890 (fig. 142).[21] In contrast to the Aransas building, but in emulation of Richardson's Allegheny County Courthouse in Pittsburgh, Gordon shifted the clock tower at LaGrange from its more traditional central location to a position over the main entry portal. In an attempt to increase light and ventilation, and likewise following the Allegheny County Courthouse precedent, Gordon also placed an open courtyard in the center of the building. Around this he constructed the body of his structure in the form of a double-armed Greek cross.

The exterior of Gordon's building was covered with richly polychromatic Richardsonian checkerboard patterns and voussoirs of blue Muldoon and red Pecos sandstones and white Belton limestone (fig. 143). The entries were flanked with clustered colonettes of polished, pink Burnett granite. Even more than in the work of Clayton, this colorful lithic display, which was unprecedented in Texas, evokes Richardson's "High Victorian" designs of the 1870s. This relationship is especially evident in the heavy geomorphic quality of Gordon's polychromatic voussoirs, which recall those on the porch of Richardson's Winn Memorial Library in Woburn, Massachusetts, or the arcades of his R. and F. Cheney Building in Hartford, Connecticut. Gordon's north and south entryways, too, with their banded arches set beneath gables with curling dragons at the eaves, seem directly to mimic the entries to the

Cheney block. At the same time Gordon's polychromatic voussoirs and stilted arches still can be related, at least in part, to his Moorish projects of the late 1880s.

In spite of the intensely lithic character of these masonry details, the overall massing of Gordon's Fayette County Courthouse, as well as of the Yoakum and Smith residences, incorporated few of the lessons of mature Richardsonian composition. The walls of the Fayette County Courthouse, in particular, in spite of their massive voussoirs and rusticated masonry, appear thin and two-dimensional and the water table too weak to support the superstructure. The individual pavilions, as well, seem awkwardly clustered and their insistent verticality closely related to several other early, if less exotic, Texas excursions into the Richardsonian Romanesque, such as the Driskill Hotel or Orlopp and Kusener's Dallas County Courthouse (fig. 144), which, like Gordon's LaGrange building, was begun in 1890.[22]

In this latter structure, Orlopp and Kusener, who at the time were working out of Little Rock, Arkansas, attempted to emphasize both the volume and weight of their massive red sandstone building by setting it on a monumental, battered foundation and by reinforcing this at the corners with huge, buttresslike turrets. In the tradition of Richardson, the whole composition is visually bound together by a proliferation of horizontal string courses and window transoms of blue granite, as well as by the continuous arcades that wrap themselves around the structure. Unfortunately, even these Richardsonian devices cannot overcome the disquietude caused by the profusion of fanciful towers, turrets, gargoyles, and dormers and the fussiness of the Queen Anne lantern that once crowned the roofline.

Gordon, too, attempted to place more emphasis on horizontality in his next Texas courthouse, which was begun in Victoria in 1891 (fig. 145). Here, he and his new partner, D. Ernest Laub, added a one-story arcade around the base of the building.[23] Awkward as this may have been, the horizontality of this loggia, combined with that of the prominent checkerboard frieze encircling the central cube of the composition, helped to counter the verticality of the pavilions and tower and to tie together the still disparate elements of the main body of the structure. This addition of the arcade appears to have resulted from Gordon's continuing attempt to cope with the difficult Texas climate. This particular motif, in fact, may have been suggested to him

▲ **143 Fayette County Courthouse, entry elevation detail**

▶ **144** *(opposite top)* **Orlopp and Kusener, Dallas County Courthouse, Dallas, Texas, 1890-91**

▶ **145** *(opposite bottom)* **Gordon and Laub, Victoria County Courthouse, Victoria, Texas, 1891-92, unsigned office watercolor rendering**

by Shepley, Rutan and Coolidge's adoption of Mission-inspired arcades for Stanford University in California only a few years earlier.[24] Arcades on the San Antonio Missions, as well as on Mifflin Bell's design for the San Antonio Federal Building which Gordon helped to erect, could also have served as models for this concept. This overt Hispanic association, as in San Antonio, would have been perfectly appropriate in Victoria, a town founded in 1824 and named to honor Victoria Guadalupe, the first president of Mexico.

In 1892 Gordon and Laub's crosstown rival, Alfred Giles, also added an arcaded loggia and heavily decorated porch, which, likewise, seem to have been inspired by the Spanish missions of the Southwest, to the facade of the Major Ira H. Evans Château in Austin (1892-94). Three years later, in 1895, his remodeling of the Charles Schreiner Mansion in Kerrville wrapped a series of broad, arcaded verandas around its facade (figs. 146 and 147). Both of these buildings were accented with lush, organic ornament. At the Schreiner Mansion, in particular, the exotic decoration seductively, yet sparingly, entwined itself around the key constructive elements of the building in an almost Moorish manner. Gordon himself ornamented his contemporaneous J.J. Steven's Residence (c.1892-93) in San Antonio with similarly lush botanical forms (fig. 148).[25]

At the same time that they seem to have been turning to the Spanish missions as the inspiration for their Victoria County Courthouse arcade, Gordon and Laub were also toning down the more exotic polychromatic quality of Gordon's earlier work by eliminating the richly banded voussoirs that had featured so prominently at LaGrange. In Victoria, Gordon and Laub rather unsuccessfully replaced these voussoirs with cut stone arches, while in a second related design for a courthouse erected in 1891 in Stephenville in Erath County, they returned to more Richardsonian rock-faced voussoirs (fig. 149). Because of local budgetary constraints, this latter building was stripped of its intended arcades and much of its ornamentation. Likewise, the tower was reduced in scale and shifted back over a central foyer to act as a ventilating shaft.[26] These changes gave the building a simpler and consequently somewhat more unified appearance than either of the courthouses at LaGrange or Victoria.

A similar unification of form occurred in three other West Texas courthouses begun in 1891 or

early 1892 in Archer (fig. 150), Dickens, and Edwards counties. As in the Stephenville courthouse, all three were constructed of local building stone with very little, if any, Richardsonian ornamentation. They also exhibited no polychromatic stonework, relying for effect on the pure geomorphic qualities of their massive, Richardsonian arches; rugged, rock-faced ashlar surfaces; and simple, yet monumental, forms.[27] These structures serve to recall the close affinity that existed between the new Richardsonian idiom and an already well-established vernacular tradition of stone-masonry building, which itself often employed somewhat less massive round-arched openings and rock-faced ashlar walls. Buildings in this tradition can be ob-

served in cities and towns all across Texas, but especially in Germanic settlement areas and in the west and west-central regions, where varieties of native limestones were found in abundance. These stones were further augmented during the 1880s when the red and pink granites of Burnett county and red Pecos sandstone became commercially available.[28] The Burnett and Pecos stones, in particular, were very similar in character to the New England granites and sandstones commonly utilized to great effect by Richardson and his followers in the East and thus became popular as a building material for Richardsonian structures in Texas. As was the case elsewhere in the country, the local stones, especially when employed in courthouses, frequently served as a source of significant community pride. They also, in a manner that John Ruskin as well as Richardson might have applauded, evoked geological associations that intimately tied these monuments of law to the landscapes they themselves symbolically ordered.[29]

The increasing emphasis in Gordon's work on the more Hispanic character of Richardson's designs, which first appeared in the early 1890s, seems to have been motivated by a similar aim. This shift coincides with a rejection of what James Wahrenberger labeled as a "peculiar misapplication of the misunderstood Byzantine and Moresque forms"[30] in buildings such as the Aransas County Courthouse of 1889. It also parallels the development of a more sophisticated understanding on Gordon's part of mature Richardsonian composition and monumentality. This new sophistication surfaced most forcefully early in 1891 in designs for the Bexar County Courthouse in San Antonio (fig. 152), which Gordon

◄146 *(opposite top)* Alfred Giles and Guindon, Charles Shreiner House Alterations, Kerrville, Texas, 1895

◄147 *(opposite bottom)* Charles Shreiner House Alterations, ground floor veranda detail

▲148 *(left)* James Riely Gordon, J.J. Stevens residence, San Antonio, Texas, c. 1892-93 (demolished), detail of veranda shortly after completion

▲149 *(right)* Gordon and Laub, Erath County Courthouse, Stephenville, Texas, 1891

◄150 A.N. Dawson, Archer County Courthouse, Archer City, Texas, 1892, main facade detail, third story altered

appears to have prepared in collaboration with his new partner, Laub.[31] This commission represented a much larger project than any of Gordon's previous courthouse commissions and thus required a radically different approach to the arrangement of the building. The secondary elevations of the designs for this structure, for example, especially those depicted in the earlier sketches, with their two-story arcades set on a massive basement surmounted with an attic colonnade, thus seem to derive from Richardson's Marshall Field Wholesale Store (1885-87) in Chicago or his Allegheny County Courthouse of 1883-88.

Gordon and Laub's designs also mixed Spanish Renaissance and Moorish themes with these Richardsonian motifs and was labeled in contemporary accounts as both Richardsonian Romanesque and "something after the Spanish and Moorish style… [with] a recessed court on the east side, and a Moorish gallery on the front, the second story resembling that of the United States courthouse…."[32] Hispano-Moorish and Richardsonian precedents, in fact, existed for all of these motifs. There are definite similarities, for example, between the towers of the Bexar County Courthouse and those that appear in Carrère and Hastings's designs for the Alcazar and the Ponce de Leon Hotel of 1888 in St. Augustine, Florida, buildings which were themselves described as having been "built in the style of the early Spanish Renaissance, which was strongly influenced by

the Moorish spirit."[33]

Certain other features of the San Antonio structure, such as the two-tower facade (fig. 151), may reflect the influence of Laub who had been trained in the Office of the Supervising Architect of the Treasury. Beehive domes similar to those that appear several times in the final configuration of the courthouse facade, for example, had featured prominently in an early design that had been sketched by Laub for the Galveston Custom House.[34] The building as depicted in this drawing also displayed a hip-roofed palazzo with a Richardsonian arcade on the first floor supporting a series of open Palladian porches on the second. Rising from the left-hand side of the building is a small, early Spanish Renaissance campanile, while the right corner is dominated by a large octagonal minaret with a prominent beehive dome of Moorish derivation.

Spanish and Richardsonian archetypes likewise existed for the entryway to Bexar County Courthouse, which consisted of a colonnaded gallery supported by a broad elliptical arch set between two towers (fig. 153). The most prominent precedent for this, although the arch does not appear over an entry, can be found in Richardson's sketch for the Young Men's Association Building in Buffalo, which was reproduced in the *American Architect and Building News* in April 1887 (fig. 154).[35] C.A. Rich in his article, "A Run through Spain, III," which appeared in the January 3, 1891 issue of the *American Architect and Building News,* moreover, re-

▲ 151 Gordon and Laub, Bexar County Courthouse, San Antonio, Texas, 1891-96, tower detail

▼ 152 *(left)* Bexar County Courthouse, unsigned office drawing showing early tower design

▼ 153 *(right)* Bexar County Courthouse, unsigned office watercolor rendering of entry

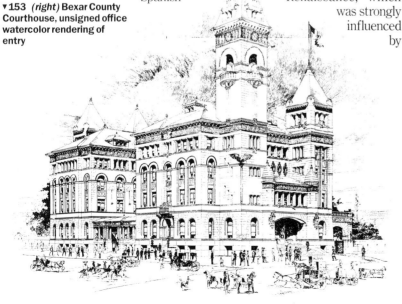

produced two, specifically Spanish precedents for this motif: a gateway to the city of Avila and the facade of the church of San Tomás in the same city (fig. 155). The first of these pictured a crenellated barbican bridging two towers and the second, a colonnaded gallery—what Rich rather freely called a *coro*—"upheld by a beautiful elliptical arch."[36]

To further enhance its Spanish character, Gordon and Laub's gallery in San Antonio was flanked by two small tourelles with Moorish domes. And in the original scheme, the entire entryway was set beneath a row of quatrefoil lights, apparently modeled after the eighteenth-century rose window of Mission San José y San Miquel de Agnayo on the San Antonio River. In addition, a bracketed cornice supported an overhanging hipped roof, covered with Spanish tile, and rich terra-cotta rinceau friezes everywhere decorated the building. This decoration had precedents in the work of Richardson, Root, and Sullivan, as well as in contemporary illustrations of Spanish ornament.[37]

Another, more generic Spanish feature of the Bexar County Courthouse was its courtyard, which like that of the Driskill Hotel in Austin has, unfortunately, since been filled in. On the ground level this courtyard was originally flanked on two sides with low verandas set on groups of tapered, octagonal columns, reminiscent of a type employed by Louis Sullivan in his Auditorium Theater in Chicago, while its upper stories opened into a series of hallways sheltered behind a variety of Richardsonian arcades (figs. 156 and 157). In the center of the courtyard was a large fountain, "surrounded by various kinds of tropical plants." According to the architects, this was "especially designed with reference to the peculiarities of the climate....With wings projecting out it catches all the breeze that strikes between them upon the principle of a funnel, and forces

American Architect and Building News, 1891

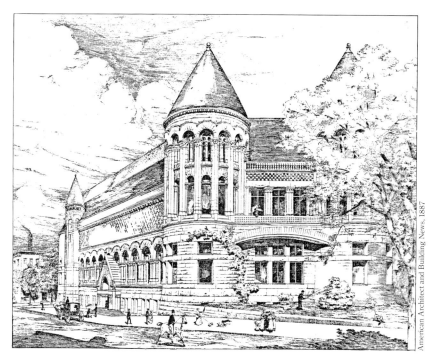

American Architect and Building News, 1887

▲ **154 H.H. Richardson, proposed design for Young Men's Association Building in Buffalo, New York, 1884, unsigned competition drawing**

◄ **155 C.A. Rich, sketch of San Tomás Church, Avila, Spain**

it through the entire structure, and the natural breeze is not wasted, thereby securing a thorough system of ventilation."[38]

According to Gordon, he had first conceived of this idea of using an open court with a fountain as a ventilating device in his design for the Fayette County Courthouse in 1890, where he had intentionally set out "to originate a plan and design that would be an innovation to courthouse architecture, and particularly adapted to [the Texas] climate." For his Victoria County Courthouse plan, which must have been on the drawing board almost concurrently with that for Bexar County early in 1891, he had added exterior colonnades to this scheme. And finally, at San Antonio he "modified [this] plan by uniting the open court, tower and ventilating shaft and changed the exterior design."[39]

While representing a surprisingly rare evocation of Richardson's Allegheny County Courthouse plan, Gordon and Laub's Bexar County courtyard also recalls the courtyard of J.N. Preston's Driskill Hotel in Austin, which was described in 1894 as "a courtyard with a fountain in the center quite similar to many Spanish places of the kind."[40] Both, too, remind one of a description of Spanish homes by Rich that appeared in the *American Architect and Building News* in February 1891. "The planning of the houses is peculiar," he wrote, "and in many ways charming, at least it is admirably adapted to the country and hot climate…as you enter and pass through a small hall you look directly into the *patio* or courtyard…often with an arched colonnade all around, and always full of plants and folliage, with the central fountain. Off from this court are the rooms in a variety of arrangements…."[41]

In combining these Richardsonian and Hispano-Moorish motifs in a regionally appropriate configuration, such as he evolved at San Antonio, Gordon seems to have felt that he had arrived at something new. In late 1891 or early 1892, for example, he stated: "I have tried for years in the treatment of designs to depart from the old style so strictly adhered to, but only in the last year or two have my efforts met with much success, and we now feel greatly encouraged at the outlook for more artistic studies."[42]

In addition to his Bexar County Courthouse, another of the "more artistic studies" that Gordon was referring to must surely

▲156 Bexar County Court-
house, detail of interior
court arcade

▼157 Bexar County Court-
house, unsigned office
watercolor rendering of
interior court

▶158 James Riely Gordon,
Texas Pavilion, World
Columbian Exposition,
Chicago, Illinois, 1893, view
shortly after completion

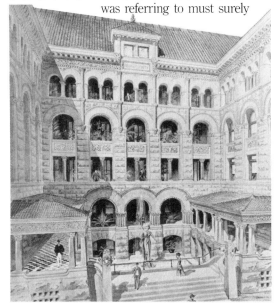

have been his design for the Texas Pavilion for the World Columbian Exposition of 1893 in Chicago (fig. 158). Late in 1891, he proposed constructing a large rotunda in the "Italian Renaissance style" with small turrets of a Moorish derivation, similar to those on the Bexar County Courthouse, flanking the entryways. By February of the following year, however, in keeping with the neoclassical theme of the Fair, the design for this building had evolved into a rectangular pavilion, more Spanish Renaissance than Italianate in character, with two-story open arcades stretching between square corner towers reminiscent of the type of belvedere that Gordon had first employed on the Clifford Building in San Antonio.[43]

That same February the California World's Fair Commission announced that the winning design of its competition for a California State Building was A. Page Brown's Mission-style pavilion, and in March of that year Daniel Burnham published the official guidelines for the state buildings at the exposition. These read in part: "The architecture should be dignified in style, formal rather than picturesque….The earlier styles that prevailed in this country such as the architecture of the Old Spanish Missions in Lower California and Mexico, can with propriety furnish the motives for the buildings of the western and southwestern states."[44] Gordon's designs for the Texas Pavilion no doubt also reflect this sentiment.

In the scheme that was actually built only a single tower was set into the re-entrant angles of a Greek cross plan, which—as in the Victoria County Courthouse—was superimposed on a cube with one-story peristyles at the corners, almost

◀159-62 James Riely Gordon, Ellis County Courthouse, Waxahachie, Texas, 1894-96, details

as if Gordon had turned the Bexar County Courthouse patio inside-out. "In the treatment of this design," wrote the *San Antonio Express,* in a statement that can probably be attributed to Gordon himself, "the architecture has not deflected from the history of the Lone Star State, which from the initial has been marked with a Spanish tinge, whose architectural feeling, and beautiful botanical effects, lay down a charm of thought far too beautiful to forsake for that of the modern day. The building, colonnade, grounds, etc., have been designed to present a Spanish vista, or bower of beautiful Texas foliage, comprising all the tropical plants so common to Texas."[45]

During this same period of about 1891 to 1894,

Gordon's firm was working on other projects within a Richardsonian idiom, which nevertheless borrowed a "Spanish" decorative vocabulary, square, hipped-roof belvederes, and open colonnaded and arcaded verandas from similar Spanish Medieval and Renaissance as well as Mission sources. The most lavish and Richardsonian of these was the Ellis County Courthouse, which was erected in Waxahachie between 1894 and 1896 (figs. 132 and 159-162).[46] This, next to the 1891 Bexar County Courthouse in San Antonio, was also one of Gordon's designs that was most clearly "marked with a Spanish tinge."

As in Gordon's courthouses at LaGrange and Victoria or his Texas Pavilion in Chicago, the basic form of the Ellis County Courthouse was generated

▲163 James Riely Gordon,
Gonzales County Court-
house, Gonzales, Texas,
1893-96, detail of front
elevation

from a cruciform plan. But the building was now literally turned inside-out, with open, two-story arcaded and colonnaded porticos, such as those employed in the courtyard of the Bexar County Courthouse, situated on the exterior in the re-entrant angles of the cross. These porticos were segmental or polygonal in plan and acted as entryways, funneling both people and breezes into the building. Inside, an open central core, around which were grouped the offices and courtrooms, similarly functioned as a ventilating shaft dramatic climax to the careful piling up of elements on the exterior. The form of this central tower looks back to Richardson's Trinity Church in Boston, which itself—as was well known at the time—was modeled on the Spanish Romanesque lantern of Salamanca Cathedral in western Spain. The structure's overall pyramidal configuration, as well, seems to have been inspired by Richardson's Boston church.

In the Richardsonian tradition, too, the Waxahachie structure was set on a heavy, battered foundation and "bound together" with repeated horizontal bands of stone. In this it exhibits a mastery of Richardsonian design principles not evident to the same degree in Gordon's work, or anywhere in Texas, only a few years earlier. To accomplish this Gordon exploited what Marianna Griswold Van Rensselaer

identified as the main characteristics of Richardson's own best work: "Strength in conception; clearness in expression; breadth in treatment; imagination; and love for repose and massive dignity of aspect, and often for an effect which in the widest meaning of the word we may call 'romantic.'"[47] These qualities were further enhanced at Waxahachie by the extravagant richness of the stonework. Here again, as at LaGrange, were intensely lithic forms and rich polychromatic surfaces, but now with a new refinement and balance. At the same time, the two-towered west elevation with its elliptical arch, the richly foliated friezes, and colonnaded porches set over each entryway of the Waxahachie building all seem to derive from Gordon and Laub's "Moorish" design for their Bexar County Courthouse.

Between 1894 and 1898, Gordon constructed eight more Texas courthouses using various applications of the Richardsonian style and produced sketches for at least two more. All of these follow closely the paradigm that he evolved at Waxahachie, and most of them also incorporated at least some Spanish or Moorish "references" into their designs. This is especially true at Gonzales (1894-96) where the building was ornamented with Spanish tiled roofs, Moorish arcades on the second story, and "beautiful botanical effects" in the form of decorated capitals, friezes and voussoirs (fig. 163). His unbuilt design for Karnes County (c.1896) exhibited a Mission parapet set between small, square turrets with miniature hipped roofs; that at Somerville (c.1896, also unbuilt) incorporated a beehive dome, while the courthouses in both Van Zandt (1894-96) and Hopkins (1894-95) counties displayed Mission-style, quatrefoil windows and escutcheons similar to those in the first designs for the Bexar County Courthouse. Though less elaborately decorated, Gordon's Lee County Courthouse of 1898-99 still exhibited the same cruciform plan that he had evolved at Waxahachie and corner entryways featuring prominent Richardsonian arcades (fig. 164).[48] All of Gordon's presentation drawings, moreover, depicted these buildings with verandas and roof gardens covered with "beautiful Texas foliage," designed, no doubt, "to present"—as he had in Chicago—"a Spanish vista."

So successful was Gordon's new courthouse paradigm that it was almost immediately imitated, albeit with limited success, by a number of his colleagues. The most flagrant of these imitations were fabricated by the Austin architect, Arthur O.

◄164 James Riely Gordon,
Lee County Courthouse,
Giddings, Texas, 1898-99,
re-entrant angle arcade

Watson, who produced at least two designs for county courthouses that were directly indebted to Gordon's fully developed cruciform scheme. Though never constructed, one or both of these probably formed the basis for a lawsuit that Gordon filed against his colleague in 1895, charging him with infringement upon a courthouse design copyright that he claimed to hold.[49]

Another courthouse based on Gordon's model was constructed by the Fort Worth firm of Messer, Sanguinet and Messer at Paris in Lamar County between 1895 and 1896 (burned in 1916). Marshall Sanguinet had supervised the construction of Gordon's Ellis County Courthouse, which would account for his familiarity with the San Antonio architect's designs. During the mid-1890s, Messer, Sanguinet and Messer were also erecting the Citizen's National Bank in Waxahachie, a fine Richardsonian building that, ironically, has often been attributed to Gordon (fig. 165). It was here that Sanguinet cemented a friendship with Gordon's draftsman, Carl G. Staats, who became his partner in 1896.[50] Working out of Fort Worth and Dallas,

Sanguinet and Staats went on to become one of the major twentieth-century architectural firms in the state, though subsequently they did not do much work in the Richardsonian idiom.

In 1896, the same year that Messer, Sanguinet and Messer were finishing work on their courthouse in Paris, Eugene T. Heiner was completing a more typical Richardsonian courthouse in Cuero, DeWitt County (fig. 166). Although this had been designed two years earlier by Arthur O. Watson, he appears to have had some difficulty carrying through the construction of the building. The County Commissioners, therefore, called in Heiner to finish it.[51] With a tower set behind an arcaded entry porch, this courthouse seems to be a smaller and somewhat simplified version of Willoughby J. Edbrooke's Post Office Building (1891-99) in Washington, D.C., which itself followed Richardson's important prototype, the Allegheny County Courthouse in Pittsburgh. Unusual and somewhat exceptional, however, is the stonework, which features a delicate play of pink granite trim against a local, cream-colored, Leon sandstone.

Although he himself did not design the DeWitt County Courthouse, Heiner, who worked out of Houston, was responsible for the design of the Lavaca County Courthouse in Halletsville, erected between 1897 and 1899 (fig. 167).[52] Although Richardsonian in style, the plan and form of this building looked back to the earlier Italianate and Second Empire courthouses of men like W.C. Dodson, who himself had attempted—somewhat less successfully than Heiner—to meld Romanesque, neoclassical, and Second Empire forms into his design for the Denton County Courthouse (1895-96) in Denton. Both Dodson and Heiner, moreover, seem to have been more interested in Richardson's ornamentation than in his system of design and the possibilities it offered for evolving new regional variations on his work.

More closely related to the "clearness of expression" and "massive dignity" of Richardson's as well as of Gordon's work of the mid-1890s is Alfred Giles's design for a coachhouse and stable erected for Daniel Sullivan in San Antonio in 1896 (fig. 168), a building that exudes both the monumentality and whimsy of Richardson's Ames Gatehouse in North Easton, Massachusetts. A similar monumentality can be observed in the designs for a number of county jails erected in the state during the mid-1890s. The Llano County Jail, constructed in 1895 by F.B. and W.S. Hull, is a particularly fine example of this trend

(fig. 169).[53] Notable here, in addition to the excellent Richardsonian masonry work, is the prominent use of Richardson's great Syrian arch. This form continued to appear in Texas architecture until well into the first decade of the twentieth century in structures such as the Hillsboro Western Union Building (c.1905); Glenn Allen's Artesia Manufacturing and Bottling Company Building, "The Home of Dr. Pepper," in Waco of 1906 (fig. 170); or the University Methodist Church in Austin (1907) by Frederick Mann.[54]

With its Spanish belvedere and red tile roof, Moorish tourelle and heavy arcades, the Dr. Pepper Building still spoke with the same regional accent as Texas buildings such as the Bexar or Ellis county courthouses, buildings that were themselves now more than a decade old. That Allen himself was more than aware of this regional tradition was evidenced by his "Spanish" Romanesque design for a mess hall

◄ **166** A.O. Watson, DeWitt County Courthouse, Cuero, Texas, 1894-96

▼ **167** Eugene T. Heiner, Lavaca County Courthouse, Halletsville, Texas, 1897-99

at Texas A&M University of 1895-97, which appeared to pay direct tribute to both Gordon's Bexar County Courthouse and his Mission Revival Waco Cotton Palace (1894). At the same time, the west elevation of the Dr. Pepper Building probably derived from Richardson's Crane Memorial Library in Quincy, Massachusetts (1880-82) or his design for the Howard Memorial Library in New Orleans (1886).[55]

Yet by the early 1900s, the leading practitioners of the Richardsonian Romanesque style in Texas, men such as James Riely Gordon or Alfred Giles, had long since abandoned Richardson's idiom and its regional variations for Beaux-Arts classicism, a shift which, for Gordon, became complete with his move to New York in 1902. Only two years later his most talented draftsman of the 1890s, Frank O. Witchell, initiated an illustrious partnership with Otto Lang, and they, along with Sanguinet and Staats, became the leading interpreters of

▸ 168 *(left)* Alfred Giles and Guindon, Daniel Sullivan Stable, San Antonio, Texas, 1896, working drawing of side elevation

▸ 169 *(right)* F.B. and W.S. Hull, Llano County Jail, Llano, Texas, 1895

the new Progressive style in Texas. Soon thereafter, a third Gordon protégé, Henry T. Phelps, began work on the first of many neoclassical courthouses that he erected in the state. With this, the era of the Richardsonian Romanesque Revival in Texas drew to a close, not, however, without having left a significant mark on both the Texas architectural profession and the landscape.

Having arrived on the scene at a signal moment in the development of both Texas and its architectural profession, the Richardsonian Romanesque idiom had filled a need for a new mode of design that could replace, with authority and meaning, the babel of architectural language then in common use in the state. Although a brief attempt was made in the late 1880s to adapt a more exotic Moorish style to this task, this movement was quickly squelched by criticism from within, as well as from outside, the architectural profession. Richardson's language, though conceived in New England, seemed to strike a more responsive chord. This was perhaps in part, as Mrs. Van Rensselaer noted, because the temperament of its creator "was essentially a southern one—loving breadth and light and color, variety and luxuriance...." As a consequence, "when he recognized the serviceableness of...forms he instinctively preferred to study them in their southern developments."[56]

Richardson's work, then, naturally met many of the climatic and aesthetic requirements of the southwestern region. This acceptability was reinforced by the fact that in his most widely acclaimed monument, Trinity Church, he himself had looked to an Hispanic precedent for part of his design. The Southern French Romanesque architecture to which he and his followers frequently turned for inspiration, as well, was also in close sympathy with the buildings of medieval Spain. Richardson's work, therefore, carried associations sympathetic to the

heritage and climate of Texas, which, as Gordon noted in 1893, "from the initial has been marked with a Spanish tinge." [57] By emphasizing this aspect of the master's oeuvre, men such as Gordon and Giles managed to evolve a recognizable and successful regional variation on Richardson's style, a variation that imparted a monumentality and depth of meaning to the architecture of this period that never had, or has since, been achieved by any other architectural fashion in the Lone Star State. ✠

▲ **170 Glen Allen, Artesia Manufacturing and Bottling Company Building ("The Home of Dr. Pepper"), Waco, Texas, 1907**

The Prairie City Comes of Age:
Ambitions and Expectations in the Richardsonian Era

Judith A. Martin

The midland prairies have a strong image in American culture. O.E. Rölvaag's *Giants in the Earth,* the Laura Ingalls Wilder stories, Sinclair Lewis's *Main Street,* and countless other sources have reinforced the perception of this region as one of endless farmland interspersed with small towns. But name the cities in this part of America—Chicago, St. Louis, Omaha, Minneapolis, St. Paul, Kansas City, San Antonio—and a different picture takes form. Two of these cities (Chicago and St. Louis) have been among the ten largest in the entire country for a hundred years, and another (San Antonio) has recently joined this ranking. The midland prairies' rural image ought to be tempered by the real experiences of urban growth there, especially in the latter years of the nineteenth century.

The 1880s and 1890s were an unprecedented time of city building in the middle section of the United States. As far north as Minneapolis and St. Paul, and south to San Antonio, a similar pattern repeated itself. One can begin as early as 1820 or as late as 1850, choosing a place that was empty or had only a few hundred residents. Look at it again in 1890, and discover that it has over 100,000 residents, or a half-million, or even a million. To ignore this phenomenal growth of these midland cities is to ignore one of the central experiences of American history: the creation of a system of transportation and commerce that linked cattle ranches of Texas and Colorado and wheat farms of the Dakotas with merchants and customers in the industrial cities of the East and with Europe.

The prairie cities made this "system" possible. Railroad lines crisscrossed these cities. Products and goods moving east and west were stored in them, and industries that processed the raw goods of the prairies quickly assumed economic importance for these cities. Within a single generation, the cities of the midland prairies sprouted huge brick and granite warehouses or massive stockyards and milling complexes. Such structures expressed the economic rationale for these cities. Similarly, their churches, libraries, and fine hotels, built in the most current styles of the day, bespoke the civic and cultural aspirations of their eager new residents.

Urban Development on the Prairie

Older American cities, like Boston and Philadelphia, developed rather gradually. For the prairie cities, whose growth coincided with a nationwide period of economic growth, the story was quite different. Omaha had 4,000 residents in 1860 and

◄**171** *(opposite)* **Leroy S. Buffington, Pillsbury Hall, University of Minnesota, Minneapolis, Minnesota, 1888**

▼**172 Long and Kees, Free Will Baptist Church, Minneapolis, Minnesota, 1890 (demolished)**

over 100,000 in 1890; Minneapolis had about 500 citizens in 1850 and over 200,000 by 1900; Chicago went from 200 residents in 1830 to over a million in 1890.[1] By the late 1890s, Chicago was the second largest city in the U.S., and St. Louis was the fourth largest. Even more impressive than the sheer numbers was the frantic pace of growth, especially in a pivotal decade like the 1880s (see Table I).

As the prairies' urban population exploded decade after decade, decisions had to be made quickly. What to build and what models to follow? With thousands of new residents arriving annually, all needing housing and most needing jobs, there was little time to plan what should go where. Almost as soon as money was made in this region, great sums were directed toward expressing an urban presence on the prairie.

Table I. Population Growth of Selected Prairie Cities, 1880-1890

	1880 Pop.	1890 Pop.	% Change
Chicago, Il.	503,185	1,099,850	118%
St. Louis, Mo.	350,518	451,770	28%
Kansas City, Mo.	55,785	132,716	137%
Minneapolis, Mn.	46,887	164,738	251%
St. Paul, Mn.	41,473	133,156	223%
St. Joseph, Mo.	32,431	52,324	61%
Omaha, Neb.	30,518	140,452	360%
Dubuque, Ia.	22,254	30,311	36%
San Antonio, Tx.	20,550	37,673	83%
Topeka, Ks.	15,452	31,007	100%
Sioux City, Ia.	7,336	37,806	413%
Kearney, Neb.	1,172	8,074	353%

Ambition, hard work, and explosive growth defined the experiences of most prairie cities, and there was not enough time to evolve a tradition of city life. Unlike Philadelphia, few prairie cities had someone like William Penn to insist on a "proper" physical format. Still, the midland prairie cities fast assumed a form and shape that suggested permanence, as well as large civic ambitions. The streets of these cities were filled with monumental structures long before they were ever paved. This was one measure of how quickly investments were put back into these communities. If style sometimes seemed less important than the simple fact of building, that was understandable. The goal was demonstrable growth.

Civic boosters of places large and small had extravagant hopes for their new homes. While tiny Kearney, Nebraska, planned to be as well known "...as Lowell in Massachusetts or the more modern Minneapolis" by the early 1890s, Chicago meant to overtake New York as the largest city in the country.[2] Prior to the consolidation of New York's five boroughs in 1893, this was not just an empty ambition.

This rapid and unplanned spurt of inland city building was fueled by four related processes, be-

ginning in the 1870s and accelerating through the 1890s:

1) Railroads were the key. In 1869, the nation's first transcontinental line, the Union Pacific, was completed, enhancing the fortunes of cities along its route, including St. Louis and Omaha. Businessmen throughout the prairie states hustled to acquire connections into the UP, while to the north and south of it, entrepreneurs started planning other cross-country lines. Throughout the 1870s, the prairie region experienced a flurry of railroad building, and several formerly small cities gained real prominence as a result. Minneapolis, for example, became the "gateway to the Northwest" with the opening of the Northern Pacific in 1883, the consolidation of the Soo Line in 1888, and the completion of the Great Northern in 1893. As new railroad lines developed, they generated supporting businesses, especially in the larger cities—numerous banks, warehouses, and insurance companies soon appeared in Minneapolis, as they had in Omaha following the success of the Union Pacific. Most prairie railroad lines, and their goods, ultimately fed into Chicago, generating even more activity for that already booming center.

Though the railroads' prominence in the prairie cities is no longer so obvious, in the 1880s and 1890s these cities were structurally and functionally transformed by rail development. St. Louis in 1870 was a relatively compact city, oriented to the river and dependent upon the steamboat trade. With the completion of the St. Louis-Illinois (Eads) Bridge in 1874, St. Louis grew quickly away from the river, and its fortunes improved dramatically. Aided by its central location in the nation's rail network, St. Louis became an important manufacturing center. By the late 1890s St. Louis humbly boasted the largest brewery and the largest shoe factory in the country, as well as the world's largest train shed, attached to Theodore Link's handsome Romanesque Union Station.[3] In its rapid and striking response to railroad expansion, St. Louis was neither alone nor unique.

2) Increases in agricultural production spurred urban development. Many people made their way to prairie towns and farms as the railroads reached across the country. In a bid for increased business, railroad owners gave away land along their routes to encourage settlement. Soon, large quantities of grain and livestock were being produced on the prairies—much more than farm families could con-

sume themselves. This surplus found its way to prairie towns and then to the cities, where it was stored or processed before being transported East. Minneapolis's grain elevators bespoke wheat and prosperity, as the enormous stockyards of Kansas City and Omaha told of meat and prosperity. Having good connections to the vast agricultural hinterlands of the West was critically important to all of the prairie cities.

3) Immigration was crucial to urban growth on the prairies, as elsewhere. The earliest prairie city residents were typically native-born migrants from eastern states. But these cities were growing during the height of foreign immigration to the U.S., and their populations reflected this process, though not evenly. In 1870 Chicago and St. Louis had the highest proportion of foreign-born residents of all prairie cities: 48 percent and 36 percent respectively; by 1910, these groups had declined to 36 percent and 18 percent.[4] The foreign populations of these two cities, as in St. Paul, Omaha, and San Antonio, were dominantly Irish and German; the Germans ranked well above the national average in both places, though both groups were actually decreasing by 1910. Like their eastern counterparts, the prairie cities experienced the "new immigration" before and after 1900. In varying combinations, Poles, Bohemians, Russian Jews, and Italians became visible in the populations of Omaha, St. Louis, and St. Paul and were even more numerous in Chicago.[5] The foreign-born population of Minneapolis was decidedly distinctive, being dominantly composed of Swedes, Norwegians, and Danes. Many migrants and immigrants intended rural lives but were trapped in the cities by economic circumstances. The prairie cities thereby gained a surplus of workers.

4) During the 1880s and 1890s, cities proved an economical location for industrial production—activities that in earlier years were concentrated on New England's waterpower sites. As steam generation of power gained importance and got cheaper, Chicago and St. Louis became important manufacturing centers. Other prairie cities held back somewhat, being still closely tied to agricultural origins and too far removed from markets for manufactured goods. Yet, there were opportunities for industrial production in these cities, especially in areas related to whatever agricultural production was already occurring. Thus, Minneapolis could tap a large hinterland for wheat, and mills in Minneapo-

lis turned the wheat into flour and simultaneously created a market for barrels and woven bags to store and transport the flour—by 1890 this former prairie hamlet was the flour milling capital of the world. Kansas City, in the center of a large cattle-raising area, was similarly able to develop a flourishing meat-packing industry, and all its attendant services, in the 1880s.

Taken together, industrial and agricultural opportunities, railroads, and immigrants fostered an impressive amount of city building on the inland prairies. These factors helped to determine *what* would get built, including railroad stations, warehouses, and mansions for the wealthy entrepreneurs who built these cities. The influence of these factors on building styles is less clear. For this, the experiences and backgrounds of those moving to the prairie cities were critical.

Urban Expectations

What did the urban pioneers on the prairies expect their cities to look like? Available photographic evidence indicates that the earliest residents of these cities had the New England town in mind. Given that many arrived in the Midwest by way of the Ohio and Mississippi rivers, after growing up in places like Maine, New Hampshire, or upstate New York, this is not surprising. Whether a nascent industrial center like Chicago, a busy river port like St. Paul, or a frontier entry point like Omaha, at the start most prairie cities featured white clapboard cottages and commercial streets with false-front wooden structures. But these early landscapes did not last very long.

Long before the 1880s, it was clear that those who had moved to the growing prairie cities had what might be called "urban expectations." These expectations were expressed in many different forms: houses clustered together on the wide open prairie to create streetscapes; the appearance of libraries, opera houses, and meeting halls to create a cultural landscape; the use of brick and stone for building materials when lumber was amply available and cheaper. The urban expectations had a social cast as well, described by one early Minneapolis resident who wrote about the civilized social life of the young community—singing and partygoing, churchgoing, political speeches. All this in a place only six years removed from Indian occupation.[6]

The urban expectations of these cities were

▲ **173 W.B. Dunnell, Main Building, Pillsbury Academy, Owatonna, Minnesota, 1889, early engraving**

based on the knowledge, experiences, and contacts of the "first families." For many prairie cities, the newcomers of the 1850s were a fortuitous catch: as they prospered, they became patrons of their cities in the 1880s. Many were the college-educated, second or third sons of middle-class eastern families. They were extraordinarily hard workers and had impeccable entrepreneurial instincts. Some set out to make their own way in the world, some were sent to extend family investments in new and more prosperous directions.

A few examples serve to illustrate:

—John S. Pillsbury arrived in Minneapolis from New Hampshire in 1855. He became a partner in a hardware store that soon burned down. Upon rebuilding, the business succeeded and was eventually incorporated into the Upper Midwest's largest hardware operation—that of T.B. Janney. Next Pillsbury invested in lumber milling, then in flour milling; he was one of the powers behind the Soo Line railroad and was a director of several banks. In the 1880s Pillsbury's nephew Charles brought the family's flour mills international prominence through his innovations in flour production. Through this and other successful investments, John Pillsbury grew very wealthy. He chose to devote much of his time to civic causes; he served in the State Senate in the 1860s and served three terms as Minnesota's governor (1875-81). Pillsbury played a crucial role for the University of Minnesota, helping to devise its organizational structure and reorganizing its finances. In the late 1880s, when H.H. Richardson's influence was at its height, Pillsbury funded several important landmarks, in whole or in part: Pillsbury Hall at the University, Free Will Baptist Church in downtown Minneapolis, and Pillsbury Academy in Owatonna, Minnesota (figs. 171-173).[7]

—The Creighton brothers, Edward and John, came to Omaha from Ohio in 1856. Edward Creighton laid telegraph lines and dreamed of connecting the Atlantic and the Pacific through these wires. Having purchased stock in the company for which he worked (Western Union), Creighton eventually became a wealthy man (fig. 174). His brother John worked in the freighting business, at first performing such basic functions as hauling supplies to gold miners in the West. Over time he built a fortune and eventually went on to found the First National Bank.[8] Like John Pillsbury, the younger Creighton donated funds for a number of building projects, the most prominent among them being Creighton

University and St. Joseph Hospital (fig. 175).

—Others came to the prairie cities without resources or connections and had to be creative. James J. Hill, for example, arrived in St. Paul in 1856 with no money but with unbounded energy and a determination to succeed. Starting as a shipping clerk, Hill quickly got intrigued with the idea of western development. He would eventually become intimately involved with the West, spending much of his middle and later years building and operating the Great Northern railroad empire.[9] Sim-

ilar stories can be told about other innovators and entrepreneurs: Philip Armour and Gustav Swift who developed the important stockyards and meatpacking industries in Chicago, as William Paxton did for Omaha; or Frederick Krug, who built a thriving brewery industry in Omaha, as other German immigrants did in other midwestern cities (Anheuser and Busch in St. Louis, Schmidt in St. Paul, Schlitz in Milwaukee, to name just the most well known). Like James J. Hill who came from Canada, many of these successful businessmen were fresh immigrants to America.

Whether coming West with financial connections or without them, this first generation of settlers was extraordinarily committed to building up and embellishing the prairie cities—to equaling or surpassing the cities of the East (fig. 176). Perhaps the raw landscapes this group confronted as young men in the 1850s fired their determination to make

◄**174** *(opposite)* **Isaac Hodgson, Jr., Pacific Express Building, Omaha, Nebraska, 1889-90 (demolished), detail of entry corner**

▲**175 Henry Voss, St. Joseph's Hospital, Omaha, Nebraska, 1890 (demolished)**

From the Bostwick-Frohardt Collection owned by KMTV & on permanent loan to Western Heritage Museum—Omaha, Nebraska.

▲176 Peabody and Stearns,
James J. Hill House, St. Paul,
Minnesota, 1887-91

a lasting mark. As mature adults with financial power, they were deeply involved in all aspects of city building. The city's form was important to them, in both its economic and cultural dimensions. Through their money, and through donating their time (as well as that of their wives and daughters), these entrepreneurs built churches, museums, and libraries, along with their homes and businesses.

By the 1880s, the expectations of the older migrants, of their children, and even of some newer immigrants had grown. Older forms of quick urban growth, exemplified by three-story frame commercial buildings, no longer sufficed. The founders of the prairie cities were ambitious, and early residents were eager to express their visions of the future. They did this, in part, by filling block after block with massive brick and stone buildings, often inspired by the designs of H.H. Richardson. By the turn of the century, the landscapes of many prairie cities had a permanent and sophisticated appearance, far beyond what would be expected of places that had been wilderness within the memory of one generation.

Urban Form—Variations on a Theme

Similar large-scale economic and social forces shaped prairie cities as widely separated as Chicago and San Antonio. But the look of these cities was really determined by internal factors like transit systems, the presence or lack of parks, and differing building materials. Each of these elements responded to differences in the landscape and local culture of each city. So the urban form of the prairie cities varied greatly and, contrary to popular belief, was not even uniformly flat or treeless.

At the start rivers shaped the prairie cities, as they did most other American cities. There was no pretense and little sense of sophistication, and the physical designs of these cities acknowledged their dependence on the river. The contours of the first streets usually conformed to the river's banks. Streets ran parallel and perpendicular to the river, and early buildings were oriented to it. Though still visible if one looks very closely, this relationship changed markedly within a short time.[10] By the 1880s, as the economies of the prairie cities became

Northwestern Architect

◄177 E.E. Joralemon,
Joseph E. Badger House,
showcase for Badger and
Penny's Addition, Minne-
apolis, Minnesota, 1885
(demolished), drawing by
Joralemon

▼178 James Riely Gordon,
Jay Adams House, showcase
for Laurel Heights, the first
addition to San Antonio,
Texas, 1890

more closely linked to the fortunes of national railroads, most effectively abandoned their riverfronts or left them exclusively to the use of industry. Important public institutions of the late nineteenth century were located well away from the rivers, while fashionable homes sprawled toward the edges of the city.

In the late nineteenth century most urban landscapes were shaped or reshaped by internal transportation systems—that is, by local streetcar networks. Prairie cities were not immune to this process. Horsecars (a carriage mounted on a track pulled by a horse) and streetcars appeared in these cities within a single generation of the initial settlement. Chicago's first horsecar began service in 1850, Omaha's in 1867, Minneapolis's in 1875. Within ten to fifteen years horses were replaced by electric power, creating systems that were faster and more efficient. These early transit systems were sometimes uncomfortable and unpredictable: in the wintertime, riders of St. Paul's Selby Avenue line often had to get out and help push the car up Cathedral Hill.[11] Still, these systems symbolized progress and opportunity.

Because prairie cities grew along with their first streetcars, they gained a distinct advantage over cities in the East, where internal transportation systems intruded into already built-up neighborhoods. Residential patterns were not severely disrupted by transit lines in the prairie cities. Instead, the transit lines usually helped determine where different groups would live. Moreover, the prairie cities did not have to endure much of the crowding and the densely packed streets that characterized older "walking" cities before the advent of transit systems.[12] Neither rich nor poor was forced to crowd together in these cities. The transit lines established expectations about the shapes of the

▼179 G.W. and F.D. Orff (probably designed by E.E. Joralemon), Pratt-Simmons House, Park Avenue, Minneapolis, Minnesota, 1891 (demolished 1959), c. 1895 view

◀180 F.R. Schock, Frank
Sturges House, Elmhurst,
Illinois, 1892 (demolished),
office drawing by
H.F. Swanson

prairie cities from a very early point; people expected to be able to live away from the center of the city, and they did.

Transportation improvements of this kind were occurring in cities all over the country. On the prairies, in combination with the prevailing flatness of the land, it sometimes led to saturation and overdevelopment. Through much of the nineteenth century, transit lines were privately owned. Starting a streetcar line where land was level and dry was relatively easy. Anyone with enough capital or enough good credit might start a line, and many real estate entrepreneurs with land scattered in disparate parts of a city did just that, primarily as a way to sell parcels of land to home builders. Sometimes these entrepreneurs would even construct a model home to demonstrate the full potential of their particular subdivision (fig. 177 and 178). In the depression of 1893, many developers lost their subdivisions, and portions of many cities languished for years because of these overextensions.

The coincidence of rapid transportation developments and urbanization had long-lasting effects on the shapes of the prairie cities. Minneapolis had a flat glacial plain south of the downtown on which it was quite easy to lay down transit lines. Residents responded to this by moving out to the edges of the city as early as the 1880s. The wealthy distributed themselves in pockets on Park Avenue and Lowry Hill, while the middle class filled in the areas between (fig. 179). Such movements began an enduring trend toward dispersal in the Minneapolis area, one that continues today. Chicago began extending residential tentacles far out into the prairie even earlier, owing to the rapid development of good transit lines. Here the middle class removed itself from the center of the city as quickly as possible. They moved eight or nine miles away from downtown to developing suburbs like Oak Park, Evanston, and Elmhurst which were already filling in by the early 1880s (fig. 180).

But not every prairie city spread out rapidly. St. Paul's growth, for example, was more contained; steep bluffs presented barriers to development in several directions that persisted for generations. Still there were clear links between transit lines

▲ 181 George R. Mann
(design attributed to Harvey
Ellis), Washington Terrace
Gates, St. Louis, Missouri,
1893, view before
construction of houses

▶ 182 H.F. Roach, James
LaPrelle House, Washington
Terrace, St. Louis, Missouri,
1896

and development even here, particularly in the six-mile-long strip of elite houses and mansions on Summit Avenue. This street attracted residents in the 1870s when wealthy families had live-in servants, and its aura of wealth has persisted. A continuous landscape of wealth and power survived even through servantless times, for the Grand Avenue streetcar one block away carried daily workers to these homes.

Transit improvements also coincided with the social ambitions of urban residents.[13] As a key entry point to the West, St. Louis took in large numbers of short-term residents and transients throughout the nineteenth century. People who had chosen to invest in St. Louis by building substantial houses wanted physical separation from the more mundane aspects of the city. Their solution, and one that was quite common, was to create exclusive neighborhoods. Vandeventer Place, developed in the late 1870s, was the first, and it contained all of the essential ingredients: a long straight street enclosed by elaborate gates; a requirement that a substantial and expensive single family home

▲ **183 T.C. Link, Portland Place Gates, west end, St. Louis, Missouri, 1891**

◄ **184 F.C. Bonsack, George W. Brown House, Portland Place, St. Louis, Missouri, 1897**

be built; and a requirement that owners maintain the public spaces and gates and pay the watchman's salary.[14]

During the 1880s and 1890s, this idea was frequently copied. By 1915 St. Louis had dozens of "Places," ranging from the exclusivity of Westmoreland Place, Washington Terrace, and Portland Place to slightly more affordable subdivisions (figs. 181-184). Such districts were, of course, intentionally beyond the reach of certain people, whatever their income might be. Depending on the religion and ethnicity of the first residents, those excluded might be Catholic, Jewish, Mexican, or black. These restricted residential districts reflected both the aspirations and the fears of their residents. Both impulses were clearly visible on the urban landscape.

Apart from transit, fire helped to determine the form of prairie cities, in sometimes unexpected ways. The Chicago Fire in 1871 frightened everyone who lived on the edge of windswept and dry open land. Chicago responded to the disaster by prohibiting frame construction in the center of the city.[15] This decision generated a completely new landscape. Residences were driven out of the downtown, and new kinds of commercial structures were built. Extremely large masonry and cast iron office buildings—such as Burnham and Root's Rookery building of 1888 and their Monadnock building of 1892—provided a bold commercial facade for Chicago's rebuilt downtown. In the wake of the fire, an architectural revolution began to take shape, and the pathbreaking fireproof technology that created the "Chicago skyscraper" was soon copied in other prairie cities.

The Chicago Fire also begat an intense interest in urban parks. Frederick Law Olmsted and Calvert Vaux, creators of New York's Central Park and Brooklyn's Prospect Park, proposed a park system for Chicago in 1869. Their plans were destroyed in the fire and revived shortly after through the work of H.W.S. Cleveland. These ideas traveled fast; Minneapolis and Kansas City quickly followed Chicago in proposing park systems, in part to provide a firebreak should disaster strike. The message about the benefits of parks was eagerly received by prairie city fathers. Cleveland came to Minneapolis after working in Chicago, and George Kessler, a protégé of Olmsted's, moved to Kansas City after working on New York's Central Park.

The park systems begun in these cities speak volumes about the foresight and sophistication that were present in the 1880s and 1890s. Long before there was a critical need—only one generation away from the first settlement—these cities embarked on a planning process comparable to, and sometimes beyond, that of contemporary eastern cities. And these prairie park systems were being built, not just planned. Kansas City's park and boulevard system was proposed in 1893 and completed by 1915. Minneapolis's much larger system started earlier (1881) and took longer to complete, but several large parks and most of the boulevards around key lakes were acquired by 1890. One consequence of city parks, wherever they appeared, was to enhance the value of real estate nearby. Parks created dramatic landscapes for the mansions of the wealthy (fig. 185). Sometimes parks could even create a demand for land parcels that had previously languished or been underused.[16]

The shapes and forms of the prairie cities changed rapidly in the 1880s and 1890s, as economic ties drew them into the orbit of their eastern counterparts. Still, the prairie cities shared something that marked them as cities of the West: expansive amounts of space. Regardless of what was being built, there was ample opportunity to spread these cities ever outward. Building styles might mimic what was done in the East, but the spatial context of the prairie cities, along with their ubiquitous tree-lined streets, set them apart.

The implications of these spatial differences, especially for monumental buildings, can be important. Two of America's great railroad stations illustrate this point: Link and Cameron's Union Station in St. Louis, a Richardsonian gem; and McKim, Mead and White's Penn Station in New York, a splendid Classical Revival structure. Union Station, a bit away from the center of downtown, languished for years, was vacated, but was finally restored in 1986, in part as a commercial center. Penn Station, in the center of New York, was deemed an underuse of valuable land; it was razed in 1967 and replaced by the third Madison Square Garden. Though not every important nineteenth-century structure in the prairie cities has been saved, their spaciousness has occasionally allowed more thoughtful redevelopment decisions to prevail.

Richardson's Influence on the Prairie Cities

The prairie cities were far distant from New York and Newport, the acknowledged centers of style and taste in the eighties and nineties. But that did not stop the prairie cities from following the most contemporary styles of architecture and design in their own development. There were conventions to be followed in architecture and in city building, as in other things. During the 1880s and 1890s, some of the most important conventions in American city building derived from the work of H.H. Richardson. Richardson's greatest moment of design influence coincided with the most rapid period of prairie city development. And this intersection yielded some rich, and richly urbane, landscapes.

To be sure, Richardson did not greatly influence the form of the American city, on the prairies or elsewhere. The works of Louis Sullivan, Daniel Burnham, John Root, and others is too amply evi-

The point to be made here is that Richardson's work had an impact on those who actually designed and built the prairie cities, even if he himself never worked in most of them. His best buildings, and especially his public buildings, set a standard that others could and did emulate. Some elements of his style—most notably his towers—were quickly transformed into local symbols of progress and achievement. By 1890, every ambitious prairie city was remodeling its Main Street, often in a recognizably Richardsonian style.

In the late nineteenth century, Richardson's work, as interpreted by other architects, prominently dotted midland city landscapes from Minneapolis to San Antonio. Richardson's style successfully envel-

◄185 Mould and McNicol, John C. Merriam House, St. Paul, Minnesota, 1887 (demolished 1960s)

A. C. Warner photo

dent in cities of this time to lay such a claim. Nor was Richardson's own work broadly democratic. It was limited to those who could afford to build in stone and to those who made decisions about "public" architecture. Moreover, within ten years after Richardson's death in 1886, the prairie cities, like their eastern counterparts, were fast adopting the steel frame skyscraper as their symbol of progress and modernity. A steel frame did not prohibit Richardson's masonry forms, as Root's Chicago buildings demonstrate, but it did imply a thrust high into the sky that would demand glass. Despite all of these qualifications, Richardson's work still can be seen as an important early influence on the look of the prairie cities.

oped sites with widely different functions, as seen in the civic, institutional, and commercial structures and residences elsewhere in this catalogue. For the prairie cities, several Richardson buildings served as important models. The Allegheny County Courthouse and Jail, for example, came almost immediately to symbolize government and all that it stood for. It also became an appropriate symbol for railroads, many of which were about to build large stations. The towers and the arches of the courthouse were copied in courthouses, schools, and railroad stations throughout the Midwest. Sometimes the entire building was replicated almost exactly, as in Long and Kees's design for the Minneapolis City Hall; sometimes it was scaled down, as in the

City Hall for Evanston, Illinois. In a similar way, Richardson's Trinity Church in Boston provided a design model for churches and libraries from Minnesota to Texas.

Perhaps an even more important influence was Richardson's Marshall Field Wholesale Store in Chicago. A monolithic but simple masonry structure, this was one of the best commercial buildings of the nineteenth century. More than Richardson's other works, this building gave form to the identity of the prairie cities. Its simplified mass quietly underscored the importance of work, and work was something these cities understood. The Field Warehouse was seldom copied exactly—its size and bulk would have been overwhelming for most prairie cities at this time. But its spirit and its message were replicated in banks and office buildings throughout the prairies, in small towns as well as in the larger cities (see figs. 17 and 19). The Field Warehouse embodied the dominant role of commerce in the midland cities. To no one's surprise, this vision resonated positively wherever it went in the Midwest.

No single Richardson house stands out as these public buildings do. Yet Richardson's influence was apparent on the late nineteenth-century residential landscape, notably in homes for the wealthy. Following Chicago's disastrous fire, entire blocks of Richardsonian masonry residences arose well away from the downtown. Prairie Avenue, for example, was developed as a stylish enclave on Chicago's south side. Anchored on one end by Richardson's 1886 Glessner house, Prairie Avenue was an oasis of large masonry homes, each symbolizing its owner's economic achievements (fig. 186). Lake Shore Drive on the north side was developed in the 1890s to succor wealthy homeowners driven from formerly elegant streets on the south and west sides by stunning social changes. This was another impressive Richardsonian landscape (see fig. 74), one that was judged "nearly prehistoric in its massive simplicity" by a contemporary writer.[17]

Richardson's mansions for the wealthy were sometimes a model for less expensive housing styles. Scaled-down Romanesque row houses could provide a Richardsonian aura at an affordable cost. Depending upon ornamentation, a 1,700-square-foot house could be had for $2,000 or less—the average cost for a middle-class house around 1890 (see figs. 34 and 75-77).[18] As architects strove to fix their professional identities in this period and disputes between architects and "mere" builders proliferated, Richardson's work became a unifying force. It appealed to both groups precisely because it "glorified economy but never cheapness."[19] A well-located Richardsonian row house or "cottage" also served the ambitions of the new middle class in the prairie cities; it shielded them from the noise and dirt of the city, distanced them from the poor, and helped promote the new idea of the nuclear family.[20]

One can speculate about the popularity of the Richardsonian style in the midsection of the country. One explanation may be wrought from the sheer amount of construction occurring in prairie cities at this time. It is normal for cities experiencing intense growth in one time period to build numerous structures in the most popular style of that time. The congruence here of Richardson's artistic influence with the boom of prairie city building cannot be underestimated.

There were, of course, other popular building styles in the 1880s and 1890s (Italianate, Gothic, and Queen Anne), and these styles were also well represented in the prairie cities. If Richardson's work had any special resonance for these cities, it may have been for its lack of ostentatious "European" ornament and for its use of stonework, a material familiar to German and Central European immigrant settlers. Richardson's style may also have proved symbolically meaningful for midwestern urban builders: while wealthy eastern magnates imported European castles and constructed massive "cottages" at Newport, there was still work to be done in Omaha and Chicago. Richardsonian structures were undoubtedly a comfortable fit for wealthy prairie residents; they could be quite large and internally elegant, yet somewhat subdued in their overall effect. In this way, Richardson's work, and that of his followers, fully encompassed the ambitions and tastes of prairie city builders and residents in the 1880s and 1890s. ✖

◄186 Prairie Avenue south
from the Glessner House,
Chicago, Illinois, c. 1925
postcard view

The Midland Prairies: Natural Resources and Urban Settlement

John C. Hudson

The built environments which we have received from our forebears are so unremarkable in most instances that there scarcely seems a need to understand them in any detail; they are simply with us, and that is enough. Americans have a long-standing tradition of ignoring—or even destroying—the past by refashioning the landscape to suit their own lives and times. The limitations of adopting such an outlook are well known, of course, and they go well beyond the poor judgment shown by those who cannot appreciate what history has given them. The past very often contains the key to understanding what a place is all about. To know a place is to know how it got that way. A cityscape is really nothing more than the longtime accumulation of decisions made by its own inhabitants or by influential outsiders. A sense of place and a sense of history are thus inextricably linked.

However much one might agree with this position, it is no easy task to trace individual links along these chains of decisions partly because so many influences and variations are involved. I would thus ask the reader's patience in what follows. The disparate topics introduced here are intended as background material for interpreting the presence of Richardson-influenced architecture in the smaller cities and towns of the midland prairie region. Setting the stage requires historical-geographic inquiry into diverse matters of geology, economy, and culture. The essay begins with an overview of geological conditions that created the supply of building stone. A discussion of the pattern of demand advances the subject on toward economic and cultural factors surrounding the urbanization process and finally to a more general analysis of the region's settlement pattern.

Regional Building Materials

A region labeled "midland prairies" might be imagined to have little in the way of accessible materials for building purposes. In fact, the opposite has always been true. Early settlers who hailed from the Upland South cut timber in the river valleys for their cabins, the Great Lakes forests to the north supplied millions of board feet of lumber for the balloon-frame structures that followed, and the clay deposits of glacial and earlier origins provided suitable raw material for brick manufacture. The progression from log to frame and then to brick construction paralleled the region's urban growth. Cities and towns evolved a new look as the frontier receded into the past. New building techniques and increased experimentation with the materials of construction reflected the aspirations of an affluent citizenry. People no longer content with the rude structures of frontier life demanded surroundings that suggested their own accomplishments as well as the future promise of their city and region.

There were still other building materials available to those who took the pains to extract them. Because of what might be termed geological happenstance, the midland prairie region is well supplied with building stone in a great variety of types, colors, and textures. In the early-to-mid-nineteenth century, stone could be used only near the site where it was quarried. Transportation barriers were largely overcome by the late nineteenth century when railroad lines reached into even the remotest corners of mid-America. Construction materials from anywhere could be ordered up by anyone with the money to do so, but there remained a tendency to rely on materials from within the region.

Granite, sandstone, quartzite, limestone, red brick, yellow brick, cobblestones, white pine, cottonwood, baled hay—one might list hundreds of materials that have been used for buildings, large or small, in one part of mid-America or another in the last two hundred years. Regional building hab-

◄**187** *(opposite)* **Portage Redstone Company advertisement, from the Chicago Architectural Sketch Club yearbook, 1892**

▲ 188 Granite quarry
distribution in the midland
prairies

▼ 189 St. Cloud, Minnesota
streetscape showing use of
local granite and brick, 1907
view of c. 1880-1900
buildings

architects and builders.

The core of the North American continent is a massive slab of granitic rock of Pre-Cambrian age (more than 600 million years old). The Pre-Cambrian granites are deeply buried under sedimentary rocks such as limestone and sandstone in most places, but in the center of the continent the ancient granitic rocks are at or near the surface in a region known as the Canadian Shield. The Superior Upland in the United States, which covers parts of Minnesota, Wisconsin, and upper Michigan, is the Shield's southern limit (fig. 188). Granite is quarried within this region and also around its southern margins where rivers carrying glacial discharge cut deep valleys into the Pre-Cambrian rocks.

These ancient granites are also within quarrying reach in several other midland localities south of the Superior Upland. Structural upwarping of the earth's crust created domes or ridges of Pre-Cambrian rock that remained after the sedimentary layers, pushed back by the uplift, eroded away and left the core of older rocks exposed. The St. François Mountains of southeastern Missouri, for example, were formed on Pre-Cambrian granites at the center of the Ozark Plateau upwarp. The highest peaks in the Black Hills of South Dakota are formed on granites that are exposed at the center of a domelike uplift. In scattered other localities, such as the Ouachita Mountains of Arkansas and the Llano Uplift in Texas, granites were being extracted for building stone by 1890. To the west, the Rocky Mountains, far more complex geologically, offered a major source of granite. Colorado led all other states west of Massachusetts in the production of granite for building purposes in 1890.[1]

Granite production in Minnesota began with operations at St. Cloud in 1867. While much of the stone was used locally, numerous courthouses and other public and commercial buildings from the Twin Cities to Winnipeg incorporated granite from the St. Cloud vicinity (fig. 189). Still older granites—more than two billion years old, the oldest rocks known in North America—were exposed in the Minnesota River valley. They were used locally, although some shipments were made beyond the region for buildings and monuments.[2]

Each formation of given rock type has its own distinctive physical and chemical properties. Rock from one formation might be useful as building stone, while that of the same type but of a different

its still reflect localisms based on what materials are at hand. The geography of building stone use has an even more strongly regional pattern because of the high transportation costs that accompanied removal over a long distance of enough stone even for a single building. The geological "basement" thus influenced the range of options open to

age (formation) might be restricted to crushing for road-building purposes. Because of its enormous weight, quarried rock had to possess some superior qualities if it was to be transported much beyond its area of production.

One of the qualities that make the Pre-Cambrian rocks desirable for building purposes is their hardness, but excessive hardness also is a limitation. Quartzite is a hard metamorphic rock formed from sandstone by the addition of silica to completely fill the interstices between grains. The fabled Sioux quartzite of the Luverne-Sioux Falls-Pipestone area of Minnesota and South Dakota is exceptionally hard even for a quartzite. Chemically, the stone is almost pure silica, but with a small percentage of iron that gives it a pink to purplish color. It is the hardest stone known to have been used for building purposes anywhere in the United States. Sioux quartzite saw limited use as a building stone outside the local region because it was not competitive with materials of lesser hardness and greater workability, but its attractive color and ability to take a polish made it marketable for facing and ornamental work[3] (figs. 190-192).

Most building stones in the Middle West are far younger than the Pre-Cambrian granites. Paleozoic-age limestones and sandstones (formed between 300 and 500 million years ago) are found beneath the surface nearly everywhere south of the Superior Upland, and they are exposed along every major river. Early white explorers making their way up the Mississippi and Missouri rivers traveled a virtual corridor between the massive bluffs of dolomitic limestone that form the bounding valley walls. Ceremonial sites, villages, and burial places of the aboriginal inhabitants dotted these bluffs that line both sides of the Mississippi valley between St. Louis and St. Paul-Minneapolis.

Because the Mississippi was the white settlers' avenue of approach to the region, many of the upper Middle West's early cities were located along the river. The valleys, which had been repeatedly deepened and broadened by the action of running water following episodes of glaciation, provided a natural corridor of penetration for the thousands of arriving migrants. The important cities along the Mississippi River and its tributaries were not located for reasons of access to building stone—it was merely a coincidence of bedrock geology and settlement history—but the coincidence is important nonetheless because of the range of building

materials that were incorporated into the local urban scene as a result (fig. 193).

Not all of mid-America has this kind of access to building stone. Settlements located near the centers of geological basins (downwarped structures that were filled with layer upon layer of sediments) sat high above the building stone formations. Areas such as central and eastern Illinois and all of the lower peninsula of Michigan, except its outer fringe, have practically no accessible building stone because the older, harder rock layers are buried be-

▲ **190 Abandoned quartzite quarry at Dell Rapids, South Dakota**

▼ **191 Quartzite streetscape, Dell Rapids, South Dakota, most of the buildings from the 1890s**

▶192 Wallace Dow, Minnehaha County Courthouse, Sioux Falls, South Dakota, 1888-90, the largest quartzite structure on the plains

▼193 Charles C. Smith, engineer, Great Northern Railway Stone Arch Bridge, Minneapolis, Minnesota, 1881

neath great depths of newer, softer rocks. The Great Plains west of about 100° has a similar geology; the present land surface is buried under newer, friable rock formations that offer no possibilities for building construction. The Gulf Coastal Plain of the southeastern United States has a geological upper story of the same sort. Its newer rock formations yield petrochemicals and stone for crushing, but building stone possibilities are practically nonexistent.

In all of these areas, the same limestone or sandstone that one might find outcropping along a Mississippi River bluff may be present, but it is so deeply buried under newer rocks that extraction is impossible. The Illinois and Michigan basins, the western Great Plains, and the Gulf Coastal Plain more or less surround the midland prairies, although, again, this is more a matter of coincidence than geological causation. The prairies were formed only during the last 10,000 years and probably owe their presence as much to human-caused fires as they do to any natural conditions

One is left, then, with a region stretching south from Lake Superior—the upper Mississippi valley, Iowa, and South Dakota, then south through Missouri and eastern Kansas to a narrow slice of Texas—that is in a uniquely favorable position for obtaining

stone. Erosion has cut the necessary valleys to expose the granite, limestone, and sandstone formations, and the rock thereby exposed is of a type that can be profitably quarried. Hundreds of limestone quarries were developed across this swath of country south of the Superior Upland (fig. 194).

As a Kansas Geological Survey bulletin noted: "Almost every municipality of any size in central and eastern Kansas has a limestone quarry nearby."[4] Such a condition reflects the widespread use, but also the short-distance travel, of most of the product. The regional bedrock geology of Kansas is revealed in some outstanding examples of stone use on the present landscape. Along the limestone bluffs of the Kansas (Kaw) River are Lawrence and LeCompton, worlds apart politically in the days when free- and slave-state forces, respectively, were headquartered there, but the two settlements shared the practice of building in stone quarried from the local formations (see figs. 106-108). Easily extracted limestones in treeless central Kansas were dug and cut for fence posts, a practice so widespread that the area became known as the Post Rock. Thin soils over bedrock made the Flint Hills grasslands south of Emporia suitable only for grazing, but the abundance of rock fragments littering the landscape were useful nonetheless and appear today as long, limestone fence walls bordering the estates of early cattle barons who came to the region a century ago.

A team of Missouri geologists reported that in their state "a majority of quarries in the sedimentary formations [were] engaged exclusively in producing stone to supply the local market."[5] Trenton limestone from the St. Genevieve area bordering the Ozarks had a marblelike appearance. The so-called "cotton rock," a light-buff dolomite quarried at Jefferson City, also had widespread local use. Sometimes a single rock formation, outcropping in a number of scattered localities, supplied stone for a broad area without requiring long-distance transportation.

The Burlington formation, an upper-Paleozoic limestone, furnished cut and sawed stone over a wide territory. The most extensive limestone quarries in Missouri were in the southwestern corner of the state, at Carthage, located on this formation. Nine quarries there shipped Burlington limestone by rail into eastern Kansas and south into Oklahoma. Banks, courthouses, schools, libraries, and business buildings as far west as central Oklahoma

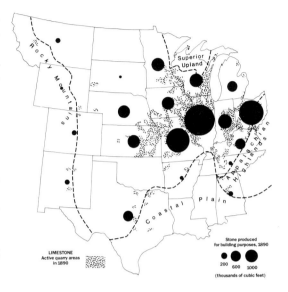

◀ 194 Limestone quarry distribution in the midland prairies

were constructed with Carthage stone. This same Burlington limestone also outcropped on the Mississippi River side of Missouri (Hannibal's quarries being one example) and at numerous other sites along the river.[6]

Practically all of the common building stone in St. Louis was obtained from the St. Louis limestone (see figs. 182-184), the same formation that forms the line of precipitous bluffs along the Mississippi River south of the city. Kansas City, likewise, had its own limestone ledge which was mined heavily for the local market. In both of these cases it was substantial on-site demand, rather than any inferiority of the stone, that caused most of the product to be consumed locally.

Sandstone, quarried at hundreds of sites from Lake Superior's wooded Apostle Islands in Wisconsin to the sagebrush mountains of West Texas, also was dispersed well beyond the scattered quarry sites (fig. 195; the map, based on data for 1890, does not show the subsequent Oklahoma and West Texas production areas). Nearly every settlement in the old Cherokee, Chickasaw, and Choctaw nations of Territorial Oklahoma had buildings of native sandstone—some of them vying for attention, perhaps, with the Carthage limestone structures in those same towns.[7] Granites and limestones were also quarried in turn-of-the-century Oklahoma, but it is the reddish sandstone, combined with the deep red hue of local brick, that lends a distinctive look to many an Oklahoman Main Street even today

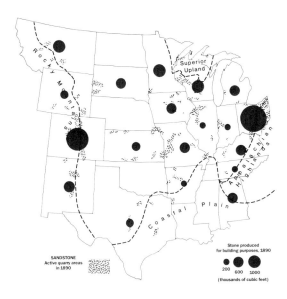

SANDSTONE
Active quarry areas
in 1890

Stone produced
for building purposes, 1890

200   600   1000
(thousands of cubic feet)

(fig. 196).

Oklahoma's deep red sandstones did not travel far to the north, but the more brownish sandstones from the Lake Superior region were shipped as far south as Kansas.[8] More than 600 million years old, sandstones quarried along the southwestern shore of Lake Superior and near Hinckley, Minnesota (fig. 197) were remnants of the sedimentary rock layers which were once deposited in the Lake Superior basin but gradually disappeared through erosion as the region underwent geologic uplift.

▲195 Sandstone quarry distribution in the midland prairie states

▼196 Joseph Foucart, De Stigner Building, Guthrie, Oklahoma, c. 1895, built of local redstone

Kettle River sandstone, quarried at Hinckley, traveled as far west as Spokane, Washington, and east to Pittsburgh, Pennsylvania, but its greatest use was for banks, business blocks, and public buildings in Minnesota, Iowa, and the Dakotas (see, for example, figs. 171 and 187).

Aesthetics, as well as cost, availability, and engineering considerations, seem to have guided those who chose to import one or another building stone from an outside location. For every exotic importation there were dozens of local shipments. The overall result was a dispersion of the more popular building stones for 100 miles or more around the quarry sites. Missouri had large sandstone quarries at Miami and at Warrensburg, south of the Missouri River in the west-central portion of the state. Warrensburg sandstone was used heavily in St. Louis and for courthouses in western Iowa and eastern Kansas, as well as in Missouri.[9] The Warrensburg and Hinckley examples are typical of the regional concentrations found in building stone use.

The sandstone hogbacks created by the Rocky Mountain uplift in Colorado and the Appalachian Plateau formations of eastern Ohio were the most important sources of sandstone for building purposes in mid-America in 1890.[10] Stone from both of these mountainous fringes of the Central Lowland was shipped into the midland prairie region. A booming, late nineteenth-century city like Chicago had enormous demands for building material, and it had the capital necessary to command quality stone from distant locations. Unlike the county-seat towns and medium-sized commercial centers to the west, Chicago had no regional look based on a predominance of color and type of stone from a single origin. Light gray Oolitic limestone from Bedford, Indiana, Lake Superior brownstone, Sioux quartzite, New England granite, and even importations from Europe might be found side by side in the great metropolis (see fig. 77). But in the country town the scene was more likely focused on one or two structures—perhaps a courthouse, railroad depot, or business block—with scaled-down dimensions fitting local needs, which incorporated only native materials.

The geographies of building stone supply and building stone demand, then, were sometimes very different. Cities such as Hot Springs, South Dakota, with its ample supply of Dakota-Lakota sandstone quarried nearby, were too remote from other centers to see much outside demand for their local

Kettle River Quarries, 1898

◀197 Kettle River sand-
stone quarry near Sandstone,
Minnesota, c. 1895

▼198 Al Hora, mason,
Petty Building, Hot Springs,
South Dakota, 1893

product[11] (fig. 198). The best building limestone in Texas was in the thinly populated Big Bend country west of the Pecos River, hundreds of miles from the major cities of the state,[12] and good sandstone was rare east of the Pecos. Commercial exploitation of these sources had not even begun in 1890, but in the following years West Texas's towns be-

gan to incorporate a variety of native stone buildings. This trait remains today as a feature of the urban scene, demarcating east from west across the broad plains of Texas.

Only two midland prairie states—Nebraska and North Dakota—were notably poor in terms of building stone resources. Both states imported theirs

(North Dakota received stone from Minnesota, Nebraska turned to Missouri as well as to Minnesota), but the lack of native materials was reflected in a less diversified array of building facades in the two states' cities. Southwestern North Dakota had some clays that were suitable for brick manufacture, but the rest of the state was short of this resource as well. Nebraska, in contrast, had a widespread pattern of brick clay deposits and manufactured more brick per inhabitant than any other state in the midland prairie region in 1890.[13] The rows of red-brick storefronts lining the Main Streets of Nebraska have their origins in this period. Their large-city equivalents were the phalanxes of brick warehouses and office buildings that once dominated Omaha's commercial district (fig. 199).

Regional Patterns of Urbanization

The brick production statistics for 1890 reveal substantial state-to-state variations which must be explained by many other factors than the availability of brick clay. Excluding bricks produced for paving purposes, ten of the twenty-four states from the Appalachians to the Rockies produced more than 1,000 bricks per capita in 1890. From east to west, they were: Ohio, Tennessee, Indiana, Illinois, Wisconsin, Minnesota, Missouri, Nebraska, Colorado, and Montana. Because cities had such voracious appetites for building bricks, the degree of urbanization of the various states should partially explain the pattern. The southern states, all of them

overwhelmingly rural, were represented only by Tennessee. The Dakotas, Oklahoma, New Mexico, and Wyoming were in the frontier category in 1890 and would not be expected to have had such industries. Colorado and Montana were mining frontiers at that time, and, as such, they had much greater urban concentrations than did the more agricultural states to the east.

The block of states from Ohio to Nebraska stood out most clearly; only Iowa and Michigan, which narrowly escaped inclusion, were absent from the list. These middle western states were scenes of rapid urban growth during the late nineteenth century. Frontier times were only a memory by then, the agricultural system was well established, most of the railroad network had been built, and the Middle West was becoming more industrial. Urban populations were growing as a result of off-farm migration within the region and a general westward shift of the population from the older, industrial Northeast.

When the national economy boomed, so did the regional economies focused upon the major urban centers. Each wave of new economic growth was accompanied by outward city expansion and by intensified building activity in the older business, industrial, and residential neighborhoods of every city. Economic boom periods thus left their mark. Earnings led to profits, profits to investments, and investments to an increasingly elaborate built environment. Building styles in vogue during a recession were thereby reproduced less often, while those in style during a boom saw many reproductions across the urban landscapes of mid-America.

The alternating booms and recessions that characterized the American economy during the late nineteenth and early twentieth centuries were felt not only in the major cities but also in every smaller place linked through the urban hierarchy to the national system. Country towns that began with a scatter of small, frame structures saw the initial stock of buildings replaced by brick business blocks, new courthouses and schools, and more elaborate residences. Towns that had no prospects for growth beyond their early boom periods did not participate in the successive waves of building and rebuilding. They became increasingly redundant as sites for business activity, and, as that happened, their initial buildings underwent adaptive reuse or were simply abandoned as the town's economy shriveled. The built environment is a semipermanent

▼199 Farnam Street,
Commercial district,
Omaha, Nebraska, c. 1900

E. C. STERLING,
President.

S. J HEWSON,
Gen'l Manager.

H. W. ELIOT,
Sec'y & Treas.

R. F. JACKSON.
Asst. Sec'y &Treas.

Northern Hydraulic-Press Brick Co.

MANUFACTURERS
AND
DEALERS IN

HYDRAULIC-PRESS BRICK
AND
Lime and Cement.

BUILDING MATERIALS

◄ 200 Northern Hydraulic-
Press Brick Company,
St. Louis, advertisement
showing W.B. Dunnell's Red
Wing Training School for
Boys

Sewer Pipe.
Plaster Hair.
Pecora Mortar Stains.
Ornamental Terra Cotta.
Wire Lath Mineral Wool.
"Sterling" Mortar Colors.
Salt Glazed Wall Coping.
Dexter Bros.' Shing'e Stains.
Passenger and Freight Eleva-
tors.
Ottawa and St. Louis Fire
Brick.
Hansen's Patent Chimney
Tops.
Two and Three Ply Ready
Roofing.
Sheathing Papers and Pipe
Covering.
Lederer's and Ricketson's Mil-
waukee Mortar Colors.

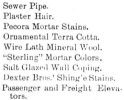

St. Louis and Chicago
Hydraulic-Press Brick.
In Red, Buff and
Mottled Shades.

Northern
Hydraulic
Press
Brick

In red or
Brown
Shades.

STATE REFORM SCHOOL, RED WING, MINN., W. B. Dunnell, Architect.

Pressed Brick in this Building and Cottages
FURNISHED BY
Northern Hydraulic-Press Brick Co.
COMMON AND VENEERING BRICK.

Prices made delivered to any railway station in the Northwest!

General Office and Exhibit Rooms:

No. 10 North Third St. Minneapolis, Minn.

TELEPHONE 823.

WORKS AT { MENOMONIE, Wis.
{ WRENSHALL, Minn.

OTHER OFFICES: { ST. PAUL, DULUTH,
{ WEST SUPERIOR.

▲ **201 H.C. Koch, Montgomery County Courthouse, Red Oak, Iowa, 1890-91, carved detail**

▶ **202 Montgomery County Courthouse, sited on a second central square**

record of these ups and downs, preserving economic history in a visible rather than statistical form, one that equally remains for succeeding generations to read.

Regional Patterns of Settlement

While the "look" of a town can be explained partly by the availability of certain materials and by the vicissitudes of economic history, closer inspection often reveals similarities and differences from place to place unrelated to such factors. Within the midland prairie region there is a cleavage between north and south, based on the cultural backgrounds of early inhabitants, that reveals itself in the layout and structure of cities both large and small.

The native-born settlers of mid-America moved nearly straight west, one generation at a time, beyond the Appalachians, into the Ohio and Mississippi valleys, and west into the grasslands. Dakotans, Minnesotans, and Wisconsinites with long family histories in the United States generally trace their ancestry back to New York and New Eng-

land; Kansans, Iowans and mid-Illinoians go back to Ohio and Pennsylvania; Missouri's early population came from Kentucky and Virginia, as did Indiana's. There were significant blurrings of lines here and there, especially across central Iowa, southern Nebraska, and Kansas, but the north-south sorting of population continued through each successive stage of westward migration.[14]

Part of this geographical zonation is explained by differences in timing of westward population surges. The Virginia-rooted population (via Kentucky) that settled southern Illinois and northern Missouri formed the first wave; the present-day communities along this southern margin of the prairie were well established by 1840. Ohio-born farmers, whose ancestors came from Pennsylvania, constituted the next wave into the prairies (1835 to 1850), and they extended their system of farming and settlement into Kansas and southern Nebraska by 1860. Yankees from New England were the third and latest to arrive, although the Yankee frontier spread so rapidly that it had reached western Minnesota by 1870.

Here, then, was a broad swath of the most fertile grassland in America that was settled by three separate frontier populations during roughly the four decades prior to 1870. By 1890, this section of the midland prairies had achieved considerable economic maturity. County-seat towns and other medium-sized places—in addition to the handful of true cities that had grown up—were ready to add to their Main Streets and courthouse squares an architecture that would reflect their newfound urban prosperity. Architects in nearly two dozen midland prairie cities had, by this time, fallen under H.H. Richardson's influence. Chicago, Minneapolis, Omaha, Topeka, Wichita, Sioux Falls, Sioux City, Davenport, Dubuque, and Mankato became local centers of Richardsonian style. Their architects soon began receiving commissions from other urban centers in their vicinity as well, resulting in a suffusion of Richardsonian buildings into numerous smaller cities. By the turn of the century, Richardsonian courthouses and business blocks were found in more than 150 prairie cities, ranging from north-central Minnesota to southern Texas.

The Influence of Migration Routes

While it was the architect, on the approval of local influential citizens, who produced a Richardsonian design, the siting of buildings and the prominence given to public versus private space in the city center provided the local context within which the architect worked. Yankees held ideas about urban settlements that set them apart from the others, especially from those who traced their roots back to Pennsylvania or Virginia.

Business was the centerpiece of the Yankee town because it was the most important function that the town performed. Yankee-stream urban designers sometimes reserved a square-block park or green at the city center, but this land generally was left open and was rarely used for anything except green space; public buildings or even public marketplaces were rarely found there. Business buildings occupied all the rest of the central downtown space. The emphasis was on private property. Public institutions were kept on the back streets or at least away from the town center.

Yankees had an aversion to placing the county courthouse in the center of town, perhaps because it suggested too prominent a role for government. Like churches and schools, courthouses in the Yankee town were set to one side a bit, off-center with

respect to the business district, and sometimes even occupying part of the residential portion of the plat. This stands in sharp contrast to the preferences of settlers whose roots went back to Pennsylvania or Virginia.

The American courthouse square probably originated in colonial southeastern Pennsylvania.[15] From there it spread westward into the midsection of the country and throughout much of the South. The county courthouse is overwhelmingly the most obvious, and usually the most elaborate, building in town when it occupies the center square. The more symmetrical and concentric the layout, the greater the attention focused on the government as centerpiece. In such an arrangement, businesses lined themselves up on the four enclosing block faces. The space between the courthouse grounds and the bracketing business square often was kept large enough so that a weekly market might be held there. Such an arrangement, but with a church substituting for the courthouse, harks back at least to the distant European past.

Whether or not ideology played a great role in

◄ 203 C.A. Dunham, Faribault County Courthouse, Blue Earth, Minnesota, 1891-92, early view toward town

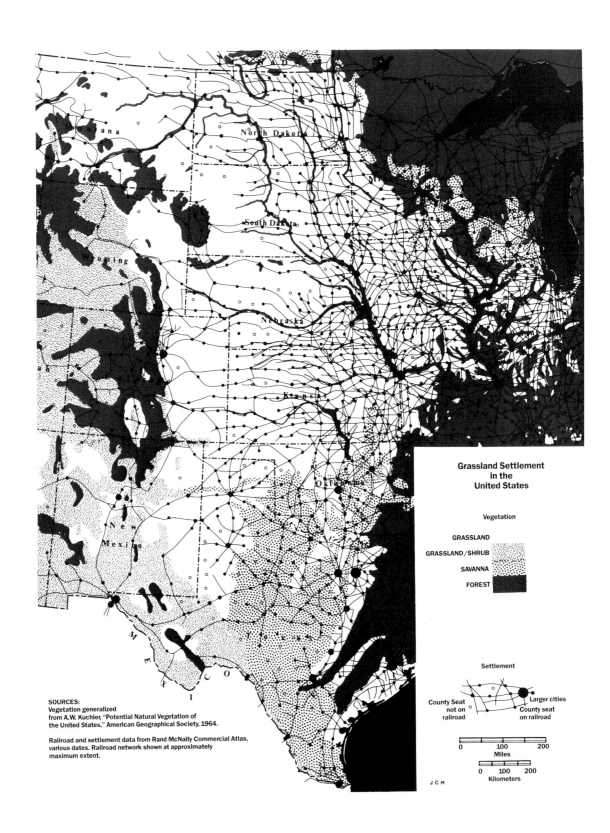

**Grassland Settlement
in the
United States**

Vegetation

GRASSLAND

GRASSLAND/SHRUB

SAVANNA

FOREST

Settlement

County Seat
not on
railroad

Larger cities

County seat
on railroad

0   100   200
Miles

0   100   200
Kilometers

SOURCES:
Vegetation generalized
from A.W. Kuchler, "Potential Natural Vegetation of
the United States," American Geographical Society, 1964.

Railroad and settlement data from Rand McNally Commercial Atlas,
various dates. Railroad network shown at approximately
maximum extent.

J C H

this Yankees-versus-others split in ideas about town form remains a subject for speculation. Eventually, in any case, the two models were repeated habitually, in county after county, as settlement spread to the west. Because migration streams were largely sorted along the north-south dimension, the courthouse-versus-business centerpiece was effectively regionalized as well. Habit and familiarity, rather than conscious decisions based on different world views, probably was the factor that kept the two types separate and confined to their respective migration streams.

The result is a spectacular series of county courthouses on center squares across the midsection of the country; the southern tier of Iowa counties probably is the best single concentration, but examples abound in every direction away from there. Richardson-influenced courthouses from southern Illinois to central Kansas are located precisely where settlers whose ancestry traces to southeastern Pennsylvania (via Ohio and Illinois) dominated in the early years. Paris, Carrollton, and Pittsfield in Illinois; Greenfield, Knoxville, and Fairfield in Iowa are half-a-dozen examples of this particular Richardsonian context (figs. 201 and 202).

There are some impressive courthouses in Yankeeland, to be sure, but their locations are not nearly as effective in terms of prominence and visibility. The Richardson-inspired courthouse in Blue Earth, Minnesota, is an example of one such imposing structure occupying a relatively obscure site a few blocks from the business district (fig. 203). Other Yankeeland examples, including Winona, Minnesota, and Sioux Falls, South Dakota, have a central city-block for their courthouses, but the four facing rows of business fronts that make the courthouse the visual center are lacking.

Influence of the railroads

Every innovation of transportation or communication, from the ox cart to television, has had the effect of homogenizing the human condition. New forms of interaction always represent a jump in society's ability to spread goods or services or ideas more widely and more cheaply than before. The railroad happened to be the innovation which transformed the prairie region because its technology was developed during the settlement period in mid-America.

Railroad builders in the 1850s stood to earn huge profits, for as many years as any investor cared to

◄ 204 *(opposite)* Grassland settlement in the United States

▲ 205 Buechner and Jacobsen, Lac Qui Parle County Courthouse, Madison, Minnesota, 1889, sited at the end of Main Street and facing the railroad tracks

project, simply by constructing across the prairies the lines of track which would carry the products of agriculture out to urban markets. But this required the addition of a new sideline to the railroad business. The only towns *in* the prairie region were not really *on* the prairie at all. They were river towns, located along the navigable streams by the region's early settlers at a time when water transportation was all there was. A few cities had been founded out on the plains between the river valleys, but their number was scarcely sufficient to constitute even a beginning for the kind of settlement system the railroads would need. Therefore railroaders took it upon themselves to create new towns along their lines of track which would serve as the marketing and collection points for the surrounding agricultural population.[16]

There was no single guiding hand behind these efforts. Rather, railroad corporations competed with one another, extending lines of track into one another's territory, crisscrossing the countryside, until every pocket of land had been placed within access to one or more railroad lines. In some areas the competition was intense, in others, less so, but the grid of railroad lines dotted with trade-center towns eventually blanketed the entire prairie-plains region (fig. 204).

The thousands of North American towns founded by railroad companies during the late nineteenth and early twentieth centuries used no more than two or three basic designs, copied and recopied from one railroad company to the next. Yankees were prominent in the railroad business all over the United States, and perhaps this is why the railroad town developed more or less along the lines of the business-centered Yankee town.

The typical railroad town Main Street either paralleled or was perpendicular to the tracks. Every 300-foot block face was divided into twelve 50-foot business lots that were 125 feet deep. With few exceptions, every business lot on every block in every town had these dimensions. The design was favored by townsite agents who wanted to sell lots. One result was that the typical railroad-town Main Street was lined by rows of identical-looking false-front store buildings, each one housing a small business. Substantial business blocks, if they came at all, came somewhat later, after the town had a chance to grow and to attract further investment. Corner lots in the heart of the business district always brought the highest prices when railroad townsite agents held their town-lot auctions. And these sites, in later years, offered the only locations where business buildings of greater architectural interest could show anything but a facade to passersby.

Here, then, is another contextual dimension within which the geography of Richardson-influenced architecture must be understood. The formative design element of the railroad town was the railroad itself. Business districts, parks, squares, and all other elements of the urban fabric were

located with respect to the railroad because the railroad company had priority in determining the design. In many early railroad towns, platted symmetrically around the railroad tracks, there was no possibility for a central focus that would hold a major public or private building.

The most common railroad-town design, known as the T-town, was based on a single, major business street projected at an angle away from the tracks. The railroad depot generally was located at one end of the street; business buildings lined both sides of the street for several blocks beyond it. Local citizens usually asked the railroad to donate townsite land for courthouses and other public structures, and most such requests were honored, only, the railroad rarely chose to give away valuable land near the town's center that otherwise might be sold. As a result, courthouse squares were located a half-dozen or more blocks away from the center in a typical railroad town. Their locations were visually prominent in those cases where the principal street had been deliberately truncated, ending at a courthouse or school, thus creating a long vista down Main Street from the tracks (fig. 205).

Probably more than half of the towns founded by railroad companies were outright failures that saw the largest share of their initial business people disappear within five or ten years of the town's founding. As the economics of retailing changed and, especially, after good roads and automobiles made the tight network of small trade centers redundant, there emerged an increasingly competitive struggle between towns to maintain their share of local business. County seat towns, with their expanded sphere of business and social relationships, were especially likely to survive. Growth was more a multiplicative than an additive process: growth begat more growth; failure, more failure. A town had "arrived" when its leading merchants and professional people were able to contemplate construction of new, substantial brick or stone edifices that would replace the one-and-a-half story frame false-fronts. Competition, pride, and envy, when backed by money in the bank, led to more handsome new buildings once somebody had built the first one (figs. 206 and 207).

Here, then, we arrive back at the starting point of this essay. The midland prairie region happens to have been endowed with building material resources sufficiently dispersed—and, equally important, sufficiently diverse—to make possible both

▼ 206 **Main Street, Ida Grove, Iowa, from bank of 1888 to Masonic Building of c. 1892**

◄ 207 Third Street, Yankton, South Dakota, from John H. Coxhead's Wilcox block of 1890 to I. J. Galbreath's Yankton National Bank of 1893

local/regional type-concentrations as well as broad, place-to-place similarities in building material choices. Pioneer migration fanned out into the midland prairies as families rooted in New England, Pennsylvania, or Virginia moved westward, but latitudinal belts were followed so closely that it is possible to discern strong cultural similarities over hundreds of miles of east-west distance today, just as it is possible to discern regional differences along the north-south axis of the prairie region. The major agency responsible for spreading a homogeneous urban network was the railroad and its practice of town-founding. The consequence of all of these factors, in combination, was to blanket the midland prairies with hundreds of settlements that might be expected to harbor remarkably similar ideas of what a city ought to look like and which, therefore, might be expected to make similar choices when new forms of architectural expression came within their grasp. ✜

Notes

In the notes, periodicals frequently cited have been identified by the following abbreviations:

AABN   *American Architect and Building News*
BB   *The Building Budget*
IA   *The Inland Architect and Builder, succeeded by The Inland Architect and News Record*
JSAH   *Journal of the Society of Architectural Historians*

Larson

1. This and all other generalizations regarding the dating of the various phases of Richardson's influence on the prairies are based on an exhaustive survey of the regional trade periodicals listed on page 30; consultation with state historic preservation officers, city landmarks commission officers, and regional specialists; and NEH-funded travel to hundreds of sites in the ten states surveyed.

2. The Cable House was evidently planned a year earlier; see *BB* 1: 8-85. Burnham and Root's quasi-Richardsonian Edward E. Ayer House went up at the same time (1885, demolished), but was built of rubble rather than ashlar.

3. The earliest example of which I have been able to find photographic record is Barnett and Haynes's A. Brocaw House in St. Louis (1886), published in an undated office brochure, *Examples From the Recent Work of Barnett, Haynes, and Barnett.* St. Louis did not produce a residential design even as Richardsonian as the McNair House until the completion of Richardson's own projects there for the Lionbergers in 1888.

4. As Carroll Meeks insisted, the round-headed style was firmly in place well before Richardson. See his "Romanesque Before Richardson," *Art Bulletin* 26 (March 1953): 17-33. More recent research has been summarized by David van Zanten in "Sullivan to 1890" in *Louis Sullivan: The Function of Ornament,* ed. Wim de Wit (New York: W.W. Norton and Co., 1986), 40. Pitch-faced ashlar had also been used extensively by both James Renwick and Cyrus Eidlitz, albeit in a Gothic mode, many years before Richardson's popularization of it.

5. Architect's report, *BB* 1 (August 1885 Supplement).

6. See, for example, Schuyler's sardonic description of E.P. Bassford's St. Paul City Hall and Courthouse (1883-84, demolished): "a congeries of unrelated and unadjusted parts [which] may be admitted to be characteristically W--n" [ellipses his], "Glimpses of Western Architecture: St. Paul and Minneapolis," *Harper's Magazine* 83 (October 1891): 736-55; reprt in *American Architecture and Other Writings,* ed. William H. Jordy and Ralph Coe (Cambridge, Mass.: Belknap Press of Harvard University, 1961), 296.

7. "The Romanesque Revival in America," *Architectural Record* 1 (October-December 1891): 192.

8. "St. Paul Correspondence," signed "Doric," *BB* 6 (May 1890): 60.

9. Ibid.

10. Unsigned article in the *Chicago Sun Times,* 30 May 1886, quoted in *BB* 3 (May 1887): 72-73.

11. Unsigned editorial in *BB* 3 (May 1887): 72-73.

12. In reviewing the competition sketches, McLean slyly called the most transparent copy of Richardson's masterpiece, which would soon win second place (by local architect W.H. Dennis, who also knew much better), "worthy of the great master himself." *IA* 11 (April 1888): 34.

13. The winning design, sketched for the competition by *American Architect and Building News* renderer D.A Gregg, was published in that magazine on April 7, 1888. Call for a final design from the architects after the commission had been awarded resulted in a number of changes recorded in a sketch by office draftsman A.B. Chamberlin. This was published as a "preliminary sketch" by the local *Real Estate Review* in its July-August 1888 issue and as the "final sketch" in *Northwestern Architect,* November 1888. The truly final sketch by freelance draftsman/designer Francis Fitzpatrick, which reorganized the window scheme, altered the main towers, and moved the city hall entry to the side opposite the county courthouse entry, was not published until early

1889 (*Real Estate Review*, December-January-February 1889). Since both Chamberlin's and Fitzpatrick's rendering styles had undergone a radical Ellisian transformation in the prior year, it is quite possible that some of the innovations on the Allegheny County Courthouse design that appeared may have been influenced by local draftsman Harvey Ellis's treatment of Richardsonian themes. The theatrical insertion of bold Egyptian columns into the base and belfry of the tower is a case in point

14. Shepley, Rutan and Coolidge's Shadyside Presbyterian Church (extant) and Halsey Wood's Christ Church (demolished), both from the late 1880s, proved strong enough designs to establish reputations in their own right.

15. Patton and Fisher, First Baptist Church of Hyde Park (1895). The earlier and much more elegant brownstone version was Burling and Whitehouse's St. Paul's Universalist Church on the west side (1891, demolished). For illustrations, see *IA* 23 (June 1894) and *Northwestern Architect* (April 1891) respectively. Burling and Whitehouse's Church of the Epiphany (1885, extant) was the first church in the midland states to borrow heavily from Richardson's work, though it imitated no particular ecclesiastical design.

16. A magnificent rendering of local architects James and James's design appeared in *AABN* 29 (16 May 1891). The brick, brownstone, granite, and terra cotta behemoth was never built. A much more prosaic Richardsonian pastiche originally slated for a suburban station went up instead.

17. This little-known structure, cowering for a few short years beneath the gargantuan city hall, set its tower at the crossing of what was little more than an L-shaped shed. For a photograph, see *Artwork in Kansas City and Vicinity* (Chicago, 1900).

18. "The Romanesque Revival in America," 159.

19. A photograph is contained in Scrap Album #1 in the Hennepin County Historical Society Collection, Minneapolis.

20. For Schuyler's comments, see Schuyler, *American Architecture*, 310. The Minneapolis commentator's letter was published in *BB* 6 (May 1890): 60.

21. Jones became the first professor of architecture at the University of Minnesota in 1892-93. He continued to be influenced by Richardson's handling of scale and volume well into the twentieth century, e.g., in his great Butler Brothers Warehouse (1906).

22. *IA* 16 (October 1890).

23. Carolyn Hewes Toft, "Who Designed Union Station?" *Landmarks Letter* 20 (May 1985): 4-5. These newsletters, published by the Landmarks Association of St. Louis, are excellent sources of information about early St. Louis architects.

24. For this and other details about van Brunt's Kansas City career, see Sherry Piland, "Henry van Brunt of the Architectural Firm of van Brunt and Howe: the Kansas City Years" (Master's thesis, University of Missouri, Kansas City, 1976).

25. For brief descriptions and renderings of these early (for Kansas City) Richardsonian blocks, see *AABN* 20 (20 August 1886) and *IA* 11 (June 1888). Longmeadow brownstone was also used by Shepley, Rutan and Coolidge for their Lionberger Warehouse in St. Louis and by Peabody and Stearns for their James J. Hill House in St. Paul, in spite of an abundance of readily available Lake Superior brownstone. Since the Norcross Brothers contracted for all of these jobs (as they had for much of Richardson's work), it may be that their ownership of a Longmeadow quarry was instrumental in such decisions to ship coals to Newcastle.

26. This Union Pacific depot, severely reduced from its 1885 plan bid out at $50-75,000, was still the firm's largest railroad project in a Richardsonian vein. A rendering of the building as executed was published in *IA* 9 (July 1887).

27. J.L. Silsbee and Frederick Perkins were the most prominent among these to pick up on Richardson's work.

28. Marlys Svendsen et al., *Davenport: Where the Mississippi Runs West: A Survey of Davenport History and Architecture* (Davenport, Iowa: City of Davenport, 1982), 13:2.

29. Richardson's possession of a copy of Revoil is well known; it was also included in B.T. Batsford's list of 100 essential books for an architect's office in *AABN* 22 (30 July 1887): 52. The Alsatian architect Joseph Eckel's copy survives in the archives of his successor firm in St. Joseph, Bruner and Bruner, architects and engineers. Revoil's measured drawings were also reprinted in this country by The Architectural Book Publishing Company.

30. The translator was W.A. Otis, a Chicago architect who had graduated from the Ecole des Beaux Arts in 1881 and was with W.L.B. Jenney at the time of publication. Jenney's very few Romanesque designs can possibly be attributed to Otis, who was his draftsman for several years before becoming his partner, or to W.B. Mundie, who made the same transition from draftsman to partner in 1890.

31. The original sketch appeared in the 1864 *Syrie centrale*, of which Richardson's library had a copy. It achieved much wider circulation through reprints in *IA* 9 (July 1887) and *AABN* 27 (28 June 1890).

32. See, for example, C.H. Blackall's "Notes of Travel: Salamanca," *AABN* 20 (28 August 1886): 95-96. Blackall, a Rotch Traveling Scholar, commented that "nowhere else in Spain is the simple, round arch used as effectively" and commended a house for its "wide arch-stones which are full of quiet interest."

33. For a balanced review of the status of San Marco at the time, see *AABN* 20 (4 September 1886).

34. The results were originally published in foreign archaeological journals (French for Sta. Sophia in 1885 and German for St. Sergius in 1895), but presumably found their way into a wider press as well. See H. Swanson, *Byzantinische Zeitschrift* 4 (1895), 106-8.

35. For a more complete account of the role of *IA* in championing a Richardsonian style, see Robert Prestiona, *The Inland Architect: Chicago's Major Architectural Journal, 1883-1908* (Ann Arbor: UMI Press, 1985), 130 ff.

36. Reviewed in *BB* 2 (April 1886) and *BB* 3 (March 1887) respectively. I have been unable to find copies of either brochure, though specific designs drawn from each were frequently published in *Northwestern Architect* and *BB*, and several of the schoolhouse designs were also published in *Scientific American, Architects and Builders Edition* (September 1886), reprinted in Eugene Mitchell, ed., *American Victoriana* (New York: Van Nostrand Reinhold, 1979), 48-49.

37. Other South Dakota schools were at Huron (1886), Pierre (1889), and Yankton (c. 1890); all have been demolished. The Brookings High School was a double version of a design first worked out for a school in Oregon Territory.

38. Freeborn County Courthouse, Albert Lea (1887-89); Morrison County Courthouse, Little Falls (1890-91); and Faribault County Courthouse, Blue Earth (1891-92).

39. *IA* 3 (July 1884).

40. *IA* 2 (January 1884); *IA* 5 (April 1885); *BB* 2 (February 1886).

41. See, for example, the debate at the Illinois Association of Architects meetings in 1887, published in its entirety in *BB* 3 (May 1887): 70-74.

42. Membership and annual meetings' attendance lists were published regularly in *IA*. See for example v. 12 (December 1888): 80. George Beaumont's "History and Development of the Chicago Architectural Sketch Club" was presented to the Illinois Association and published in *IA* 13 (April 1889): 57-58.

43. Reported in a notice submitted by Edward H. Allen, president of the Exchange Building Association, and architectural advisor William R. Ware, *IA* 8 (August 1886): 4-5. This was the first competition under the code developed by members of the Western Association in 1885.

44. A circular went out in late 1887, with plans due in February 1888. See n. 13 above.

45. These were published in *Northwestern Architect* 6 (Supplement to n. 4, 1888).

46. Paul Goeldner, "Our Architectural Ancestors," *Texas Architect* 24 (July-August 1974).

47. Root's Chicago contemporaries were insistent on his independence from Richardson's influence in spite of Root's frequent use of such common Richardsonian devices as low-sprung arches, battered foundations, and raised arcades with Romanesque ornament. A modified version of this view is developed by Donald Hoffmann in *The Architecture of John Wellborn Root* (Baltimore: The Johns Hopkins University Press, 1973).

48. Similar grotesques, but without such pained looks, flank the central entries of the west portals of St. Gilles du Gard and St. Trophime. Both were illustrated by Revoil.

49. *AABN* 18 (12 December 1885)

50. Interview with Josiah Moss in "J.B. Moss—Medieval Castle for Frontier Baron," *St. Joseph News-Press*, 12 June 1938. I am indebted for this and other material regarding the Moss house to his nephew, Preston Moss.

51. Joseph Eckel's widow complained repeatedly and bitterly about the inflated role accorded to Ellis by his later admirers. Her memory of him, as a draftsman absent during the planning stages of the designs he drew, was likely correct.

52. See Mary Carolyn Jutson, *Alfred Giles: An English Architect in Texas and Mexico* (San Antonio: Trinity University Press, 1972). Giles's other ambitious San Antonio residential commission was dubbed the "Evans Chateâu" shortly after it was built.

53. See, for example, his "Architectural Ornamentation," *IA* 5 (April 1885): 55.

54. N. Clifford Ricker, "Possibilities for American Architecture," *IA* 6 (November 1885): 63.

55. Hoffmann, *Architecture of J.W. Root*, 95.

56. "The Romanesque Revival in America," 198.

57. See, for example, the editor's scathing attack on "the American Romansque" as "bald in treatment, clumsy in mass, brutal in detail" in *Architectural Review* 1 (14 December 1891):14.

58. Promotional brochure privately printed by Link and Cameron, "St. Louis Depot Competition, 1891," 15.

59. Letter to Claude Bragdon dated November 8, 1903; published by Bragdon in *More Lives Than One* (New York: Knopf, 1938), 157.

60. For a recent visual analysis of the relation between the Marshall Field Wholesale Store and the Auditorium Building fenestration schemes, see William H. Jordy, "The Tall Buildings," in *Louis Sullivan: The Function of Ornament*, ed. Wim de Wit (New York: W.W. Norton and Co., 1986), 73.

61. Quoted in a letter written by David Gibson to A.W. Sullivan; copy on file in the Getty Tomb notebook, Commission on Architectural Landmarks, Chicago.

62. Dunnell had no official state post but designed precisely the same class of buildings—schools, hospitals, penal and welfare institutions—as his successor in the first state architect's office, Clarence Johnston.

63. "Architectural Ornamentation," *IA* 5 (April 1885):54

64. Unsigned comment in the Minneapolis-based *Improvement Bulletin*, 8 June 1898.

65. Bell's Richardsonian designs for federal buildings ran the gamut from crude assemblies of boxy volumes with meretricious ornament (Carson City United States Courthouse and Post Office) to doctrinaire renditions of the master's style (Rochester United States Courthouse and Post Office), with the Bexar United States Courthouse and Post Office in San Antonio falling somewhere between.

66. A favorite device of Aiken's was to substitute an elegant Florentine campanile for Richardson's rude shaft. See, for example, his United States Courthouse and Post Office in Sioux City, Iowa, which was begun under Edbrooke in 1892 but not completed until 1896 under Aiken's direction.

67. For side-by-side comparison, see Philip Larson, *World Architecture in Minnesota* (St. Paul: Minnesota Museum of Art, 1979), 4.

68. See Henry-Russell Hitchcock, *The Architecture of H.H. Richardson and His Times* (New York: Museum of Modern Art, 1936; 2d ed. Hampden, Conn.: Archon Books, 1961; rpt. ed. Cambridge, Mass.: The MIT Press, 1966) and Lewis Mumford, *The Brown Decades* (New York, 1931). Hitchcock has since given more attention to the Victorian roots of Richardson's work but continues to see his impact as directly modern, i.e., without the intervening work of the Renaissance Revivalists.

Schlereth

1. Marcus Whiffen and Frederick Koeper, *American Architecture, 1607-1976* (Cambridge, Mass.: The MIT Press, 1981), 227.

2. Thomas E. Tallmadge, *Architecture in Old Chicago* (Chicago: University of Chicago Press, 1941), 145-69. Montgomery Schulyer, *American Architecture and Other Writings*, ed. William H. Jordy and Ralph Coe (Cambridge, Mass.: Belknap Press of Harvard University Press, 1961), 200-225; 246-81.

3. Whiffen and Koeper, *American Architecture*, 233; Schuyler, *American Architecture*, 191-330.

4. Two Richardsonian influences in Chicago and on Chicago architects are not traced. No attention is given to Richardson's three able assistants—George Foster Shepley (1858-1903); Charles Hercules Rutan (1851-1914); and Charles Allerton Coolidge (1858-1936)— who not only saw several of his Chicago and other midwestern projects to completion after his death in 1886 but also had Chicago careers of their own. Similarly, the important indebtedness of Frank Lloyd Wright to an earlier master builder (particularly in the Shingle Style) of the custom-designed, one-family residence is not discussed. On the role of Shepley, Rutan, and Coolidge in Chicago architectural history, see the entry "Charles Allerton Coolidge," in Henry F. Withey and Elsie R. Withey, *Biographical Dictionary of American Architects* (Los Angeles: New Age Publishers, 1956), 136-37. Richardson's influence on Wright is traced in James O'Gorman, "Henry Hobson Richardson and Frank Lloyd Wright," *The Art Quarterly* 22 (Autumn 1969): 308-11.

5. Marianna Griswold Van Rensselaer, *Henry Hobson Richardson and His Works* (Boston: 1888; rpt. ed., New York: Dover, 1969), 169-70, lists Richardson's commissioned Chicago works as being received into the office as follows: Marshall Field Wholesale Store, April 11, 1885; J.J. Glessner Residence, May 1885; Franklin MacVeagh Residence, July 1885.

6. John Jacob Glessner, a vice-president of Warder, Bushnell and Glessner, a midwestern farm implements manufacturing firm eventually merged to form International Harvester, wrote that he first spoke with "Boston friends" before approaching Richardson to do his house in May 1885. J.J. Glessner, *The House at 1800 Prairie Avenue, Chicago, 1886: H.H. Richardson, Architect,* ed. Jethro M. Hurt (Chicago Architectural Foundation, 1978), 3, reprints Glessner's *The Story of a House* (1923) and an unpublished letter to the Glessner children on how the Glessners selected Richardson as architect.

7. Henry-Russell Hitchcock, "Richardson's American Express Building: A Note" and J. Carson Webster, "Richardson's American Express Building," *JSAH* 9

(March-May 1950): 25-30, 21-24; Schuyler, *American Architecture,* 261-62; Peter B. Wight, "H.H. Richardson," obituary in *IA* 7 (May 1886): 59; Tallmadge, *Architecture in Old Chicago,* 114.

8. Henry-Russell Hitchcock, *The Architecture of H.H. Richardson and His Times* (New York: Museum of Modern Art, 1936; 2d ed. Hampden, Conn.: Archon Books, 1961; rpt. ed. Cambridge, Mass.: The MIT Press, 1966), 273.

9. Dankmar Adler, "Style," *IA* 8 (December 1886): 76; R.C. McLean, *IA* 7 (August 1886): 1-2; A.O. Elzner, "A Reminiscence of Richardson," *IA* 20 (September 1892): 15; Thomas Tallmadge, "Holographs of Famous Architects," *American Architect* 143 (March 1933): 8-12; Charles Dudley Warner, *Studies in the South and West* (New York: 1889): 184-85; Edward Atkinson, "Slow-Burning Construction," *The Century Magazine* 37 (February 1889): 566-79. See also J.B. Noel, "Modern Romanesque Architecture," *Architectural Review* 6 (August 1899): 103-7.

10. O'Gorman, now the leading American student of Richardson, has examined the Field Store in the greatest detail to date in "The Marshall Field Wholesale Store: Materials Toward a Monograph," *JSAH* 37 (October 1978): 175-94.

11. Schuyler, *American Architecture,* 264; Edward Atkinson, who knew the New England mill tradition first-hand and was Richardson's Brookline neighbor and erstwhile client, remarks that the Field Store was "but a glorified cotton factory" in "Slow-Burning Construction" 566-79. Also see Jack Quinn, "H.H. Richardson and the Boston Granite Tradition," *Little Journal,* Society of Architectural Historians, Western New York Chapter, 3 (February 1979): 20-29 and O'Gorman, "Marshall Field Wholesale Store," 191-92.

12. Harriet Monroe, *John Wellborn Root* (Boston: 1896), 119-20; J.K. Freitag, *Architectural Engineering,* (2nd ed., New York: 1912), 311; Donald Hoffmann, *The Architecture of John Wellborn Root* (Baltimore: The Johns Hopkins University Press, 1973), 45-46.

13. Louis Sullivan, *Kindergarten Chats and Other Writings* (New York: Wittenborn, 1947), 28; John Edelmann, "Pessimism of Modern Architecure," *The Engineering Magazine* 3 (April-September 1892): 44-54.

14. O'Gorman, "Marshall Field Wholesale Store," 117.

15. M.W. Newman, "Granite Hut," *Architectural Forum* (November 1972): 3; Drury, *Old Chicago Houses,* 44-45; J.J Glessner, *Should Auld Acquaintance Be Forgot?* (Chicago: 1924), 19; Schuyler, *American Architecture,* 285.

16. Glessner, *The House at 1800 Prairie Avenue,* 11.

17. L-shaped domestic plans were popular with Richardson. He had used them as early as his F.W. Andrew House (1872-73) in Newport, elsewhere in the Midwest as in the J.R. Lionberger (1885-88) house in St. Louis, and again in the Chicago city house he designed for Glessner's close friend, Franklin MacVeagh in July 1885. For more detailed discussion of these plans, see Karl Ochsner, *H.H. Richardson: Complete Architectural Works* (Cambridge, Mass.: The MIT Press, 1982), 111, 201, 407; and James O'Gorman, *H.H. Richardson and His Office: Selected Drawings* (Boston: David R. Godine, 1974), 89, 93, 94, 104, 107.

18. Frances Macbeth Glessner's Diary records various contemporary appraisals of the house; Newman, "Granite Hut," 3 and Drury, *Old Chicago Houses,* 44 document the European interest.

19. Additional discussion of the MacVeagh residence can be found in: Hitchcock, *H.H. Richardson* (1966), 280; "Entrance to the Residence of Franklin MacVeagh, Chicago," *American Buildings, Selections,* no. I, pl. 78; A.D.F. Hamlin, "The Genesis of the American Country House," *Architectural Record* 42 (October 1917): 291-99; Hitchcock, *Richardson* (1966), 179-80; "Residence of Franklin MacVeagh, Esq., Chicago," *AABN* 36 (April 15, 1893); Van Rensselaer, *Works,* 108.

20. Paul Sprague, "Glessner House," *Outdoor Illinois* (May 1973): 8-23, goes on to argue: "But however progressive Richardson's design for the street fronts of Glessner House may have been, he did not carry that same sober aesthetic to the garden fronts and the interiors. The garden walls are marked instead by a colorful combination of brick and stone erected in the form of picturesque towers, high pitched roofs, and diminutive dormers. The plan of the house is similar in its emphasis on irregularity, contrasting visual axes, and intriguing variations in the sequence of interior spaces."

21. Sullivan, *Kindergarten Chats,* 29-30. On the popular practice of sexual typing of structures, see G.L. Hersey, *High Victorian Gothic* (Baltimore: The Johns Hopkins University Press, 1972).

22. Ibid., 30; on Sullivan's changes in his Auditorium, see Hugh L. Morrison, *Louis Sullivan, Prophet of Modern Architecture* (1935; rpt. New York: W.W. Norton, 1962), 80-110.

23. Morrison, *Louis Sullivan,* 114; Drury, *Old Chicago Houses,* 480-83.

24. Morrison, *Louis Sullivan,* 115. Other projects demonstrating Sullivan's assimilation of the Richardsonian spirit and the Chicagoan's various redirections of it would include the Dooly Block in Salt Lake City built in 1890-91, the Transportation Building at the Chicago World's Fair (1893), and the Crane Company Building (1903-4) in Chicago.

25. Hoffmann, *Architecture of J.W. Root*, 38.

26. Ibid., 53. C.H. Blackwell's critique is in "Notes of Travel: Chicago—IV," *American Architect* 23 (March 1888): 142.

27. Thomas Tallmadge, *The Story of Architecture in America* (New York, 1927), 185; Schuyler, *American Architecture*, 269-70.

28. Quoted in Hoffmann, *Architecture of J.W. Root*, 67.

29. Jean Block, *Hyde Park Houses* (Chicago: University of Chicago Press, 1970), 89.

30. An elaboration of the claim for Chicago as the most "American" American city, 1870-1920, can be found in Thomas J. Schlereth, "America, 1871-1919: A View of Chicago," *American Studies* 17:2 (Fall 1976): 87-100.

31. Richardson's long-time clients included individuals such as William Dorsheimer, Richard Cheney, and F.L. Ames; Beman's were the Studebaker brothers, the Blackstone family, and George Pullman.

32. Thomas J. Schlereth, "Solon Spencer Beman: The Social History of A Midwest Architect," *The Chicago Architectural Journal* 5 (1985): 9-31.

33. Samples of Beman's smaller Romanesque projects include: the 1887 Batavia Bank and Office Building in La Crosse, Wisconsin; the United States Trust Company (1903) in Terre Haute, Indiana; and the Michigan Trust Building (1891) in Grand Rapids, Michigan.

34. Block, *Hyde Park Houses*, 81-91; also see C.M. Jenkins, "Solon Spencer Beman," *Architectural Record* 14:3 (March 1902): 91-101; "Solon Spencer Beman" in A.J. Andreas, *History of Chicago*, 3 (Chicago: A.J. Andreas, 1884-85), 72; "Solon Spencer Beman," *Construction News* (20 October 1904): 291.

35. Beman's Chicago career divides almost in half. Prior to 1893, he designed in both historical picturesque and the Richardsonian Romanesque. In the early 1890s, Beman abandoned this eclecticism. In something of an architectural about-face, he became a classicist and, for the remainder of his career, an important midwestern contributor to the Beaux Arts movement through a number of civic and ecclesiastical buildings. He turned his back on the playfulness and diversity of the Queen Anne and the Romanesque for the sobriety and unity of the Renaissance and classical antiquity. Whereas the New England of Richardson had prompted many of his designs throughout the 1880s, it was the Greece of Pericles in the fifth century B.C. that inspired his creations in the mid-1890s and thereafter.

36. Thomas J. Schlereth, "A High Victorian Gothicist/A Beaux-Arts Classicist: The Architectural Odyssey of Solon S. Beman," *Studies in Medievalism* (1987, in press).

37. On the Beman Studebaker/Fine Arts Building evolution see Joan Pomaranc, *Fine Arts Building* (Chicago: Commission on Chicago Historical and Architectural Landmarks, 1977), 2-9.

38. Carl Condit, *The Chicago School of Architecture: A History of Commercial and Public Building in the Chicago Area, 1875-1925* (Chicago: University of Chicago Press, 1964), 145.

39. Carroll Meeks, *The Railroad Station, An Architectural History* (New Haven: Yale University Press, 1956), 106-7.

40. Folke T. Kihlstedt, "Grand Central Station, Chicago," *The Prairie School Review* 11:1 (First Quarter 1974): 19.

41. Donald Hoffmann, "Chicago Architecture: The Other Side" and James O'Gorman, "America and H.H. Richardson" in *American Architecture: Innovation and Tradition*, ed. David G. DeLong, Helen Searing, and Robert Stern (New York: Rizzoli, 1986), 97, 105; Hitchcock, *H.H. Richardson* (1966), 275.

42. See, as typical testimonials to Richardson's impact and import, articles by John Root, William Mundie, C.R. Jenkins, R.C. Mclean, and Dankmar Adler in *IA* 5 (April 1885): 55; 8 (August 1886): 1-2; 8 (December 1886): 76; 12 (November 1888): 53-55; 28 (August 1896): 5. On the impact of the *Inland Architect* in promulgating the Romanesque, see Tallmadge, *Architecture In Old Chicago*, 180 and Robert Prestiano, *The Inland Architect: Chicago's Major Architectural Journal, 1883-1908* (Ann Arbor: UMI Press, 1985), 130-34.

Longstreth

I am grateful to the staffs of the Historic Preservation Department, Library, and photographic collections at the Kansas State Historical Society, Topeka; Wichita-Sedgwick County Historical Museum, Wichita City Planning Department; Kansas State University Archives, Manhattan; and National Park Service, Washington, D.C., for their assistance in compiling material for this essay. I have had the good fortune to visit most of the state's incorporated communities, many of them several times. Nevertheless, the research done by me and others must be considered preliminary.

1. Throughout this essay, "Richardsonian" is used as a general term to include buildings in the spirit of Richard-

son's own, but also those that incorporate other influences. Richardsonian design thus connotes a tendency in American architecture, one that encompasses the motifs associated with the master no less than the salient formal qualities he gave to buildings. Assessment of these different facets of Richardson's legacy is appropriate to a much broader study than the one attempted here.

2. William John Hennessey, "The Architectural Works of Henry Van Brunt" (Ph.D. diss., Columbia University, 1979), 124-87, offers a good discussion of this project and van Brunt's influential work in library design. Van Brunt's friendship with Charles Francis Adams, who became president of the Union Pacific in 1884, led to the architect's relocating his practice in Kansas City, Missouri. See also Joseph W. Snell, "The Library on Capitol Square," *Shawnee County Historical Society Bulletin* 47 (November 1970): 57-68, although it incorrectly identifies George Ropes, the supervising architect, as a van Brunt employee and designer of the building. It is worthwhile noting that Richardson himself was not commissioned since his experience with library design was greater than van Brunt's. One possible reason was that Richardson's planning was not highly regarded by librarians, while van Brunt's was considered far more attuned to the requirements of this rapidly evolving type. See Hennessey, "Van Brunt," 133-34 and Kenneth Alan Breisch, "The Small Public Library in America, 1850-1890: The Invention and Evolution of a Building Type" (Ph.D. diss., University of Michigan, 1982).

3. The change in Burnham and Root's work is quite apparent when the Topeka building is compared to their 1882-83 offices for the Chicago, Burlington & Quincy Railroad in Chicago. See Donald Hoffmann, *The Architecture of John Wellborn Root* (Baltimore: The Johns Hopkins University Press, 1973), 30-32, 36-39. A brief chronicle of the Santa Fe offices is presented in Aileen Mallory, "All Around the Town—Santa Fe General Offices," *Shawnee County Historical Society Bulletin* 56 (December 1979): 113-21.

4. The Topeka library and some of van Brunt's Massachusetts work appear to have inspired the exterior design of the chemistry building at the University of Kansas, Lawrence (1883-84, demolished) by Haskell and Wood, illustrated in John M. Peterson, *John G. Haskell, Pioneer Kansas Architect* (Lawrence: Douglas County Historical Society, 1984), 183, and, less overtly, Haskell's Boswell Library discussed in the text. Seymour Davis's Central National Bank at Topeka (c. 1888, demolished 1960) can be seen as a spirited response to the Santa Fe offices nearby. For illustration, see *The Capital City: Topeka, Picturesque and Descriptive* (Neenah, Wis.: Art Publishing Company, 1888-89).

5. The Leavenworth depot is illustrated in *IA* 11 (June 1888); the Watkins Bank in *Kansas Preservation* 4 (July-August 1982): 7; the Marysville courthouse in *Kansas Preservation* 2 (March-April 1980): 3-5; the Arkansas City High School in *Improvement Bulletin* (Minneapolis, 1895): 34; and *Kansas Preservation* 3 (January-February 1981): 1. Other Richardsonian buildings designed by out-of-state architects include: English Lutheran College, Winfield (1893-94) by Charles F. May of St. Louis; Fairmount College, Wichita (1887-88, burned 1929) by Patton and Fisher of Chicago; the Stillwell Hotel, Pittsburg (1888-90, altered) by J.B. Lindsly and Son of St. Louis; and the Russell County Courthouse, Russell (1903-4, demolished) by George Berlinghof of Omaha.

6. In 1880, Kansas City's population was 55,785 compared to Topeka's 15,452. During the next decade both cities experienced rapid growth, but the gap between them had not narrowed. Kansas City stood at 132,716 in 1890, Topeka at 31,057. Concerning Kansas City's ascendance in the region, see Charles N. Glaab, *Kansas City and the Railroads* (Madison: State Historical Society of Wisconsin, 1962); A. Theodore Brown and Lyle W. Dorsett, *K.C., A History of Kansas City, Missouri* (Boulder, Colo.: Pruett Publishing Company, 1978); and Lawrence H. Larsen, *The Urban West at the End of the Frontier* (Lawrence: Regents Press of Kansas, 1978).

7. In the eleven volumes of the *Kansas State Gazetteer and Business Directory* published between 1878 and 1908, Kansas City practitioners comprise the largest architectural contingent. Indeed, advertising to a Kansas audience appears to have been a common procedure among them. The rapidly developing metropolitan image conveyed by Kansas City's retail, financial, wholesale, and residential quarters, as well as by its institutional and public buildings, very probably did influence Kansans' notion of how a modern city should look. Nevertheless, almost no significant projects in the state were designed by Kansas City architects prior to 1900.

Concerning van Brunt's later work in Kansas, see Hennessey, "Van Brunt," 166-75, 206-8. In both cases the architect was hired as a specialist—in the first instance because of his experience with the building type, in the second, as part of his ongoing work for the railroad. The only other Kansas City architect of a Richardsonian building in Kansas that I have been able to find is L.L. Levering, who designed the Rush County Courthouse at La Crosse (1888-89).

8. John W. Reps, *Cities of the American West: A History of Frontier Urban Planning* (Princeton: Princeton University Press, 1979), 425-54, 547-56.

9. See, for example, "The Development of Kansas," in *Addresses by John A. Martin Delivered in Kansas* (Topeka: Kansas Publishing House, 1888), 119-37. Kansas's urban population (residing in communities of 2,500 or more) was 104,956, or 10.5 percent of the total in 1880; 272,201 (19.1 percent) in 1890.

10. During the 1880s, Kansas City, Kansas, annexing several adjacent communities, grew from 3,200 to 38,316, an increase of over 1,000 percent. Leavenworth had long been the largest community in Kansas, even though its population decreased from 17,872 in 1870 to 16,546 in 1880. Growth occurred in the 1880s, but only by slightly more than 3,000 people, and Leavenworth's rank statewide dropped to fourth place in 1890. Atchison's population more than doubled during the 1870s, then declined from 15,105 in 1880 to 13,963 in 1890.

11. James L. King, "A Toast to Topeka," *Radges' Topeka Directory* (1887), 20, 22, 23. See also *Topeka Illustrated, Its Progress and Importance...*(Topeka: Illustrated Publishing Company, 1887); *Historical and Descriptive Review of Kansas, Volume I, The Northern Section* (Topeka: Jno. Lethem, 1890), 9-12; James L. King, *History of Shawnee County, Kansas and Representative Citizens* (Chicago: Richmond & Arnold, 1905), 165-68; Frank W. Blackmar, ed., *Kansas, A Cyclopedia of State History...*, 2 vols. (Chicago: Standard Publishing Company, 1912), 2:811-14; and Douglass W. Wallace and Roy D. Bird, *Witness of the Times: A History of Shawnee County* (Topeka: Shawnee County Historical Society, 1976).

12. *Souvenir of Wichita...*(Wichita: P.B. Dilday, 1895); Blackmar, *Kansas*, 911-14; Constance McLaughlin Green, *American Cities in the Growth of the Nation* (reprt ed. New York: Harper & Row, 1965), 148-58; Richard Sheridan, *Economic Development in South Central Kansas, Part Ia, an Economic History 1500-1900* (Lawrence: University of Kansas School of Business, Bureau of Business Research, 1956), 150-99; and Jimmy M. Skaggs, "Wichita, Kansas: Economic Origins of Metropolitan Development, 1870-1960," in Glenn W. Miller and Jimmy M. Skaggs, eds., *Metropolitan Wichita: Past, Present, Future* (Lawrence: Regents Press of Kansas, 1978), 4-7.

13. Most of the urban fabric from this period has been lost or substantially altered in both cities; however, historical photographs afford a good sense of what existed.

14. Paul Kenneth Goeldner, "Temples of Justice: Nineteenth Century Courthouses in the Midwest and Texas" (Ph.D. diss., Columbia University, 1970), 302.

15. Besides the Capitol at Topeka (1866-1903), the courthouse at Leavenworth (1873, burned 1911) was among the most conspicuous exceptions.

16. *Kansas City Journal*, 7 September 1888, as quoted in Snell, "Library on Capitol Square," 64.

17. *Historical and Descriptive Review*, p. 17. Queen Anne design did enjoy some popularity in Kansas beginning in the mid-1880s. The mode was used for a number of large residences in Topeka, Wichita, Atchison, and other centers. Only a very few Richardsonian houses were built in Kansas, and these tend to be Queen Anne in form, Richardsonian in detail.

18. *Beloit Weekly Record*, 23 November 1877, as quoted in Grace Muilenburg and Ada Swineford, *Land of the Post Rock: Its Origins, History and People* (Lawrence: University Press of Kansas, 1975), 61; J.G. Haskell, "Stones of Kansas," Kansas State Board of Agriculture, *Proceedings* 1 (1872): 336-38. See also *History of the State of Kansas* (Chicago: A.T. Andreas, 1883), 41; *The Resources and Attractions of Kansas for the Homeseeker, Capitalist, and Tourist* (Battle Creek, Mich.: William C. Gage & Son, 1890), 46; and Walter H. Schoewe, "The Geography of Kansas," Kansas Academy of Science, *Transactions* 61 (Winter 1958): 443-52.

19. Kansas Bureau of Labor and Industry, *Biennial Report* (1901-1902), 150-53; Richard L. Douglas, "A History of Manufacturers in Kansas," Kansas State Historical Society, *Collections* 11 (1909-10): 123-26; Schoewe, "Geography of Kansas," 428-31.

20. *Directory and Shippers' Guide of Kansas and Nebraska...* (Leavenworth: T.A. Holland & Co., 1866). Listings in the *Kansas State Gazetteer and Business Directory* reflect the surge in building during the 1880s and the pronounced decline thereafter. Eleven Kansas architects are included in the 1878 edition, nineteen in 1882-83, thirty-nine in 1884-85, eighty-six in 1888-89, and thirty-two in 1894. The extent of work done by architects in the state is indicated in published biographies. The best source in this regard is *History of the State of Kansas*. Other useful volumes include: *Historical and Descriptive Review*; King, *History of Shawnee County*; Howard D. Bennett, *Who's Who in Topeka* (Topeka: Adams Brothers, 1905); *United States Biographical Dictionary* (Chicago: American Biographical Publishing Company, 1883); and *Portrait and Biographical Record of Leavenworth, Douglas and Franklin Counties* (Chicago: Chapman Publishing Company, 1899). Additional information has been compiled by the Historic Preservation Department, Kansas State Historical Society, Topeka.

21. For example, Charles Goodlander (1834-?) of Fort Scott also worked as a builder and owned a lumber business, a brickyard, and an undertaking establishment in addition to serving as mayor (*U.S. Biographical Dictionary*, pp. 390-91). Erasmus Carr (1825-1915) of Leavenworth continued to work as a builder for a period (*Portrait and Biographical Record*, pp. 788-89). Ferdinand Fuller (1815-?) of Lawrence did likewise (*U.S. Biographical Dictionary*, p. 587). George Wells (1831-?) of Leavenworth was also a contractor and a real estate speculator (*Portrait and Biographical Record*, pp. 499-500). John Pelton advertised in the 1872-73 Atchison directory as a carpenter, builder, undertaker, and architect. Jameson and Jobson advertised in the 1884 Leavenworth directory as "archi-

tects, surveyors, and sanitary engineers." Chadwick and Rawson of Wamego made a specialty of tombstones and other funerary monuments (*Kansas State Gazetteer,* 1884-85). In the 1888-89 edition of the *Gazetteer,* G.W. Cochler of Belleville, Rixon Brothers of Chanute, G.W. Blankenbeckler of Downs, and Stevens and Thompson of Garden City were among those listed as architects and builders. Excellent documentation of how important diversified interests could be in the region, even for a professionally trained architect, is given in George Ehrlich and Peggy E. Schrock, "The A.B. Cross Lumber Company 1858-1871," *Missouri Historical Review* 60 (October 1985): 14-32.

22. Peterson, *Haskell,* provides a very detailed account of the architect's career. See also J. Kurt von Achen, "Lives and Works of Early Kansas Architects" (M. Arch. thesis, University of Kansas, 1966), 26-84e. A contemporary record of Haskell's practice is contained in *The Leading Industries of Topeka, Kansas* (Chicago: Reed & Company, 1882), 50-51.

23. Cost does not appear to have been a significant factor generating these differences. Expenditures for Boswell Library ran approximately $20,000. Snow Hall, which was about two-and-a-half times larger, cost some $50,000.

24. Haskell had two other well-known associates. Louis M.H. Wood (1846-1920) studied architecture at Cornell and worked in Pennsylvania and Chicago before entering the office in 1872. He was Haskell's partner from 1875 to 1887. In the latter year, John F. Stanton (1862-1916) joined the firm. Stanton had trained as a civil engineer and worked for an architect in his native New Hampshire. From 1893 to 1895, he was a partner, then opened his own office. Both men seem to have been given charge of at least some commissions. See Peterson, *Haskell,* 81-82, 113, 116, 165-67, 204-6; *U.S. Biographical Dictionary,* 452-53; *Topeka Journal,* 14 October 1920 (Wood); King, *History of Shawnee County,* 357-58; and *Topeka Journal,* 25 May 1916 (Stanton).

25. The best contemporary account of Davis is in *Topeka Illustrated,* 118. See also his obituaries in *Topeka Journal,* 4 September 1923, and *Topeka Capital,* 7 September 1923; and Sandra L. Tatman and Roger W. Moss, *Biographical Dictionary of Philadelphia Architects: 1700-1930* (Boston: G.K. Hall & Company, 1985), 189-91. Obituaries give Davis's year of birth as 1869; however, this would make him only eleven when he studied at the Pennsylvania Academy, fourteen when he came to Topeka, and seventeen when he established his own office. Even by standards of the day, this would have been a precocious career indeed.

26. A perspective rendering and floor plans of the Adair Building are in *American Architect* 48 (27 June 1895).

27. Davis also appears to have drawn from the work of Adler and Sullivan, the most striking example of which is a project for a hotel at Messila Park, New Mexico, illustrated in *AABN* 35 (20 January 1892). Here, abstract form is employed in as bold a manner as could be found in any of Frank Lloyd Wright's designs to date. The Kansas Building at Chicago was somewhat similar, and Davis's explanation of the scheme bears note: "I have endeavored ...to get a feeling...that would be harmonious with our surroundings, that is a building that would have a Kansas feeling and [be] typical of us. For this I looked to the topography of our state, which is broad and comparatively level...." (*Topeka Capital,* 18 February 1892). Was Wright saying similar things so early?

28. Compare with the Knox (now Columbian) Building (1888) where horizontal layering predominates; the Central National Bank (cited in n. 4 above), where, in a facile Richardsonian manner, verticality is emphasized; and Davis's first known commercial design, the Keith Building (1887, demolished), which, while using some Richardsonian details, possesses neither compositional balance nor emphasis. See *Kansas Preservation* 5 (January-February 1983): 5 and *The Capital City,* n.p., for illustration.

29. Beyond a not entirely accurate account of Proudfoot in Henry F. and Elsie Rathborn Withey, *Biographical Dictionary of American Architects (Deceased)* (Los Angeles: New Age Publishing Company, 1956), 492, most of the available information on the firm has been compiled by Sondra Van Meter, copies of which are at the Wichita City Planning Office. M.I.T.'s records list a William Proudfoot, and some much later accounts also give this name. However, Willis and William appear to be the same person, and the former was used consistently while he was in Wichita. Only a brief note on the firm has been found in contemporary papers, see *Wichita Daily Eagle,* 8 November 1885. Nothing is known about Bird's training, except from a short article published shortly after his death, which states that he had been employed in a Philadelphia woodworking mill. See "George Bird Buildings Reflect Renaissance In Italian and French Styles," *Iowa Architect* (January-February 1958): 20.

30. For background on the project, see Juliet Reeve, *Friends University: The Growth of an Idea* (Wichita: Friends University, 1948). Concerning the importance many institutions in the central United States placed on having a grand, all-purpose building, see Richard Longstreth "From Farm to Campus: Planning, Politics and the Agricultural College Idea in Kansas," *Winterthur Portfolio* 20 (Summer-Autumn 1985): 156.

31. Throughout the central United States during the nineteenth century, municipal buildings tended to be cheap, modest in appearance, and often combined with other facilities such as firehouses. In Wichita, the intent

was no doubt to erect a counterpart to the grand Victorian piles in metropolises. Kansas City was probably the only other place in the region to undertake such a project at that time, see George Ehrlich, *Kansas City, Missouri: An Architectural History 1826-1976* (Kansas City: Historic Kansas City Foundation, 1979). Citizen rivalries may also have added fuel to the undertaking. Entrepreneurs owning property south of the main street (Douglas Avenue) sought to counterbalance the benefits of having a very grand courthouse erected several blocks to the north. A major public facility in their precinct, it was felt, would boost business and land values. For background, see Craig Miner, *A Souvenir History of the City Building 1888-1980* (Wichita: Wichita-Sedgwick County Historical Museum Association, 1978).

32. Concerning the City and County Building in Salt Lake City, see John S. McCormick, *The Historic Buildings of Salt Lake City* (Salt Lake City: Utah Historical Society, 1982), 48-49. Proudfoot and Bird did not remain there long either. In 1896, Proudfoot moved to Kansas City, Bird to Philadelphia. Several years later they joined forces again in Iowa, where the firm continued under the name of Brooks, Borg and Skiles.

33. Concerning Holland, see *Topeka Illustrated*, 54; Weston Arthur Goodspeed, ed., *The Provinces and the States...*, 7 vols. (Madison, Wis.: Western Historical Association, 1904), 7: 528-29; Berrett, *Who's Who in Topeka*, 57-58; William E. Connelley, *Standard History of Kansas and Kansans*, 5 vols. (Chicago: Lewis Publishing Company, 1918), 1742-43; and his obituary in *Topeka Capital*, 29 May 1919. Frank Squires (1871-?), also from Ohio but educated in Topeka, joined the office in 1898 and became a partner in 1903. The association lasted until c. 1910. See Berrett, *Who's Who in Topeka*, 114.

34. The building cost $145,000. The Sedgwick County Courthouse at Wichita, begun at the height of the building boom, cost much more: $250,000. Competition between the two cities may have induced Topeka's hefty expenditure during the subsequent depression. For its size and pretentiousness, the only other rival facility in the state was the much earlier courthouse at Leavenworth cited in n. 15 above.

35. See n. 51 below.

36. Concerning Washburn, see *Portrait and Biographical Record*, 482-483; and von Achen, "Lives," 85-139a. Upon retirement, Washburn spent much of his time making furniture. The firm continued under the direction of a son, C.A. Washburn, and son-in-law, Roy Stookey.

37. Many of Holland's and Washburn's courthouses cost between $35,000 and $50,000; however, several of Washburn's were considerably higher without significant differences in size or accoutrements. These include the

facilities for Harper County ($60,000), Butler County ($65,000), Anderson County ($75,000), and Franklin County ($70,000). The only occasion on which Washburn used stone for a courthouse was at Atchison, where the material was stipulated by the client. See Jane Price Byram, "Two Public Buildings in Atchison, Kansas: An Architectural History" (Master's thesis, University of Missouri, Kansas City, 1971), 103 and von Achen, "Lives," 112.

38. Concerning Lescher, see Berrett, *Who's Who in Topeka*, 71-72; concerning Stanton, see. n. 24 above; concerning Squires, see *Historical and Descriptive Review of Kansas, Volume II, The Eastern Section* (Topeka: Jno. Lethem, 1891), 126 and his obituaries in *Emporia Gazette*, 26 and 27 December 1934. Information on Gould was obtained from notes in the city's planning office and from Richard Chaffee.

39. The American National Bank was one of several comparatively large commercial buildings erected in Arkansas City during the second half of the 1880s. Similar work occurred in other expanding secondary centers such as Winfield, Pittsburg, Newton, and Salina.

40. These include: the Sedgwick Block (1888, demolished) by Jerome B. Legg, Getto Building (c. 1887, demolished); Martinson Block (1887, demolished) by Proudfoot and Bird; Smith-Skinner and Walter-Snively Block (c. 1887, demolished); Fletcher Block (c. 1887, demolished); and the Crawford Grand Opera House (1887, burned 1913) by George A. Masters. Most of these buildings were not Richardsonian; however, their character was distinctly that of the metropolis. For illustration, see *Album of Wichita, Kansas* (Wichita: c. 1888), n.p. and *Wichita, The Magic City, Picturesque and Descriptive* (Neenah, Wis.: Art Publishing Company, 1889).

41. For illustration, see the pictorial sources cited in n. 13 above.

42. These include: the Rock Island Depot (1887, demolished c. 1944) at Topeka; Union Depot (c. 1890, demolished) by Perkins and Adams at Atchison; the Santa Fe Depot (1890) by Perkins and Adams and the Union Depot (1886-88) at Leavenworth; the Rock Island Depot (1887) by J.T. Long; and the Santa Fe Depot (1890, demolished) by Perkins and Adams at Wichita. For illustration of the Perkins and Adams depots, see *AABN* 31 (17 January 1891). The firm practiced in Topeka for only about a year, during which time it also designed depots for Galveston and Dallas as well as a competition entry for the Arkansas City High School. Nothing is known about the background or subsequent careers of these talented men, except that Adams moved to St. Louis. His rendering of Theodore Link and Edward Cameron's winning scheme for the Union Depot there appears in *IA* 17 (July 1891), and he is listed in local directories for three years as a draftsman (1892), contractor (1893), and architect (1894).

43. Concerning the Union Pacific depots, see n. 7 above. The best general account of standardized depot design is H. Roger Grant and Charles W. Bohi, *The Country Railroad Station in America* (Boulder, Colo.: Pruett Publishing Company, 1978). See also their "Standardized Railroad Stations in Kansas: The Case of the Atchison, Topeka & Santa Fe," *Kansas History* 4 (Spring 1981): 39-47.

44. See nos. 5 and 30 above. To these institutions should be added the short-lived Wichita University (1886-87, demolished 1913) by Dumont and Hayward and Bethel College (1887-93) by Proudfoot and Bird at Newton.

45. Specifically: Midland College (c. 1888-89) at Atchison; Cooper Memorial College (1887) by William Gall at Sterling; St. John's School (1887-88, burned 1978) at Salina; University Hall (1887-88, additions 1902, burned 1902; rebuilt 1903-4) by George Washburn at Ottawa University, Ottawa; and Boswell Library (cited in the text above) and Mac Vicar Chapel (1889-90, demolished 1966) by T.M. Lescher at Washburn University, Topeka.

46. Proudfoot and Bird's contributions include the College Hill School, Kellogg School, Harry Street School, and McCormick School, all of which were erected around 1890. Only the McCormick School remains. The firm also probably designed the Third Ward School at Dodge City and schools elsewhere in the area. Even earlier (1887) Great Bend erected the East Side and West Side schools in a Richardsonian vein, and further research will no doubt yield other examples. Most of these nineteenth-century buildings were replaced in school building campaigns that occurred during the 1910s and thereafter.

47. Concerning the Arkansas City High School, see n. 5 above; the Lawrence High School (1889-91, demolished), see Peterson, *Haskell*, 177-79, 230; the Atchison County High School (1891, rebuilt 1894, demolished) at Effingham, see Sheffield Ingalls, *History of Atchison County, Kansas* (Lawrence: Standard Publishing Company, 1916), 273-75.

48. Concerning the Kansas State University buildings, see Longstreth, "From Farm to Campus." Concerning those at the University of Kansas, see Peterson, *Haskell*, 208-10, 235 and Virginia Adams et al., comps., *On the Hill: A Photographic History of the University of Kansas* (Lawrence: University Press of Kansas, 1983), 37, 52, 59.

49. Prior to 1891, architects had been appointed to design and supervise the construction of the State Capitol, during which time commissions for at least some other state projects were given to them. Haskell served in this capacity from 1866 to 1867 and again from 1885 to 1886. For a complete listing, see "Official Roster of Kansas, 1854-1925," Kansas State Historical Society, *Collections* 16 (1923-25): 703.

The influence of federal architecture and the Office of the Supervising Architect of the Treasury does not appear to have been great in Kansas prior to 1900. Richardsonian post offices were erected at Fort Scott (1887-90, demolished), Atchison (1891-94), and Salina (1895-96, demolished). Like the state's urban railroad depots, these buildings probably enhanced the mode's stature, but were not central to its initial widespread diffusion. For documentation, see Byram, "Two Public Buildings," 19-74 and *History of Public Buildings Under the Control of the Treasury Department* (Washington, D.C.: Government Printing Office, 1901), 178-89.

50. The comparative base in this instance is set by the lavish courthouses constructed throughout the Midwest during the latter half of the nineteenth century. Kansas facilities at Leavenworth (1873), Wellington (1884), Fredonia (1886), Independence (c. 1887), and Washington (1887) rivaled them, but many examples from the High Victorian era are much simpler, including those at Topeka (1867), Oskaloosa (1867), Eureka (1871), Cottonwood Falls (1871), Holton (1872), Great Bend (1873-74), Dodge City (1876), Kinsley (1886), and Tribune (1889-90). Courthouses at Lincoln (1873), Westmorland (1884), and Jetmore (1886) retained forms characteristic of work from the early nineteenth century. Utilizing space in commercial buildings was common during the early settlement period in the western part of the state; however, the same practice could be found much earlier in some eastern counties, as was the case in Manhattan until Holland's courthouse was completed in 1906.

51. Julie A. Wortman and David P. Johnson, *Legacies: Kansas' Older County Courthouses* (Topeka: Kansas State Historical Society, 1981), 29-30. The courthouse in question is at Osborne (1907-8) and is a near twin of those at Manhattan, Marion (1905-6), and Newton (1906, demolished). The same plans appear to have been used for the courthouse at Colby (1906-7), but with brick used instead of limestone for the exterior walls. Slightly greater differentiation occurred with earlier facilities at Junction City (1899-1900) and Beloit (1901-2). Other Richardsonian courthouses by Holland include those at Burlington (1900-1901, demolished c. 1963), Clay Center (1898-1901), Iola (c. 1910, demolished), and Lyons (1910-11).

Holland was not the first Kansas architect to replicate his courthouse designs—Haskell's facilities at Cottonwood Falls and Eureka are very similar—nor was he the last. Several firms followed this practice during the 1920s, although the same design was never used more than twice.

52. Washburn, in fact, never repeated a courthouse design but often let one project provide a basis for development of the next. His Richardsonian work includes facilities at: Olathe (1890-91, demolished 1951), Ottawa (1891-93), Atchison (1896-97), Paola (1897-99), Yates

Center (1899-1900), Garnett (1901-2), Erie (1903-4, demolished 1963), Troy (1905-6), Anthony (1907-8), Kingman (1907-8), and El Dorado (1908-9). For background material on these buildings, see von Achen, "Lives," 106-7, 109-15, and 117-24; Bryam, "Two Public Buildings," 111-60; and Charles L. Hall, "The Kansas Courthouses of George P. Washburn, Architect," *Journal of the West* 17 (January 1978): 74-80. Wortman and Johnson, *Legacies*, provides the best introduction to the subject generally and includes a catalogue of extant examples erected prior to 1914.

53. The state's population was approximately 1,428,000 in 1890, 1,470,000 in 1900, and 1,690,000 in 1910, by which time Oklahoma's was nearly as great. Kansas City, Kansas grew from 38,316 in 1890 to 82,331 in 1910. Topeka grew from 31,057 to 43,864; Wichita from 23,853 to 52,450. But by 1910, Kansas City, Missouri's population stood at 301,408; Omaha's at 124,096; Minneapolis's at 301,408; St. Paul's at 214,744; St. Louis's at 687,029; Denver's at 213,381; and still nascent Oklahoma City's at 64,205. Cities in Kansas lay distinctly in a second tier. In 1900 the state had nine communities with over 10,000 people, twelve in 1910; sixty-nine communities of between 1,000 and 3,000 people in 1900, eighty-seven in 1910. The percentage of urban population rose only slightly between 1890 and 1900, then increased to 29.2 in 1910; however, this remained considerably lower than figures for midwestern states. Kansas had established a clear pattern as a state of towns, not cities.

54. This tendency is quite evident in courthouse design, see Wortman and Johnson, *Legacies*, for illustration. This work bears comparison to courthouses in a newer state, South Dakota. There, twelve projects built between 1904 and 1919, adhering more or less to the same design (by Minneapolis architects Buechner and Orth), are lively classical counterparts to the more conservative Richardsonian facilities in Kansas. See C. Ross Bloomquist, "Planning and Building a Courthouse for Foster County, 1907-1912," *North Dakota History* 49 (Spring 1982): 12-21. A similar conservatism is seen in the development of the Kansas State University campus after 1900, see Longstreth, "From Farm to Campus," 173-79.

Breisch

1. For earlier discussions of the influence of Richardson in Texas, see Jay C. Henry, "The Richardsonian Romanesque in Texas: An Interpretation," *Texas Architect* 31 (March-April 1981):52-59; Willard B. Robinson, *The People's Architecture: Texas Courthouses, Jails, and Municipal Buildings* (Austin: Texas State Historical Association,

1983), 153-79; and Willard B. Robinson and Todd Webb, *Texas Public Buildings of the Nineteenth Century* (Austin: University of Texas Press, 1974), 201-7.

2. See the Dallas Morning News, *Texas Almanac 1980-1981* (Dallas: The Dallas Morning News, 1980), 192, 436, 454.

3. The populist People's Party was formed in Texas in 1891 and ran well in state and local races from 1892 to 1898, especially following the panic of 1893, in 1894 and 1896. This rise in dissatisfaction of the farmer coincides with the closing of the frontier and the more limited availability of land. As the 1893 depression lifted in the late 1890s, the Party dissolved. See Roscoe C. Martin, *The People's Party in Texas: A Study in Third Party Politics*, Austin: University of Texas Press, 1970 and the Dallas Morning News, *Texas Almanac 1986-1987* (Dallas: The Morning News, 1986), 214-15.

4. See *The Minutes of the Texas State Society of Architects: 1886-1896*, in the James Riely Gordon Archive, the Architectural Drawings Collection, the University of Texas at Austin (hereafter referred to as the Gordon Archive); and also Hank Todd Smith, *Since 1886: A History of the Texas Society of Architects* (Austin: The Society, 1983), 2-9.

5. "Address of James Wahrenberger to the Texas State Society of Architects, January 17, 1889," in *Minutes: 1886-1896*, 106.

6. "Annual Address of the President, May 13, 1890," in *Minutes: 1886-1896*, 116.

7. *Austin American Statesman* (special supplement, 17 December 1886):17. Construction began in December 1885. See *Art Work of Austin* (Chicago, 1894), 41; Robinson and Webb, *Texas Public Buildings*, pls. 64 and 65; and Roxanne Kuter Williamson, *Austin, Texas: An American Architectural History* (San Antonio: Trinity University Press, 1973), 99-100. Jasper N. Preston was born in Michigan in 1832. He studied architecture and worked in Lansing, Michigan, before moving to Austin in 1875, where he also supervised work on the new capitol. In 1886 he moved to Los Angeles, where he died. See Henry F. Withey and Elsie Rathbone Withey, *Biographical Dictionary of American Architects (Deceased)* (Los Angeles: New Age Publishing Co., 1956), 486.

8. *The Industrial Advantages of Austin, Texas, or Austin Up to Date* (Austin: Akehurst Publishing Co., 1894), n.p.

9. The impact of the Richardsonian idiom on Clayton becomes especially apparent if the Ashbel Smith Building is compared to the still much more Victorian John Sealy Hospital. This was designed shortly before his sojourn East. See John C. Garner, "HABS Photograph-Data Book Report on the Ashbel Smith Building" (1967), in the

Texas Historical Commission National Register Files (hereafter referred to as THC Files); *Art Work in Galveston* (Chicago: W.H. Parish Publishing Co., 1894), pt. v; *The Galveston Daily News*, 2 October 1891; and Howard Barnstone, *The Galveston That Was* (New York: Macmillan Co., 1966), 182-89. Clayton arrived in 1873 in Galveston, where he would dominate the building profession until his death in 1916, after working with Jones and Balwin in Memphis, Tennessee. See Stephen Fox, "N.J Clayton (1840-1916)," *Architectural Review* 164 (November 1978): 275 and "Profile: Nicholas Clayton, Architect," *Texas Architect* 26 (July/August 1976): 51-52.

10. *IA*, Photogravure Edition, 9 (July 1887). For the Gresham House, see *Art Work in Galveston*, pt. 1; Drury Blake Alexander and Todd Webb, *Texas Homes of the Nineteenth Century* (Austin: University of Texas Press, 1966), pl. 194; and Barnstone, *The Galveston That Was*, 156-57, 170-75.

11. Others might include C.W. Bulger's Slaughter Building (c. 1895), which is also in Dallas, or the Hurley Building by Armstrong and Messer in Fort Worth (1889-90). See Henry, "The Richardsonian Romanesque in Texas," 55; Robinson and Webb, *Texas Public Buildings*, 112, fig. 21; and Willard B. Robinson, *Gone From Texas: Our Lost Architectural Heritage* (College Station, Texas: Texas A & M University Press, 1981), fig. 155.

12. San Antonio Chapter of the AIA, *A Guide to San Antonio Architecture* (San Antonio: San Antonio Chapter of the AIA, 1986), 24. This small, hipped-roof tower is very similar to one used by Louis Sullivan on his Pueblo, Colorado, Opera House. See *IA* 21 (March 1893). James Riely Gordon was born in Virginia in 1863 and moved with his parents to San Antonio in 1874. From 1879 to 1882, he apparently worked in the Civil Engineering Corps of the International and Great Northern Railroad and then apprenticed with the San Antonio architect, W.K. Dobson. Gordon left this firm in 1882 when Dobson's practice was taken over by James Wahrenberger. Between 1884 and 1888, he practiced singly and in partnership with a local contractor, James Murphy. His appointment as Superintendent of the San Antonio Courthouse in 1887 at age 24 (see n. 16 below), however, in effect marks the actual beginning of his success as an architect. See "Fayette's Courthouse," *Houston Daily Post* (2 December 1891): 4; Withey, *Biographical Dictionary*, 241-42; and Lila Stillson, "James Riely Gordon, Architect," in *James Riely Gordon: Texas Courthouse Architect* (Austin: University of Texas), exhibition catalogue, January 21-March 18, 1983.

13. From James Fergusson, *History of the Modern Styles of Architecture*, 3d ed. rev. by Robert Kerr, 2 (London, 1891), 361 (quoted in *JSAH* 29 [1979]:171).

14. The Kampmann Building was published in *AABN* 43 (20 January 1894) and also in *Sketches from the Portfolio of James Riely Gordon* (privately published, 1896); *Art Work in San Antonio. Published in Twelve Parts* (Chicago: W.H. Parish Publishing Co., 1894), but was apparently never constructed. Temple Emanu-El was designed by Gordon in association with the Dallas architects H.A. and Roy Overbeck. See William McDonald, *Dallas Rediscovered: A Photographic Chronicle of Urban Expansion, 1870-1925* (Dallas: Historical Society of Dallas, 1978), 115, fig. 107. Examples of contemporary illustrations of Root's entryways can be seen in John Wellborn Root, *The Meanings of Architecture: Buildings and Writings of John Wellborn Root*, collected and with an introduction by Donald Hoffmann (New York: Horizon Press, 1967), pls. 33, 35, 49, 65.

15. For illustrations of these no-longer extant buildings, see *Sketches from the Portfolio of James Riely Gordon* and Andrew Morrison, *The City of San Antonio, Texas* (St. Louis: George W. Englehardt and Co., c.1891), 42-43. The porches on the Alamo Fire Insurance Building are also similar to the open porches that appear on Richardson's Lionberger House (1885-88) in St. Louis or his Hay and Adams Houses (1884-86) in Washington, D.C. These latter homes, no doubt, would have been familiar to D.E. Laub, who joined Gordon just as the Alamo Fire Insurance Company Building was being designed in July 1891.

16. Vol. 21 (9 April 1887) and vol. 22 (13 August 1887). Construction details were also published in the 7 April 1888 issue of this journal. See also Morrison, *The City of San Antonio, Texas*, 9-10. There is a letter, dated 17 January 1887, in the Gordon Archive from Mifflin Bell, appointing Gordon superintendent of construction for this building. He served in this capacity until June 1889, when he was apparently caught in the middle of a local political squabble and removed from this position shortly before completion of the building. In conjunction with this commission, Gordon made several small changes to the design of the building and very briefly visited Washington, D.C. early in 1887, an excursion which has given rise to the widely held notion that he worked for the Supervising Architect's Office in that city. See the *San Antonio Express* (13 March, 12 June, 23 July 1887 and 28 June, 9 and 10 July 1889).

17. Reprinted in William H. Jordy and Ralph Coe, eds., *American Architecture and Other Writings by Montgomery Schuyler*, abridged by William H. Jordy (New York: Athenaeum, 1964), 128.

18. For more on these structures see Bates Lowry, *Building A National Image: Architectural Drawings for the American Democracy, 1879-1912* (Washington, D.C.: The National Building Museum, 1985), pl. 74 and 75; Lois A. Craig and the Staff of the Federal Architecture Project,

The Federal Presence: Architecture, Politics, and National Design (Cambridge, Mass.: The MIT Press, 1984), 162-69, 195-205; and Robinson, *Gone From Texas*, 235-40.

19. Robinson, *Gone From Texas*, figs. 126, 131, 219; "The Lone Star State," *Frank Leslie's Illustrated Newspaper* (18 October 1890):4; and *Sketches from the Portfolio of James Riely Gordon*. Another Richardsonian house erected about the same time in San Antonio, which is very similar in character to the Yoakum Residence, was B.F. Trester Jr.'s home for Judge L.W. Florea. When Trester died unexpectedly in February 1891, it was announced that Gordon and Laub would complete his unfinished work (*San Antonio Express*, 12 March 1891).

20. Benjamin Franklin Yoakum was general manager of the San Antonio and Arkansas Pass Railroad at the time his house was constructed. See Morrison, *San Antonio*, esp. 3-4 and 36-39. In 1886 Cyrus L.W. Eidlitz (1853-1921) also completed the San Antonio National Bank which was built for George Brackenridge in a similar Moorish vein. See the *Architectural Record* 1 (July-September 1891):61 and AIA, *Guide to San Antonio*, 27.

21. "Fayette's Courthouse," *Houston Daily Post* (2 December 1891):4; Paul Goeldner, "Temples of Justice: Nineteenth-Century Courthouses in the Midwest and Texas" (Ph.D. diss., Columbia University, 1970), 335-37; and Henry, "The Richardsonian Romanesque in Texas," 54-55.

22. The contract for the Dallas County Courthouse was let on July 23, 1890, and it was occupied by the winter of 1892. McDonald, *Dallas Rediscovered*, 65; THC Files, "Dallas County Courthouse"; Goeldner, "Temples of Justice," 332-33; and Henry-Russell Hitchcock and William Seale, "Notes on the Architecture" in *Courthouse: A Photographic Document*, ed. Richard Pare (New York: Horizon Press, 1978), 215. Hitchcock and Seale call this "the grandest Richardsonian court house in Texas," but appear to be analyzing it minus its original cupola.

23. As was not uncommon for Gordon, he published a greatly elaborated rendering of this building in *AABN* 54 (17 October 1896) and in his own *Sketches from the Portfolio of James Riely Gordon* of the same year. D. Ernest Laub became Gordon's partner in July 1890. He had been with the Supervising Architect's Office in Washington since at least 1884, when his drawings first started to appear in the Annual Reports, and it was here that he first met his future partner. This partnership with Gordon appears to have lasted until about 1893. See undated clipping (c. January 1892) from the *San Antonio Times* in the Gordon Archive and also Goeldner, "Temples of Justice," 337-38.

24. For Stanford and the early Mission Revival in California, Paul V. Turner, Marcia E. Vetrocq, and Karen Weitze, *The Founders and the Architects: The Design of Stanford University* (Stanford University: The Department of Art, 1976), passim and Karen J. Weitze, *California's Mission Revival* (Los Angeles: Hennessey and Ingalls, 1984), 2-43.

25. See Mary Carolyn Jutson, *Alfred Giles: An English Architect in Texas and Mexico* (San Antonio: Trinity University Press, 1972), 64-68 and *Sketches from the Portfolio of James Riely Gordon*. With their open arcades and prominent corner turrets both the Schreiner and Stevens houses also recall Richardson's Franklin MacVeagh House in Chicago of 1885-87.

26. See the letter of March 27, 1893 from the Erath County Clerk, W.E. Cody, to James Riely Gordon in the Gordon Archive, where he praises "the strength of building and the appearance [which are] enhanced, rather than diminished," by this modified arrangement; and Robinson and Webb, *Texas Public Buildings*, pl. 144.

27. The Archer County Courthouse was designed by the Fort Worth architect A. N. Dawson, and the very similar Dickens County Building by E.L. Aiken. Both have been severely altered above their second floors. The Edwards County building was erected by Ben Davey and Bruno Schott. See THC Files for Archer, Dickens, and Edwards County Courthouses and Robinson, *The People's Architecture*, 180-81.

28. George P. Merrill, *Stones for Building and Decoration*, 3d ed. (New York: John Wiley and Sons, 1908).

29. In *Stones of Venice*, for example, Ruskin draws an analogy between architectural polychromy and the geological strata of mountains. See John Ruskin, *The Works of John Ruskin*, ed. E.T. Cook and Alexander Wedderburn, 9 (London, 1903-12), 85-89. For Richardson's use of stone, see James F. O'Gorman, "O.W. Norcross, Richardson's Master Mason: A Preliminary Report," *JSAH* 32 (1973): 104-17.

30. James Wahrenberger, "Annual Address of the President, May 13, 1890," in *Minutes: 1886-1896*, 116. These remarks were made at the Annual Meeting of the Texas State Architects Society, which Gordon attended. He was, of course, just completing many of his own "Moresque" buildings.

31. *San Antonio Express*, 19 May 1891 and 4 October 1896; *San Antonio Light*, 17 October 1893; NR Files, "Bexar County Courthouse"; Robinson and Webb, *Texas Public Buildings*, 247; and *Sketches from the Portfolio of James Riely Gordon*.

32. Undated clipping (c. May 1891) in the Gordon Archive.

33. *AABN* 24 (25 August 1888): 87-88.

34. *AABN* 21 (9 April 1887).

35. Similar schemes can be seen in a design by Robert Stead, for a "House at Washington, D.C." and an entryway for the Morgan Park Library of Charles Frost, in *IA* 14 (August 1889). Samuel Newson also used a similar motif over the entryway of his design for "Un Château en Espagne," which appeared in the *California Architect and Building News* (February 1891). See Weitze, *California's Mission Revival*, fig. 26.

36. C.A. Rich, "A Run Through Spain III," *AABN* 31 (3 January 1891): 5-6.

37. For a rinceau design very similar to that used by Gordon and Laub on their entryway frieze, see *Spanish Architecture and Ornament*, compiled by George H. Polley and Co.(Boston: George H. Polley and Co., 1889) pl. XXXVIII.

38. *San Antonio Express*, 4 October 1896.

39. Undated clipping in the Gordon Archive citing an affidavit sworn by Gordon on July 6, 1895 describing his copyrighted courthouse plan. This was done in order to obtain an injunction against Arthur O. Watson to keep him from using it in Lamar County.

40. *Industrial Advantages of Austin*, n.p.

41. C.A. Rich, "A Run Through Spain V," *AABN* 31 (7 February 1891): 87. Weitze feels that this series of articles was also influential in the formation of the Mission Revival style in California, *California's Mission Revival*, 32-33.

42. "Visit to Office of Gordon and Laub," *San Antonio Times*, undated clipping (c. January 1892) in the Gordon Archive.

43. For Gordon's first design see the *San Antonio Express*, 20 December 1891 and 22 February 1892. A design similar to that which was erected, but with two towers, appears in Gordon's *Sketches from the Portfolio of James Riely Gordon* of 1896. See also *IA* 20 (September 1892) and 22 (September 1893).

44. D.H. Burnham, "World's Fair State Buildings," *IA* 19 (March 1892): 25 and Weitze, *California's Mission Revival*, 39.

45. *San Antonio Express*, 17 September 1893.

46. For other discussions of Gordon's courthouses, see Robinson, *People's Architecture*, 160-74; Robinson and Webb, *Texas Public Bulidings*, 201-4; Hitchcock and Seale "Notes," 215-21; Goeldner, "Temples of Justice,"

335-43; and Molly Malone Chesney, "The Texas Courthouse of James Riely Gordon," in *James Riely Gordon: Texas Courthouse Architect*.

47. Marianna Griswold Van Rensselaer (Mrs. Schuyler), *Henry Hobson Richardson and His Works* (Boston: Houghton Mifflin, 1888; reprt, New York: Dover Publications, 1969), 112.

48. Gordon erected a total of sixteen courthouses in Texas between 1890 and 1901, fourteen of which were in a Richardsonian mode. In addition to those mentioned, these include courthouses in San Patricio (1894), Brazoria (1894-95), Wise (1895-96), and Comal (1897-98) counties. See *Sketches from the Portfolio of James Riely Gordon* and Chesney, "The Texas Courthouse of James Riely Gordon."

49. See n. 39 above. These undated drawings are in the Austin History Collection.

50. *Some Work from the Office of Sanguinet and Staats. Successors to Messer, Sanguinet and Messer, Architects, Fort Worth, Texas* (1896), n.p. (xerox copy in the Amon Carter Museum, Fort Worth). Messer, Sanguinet and Messer also erected several other buildings in Fort Worth in the Richardsonian mode. These included the Sixth Ward School (1892-93) and a Natatorium (c. 1890-95), the latter with both semicircular and horseshoe arches and open porches in the central bay that are reminiscent of Gordon's commercial buildings in San Antonio.

51. Robinson, *People's Architecture*, 156-57 and fig. 146. Watson, who worked in Austin, designed one other Richardsonian courthouse in Llano in 1892.

52. *Halletsville Herald* (17 June 1897) and Robinson and Wade, *Texas Public Buildings*, 240-41.

53. Robinson, *People's Architecture*, 184-85.

54. THC files, "Home of Dr. Pepper." Based on stylistic criteria it appears likely that Allen also designed the Hillsboro Western Union Building.

55. For the Texas A & M University Mess Hall, see *AABN* 58 (16 October 1897).

56. Van Rensselaer, *Henry Hobson Richardson*, 114.

57. Unlike in California, where a more arcadian view of the land and its Spanish past persisted, this "tinge" in Texas carried strong associations of tyranny and oppression. Consequently, it would seem, the missions never presented themselves in quite the same manner as models for a new architecture. A Texas "Mission Style" thus never gained popular currency in the late nineteenth century.

Martin

1. Adna Weber, *The Growth of Cities in the Nineteenth Century* (Ithaca, NY: Cornell University Press, 1967), 32-36.

2. Quoted in the New York *Morning Journal* (19 October 1888) from the promotional brochure, *City of Kearney, Nebraska* (published privately, 1888).

3. Selwyn K. Troen and Glen E. Holt, eds., *St. Louis* (New York: New Viewpoints, 1977), 65-66.

4. David Ward, *Cities and Immigrants* (New York: Oxford University Press, 1971), 78-80.

5. Ibid., 81.

6. Elizabeth Gale, ed., *Minneapolis 1857-59* (Minneapolis, 1922), 13-49.

7. Marion Shutter, *History of Minneapolis* 2 (Chicago: S.S. Clarke Publishing Company, 1923), 6-11.

8. Landmarks Heritage Preservation Commission, *A Comprehensive Program for Historic Preservation in Omaha* (Omaha, 1980), n.p.

9. Albro Martin, *James J. Hill and the Opening of the Northwest* (New York: Oxford University Press, 1976), 16-31.

10. Grady Clay, *Close-Up: How to Read the American City* (New York: Praeger Publishers, 1973), 42-50.

11. Ernest Sandeen, *St. Paul's Historic Summit Avenue* (St. Paul: Living Historical Museum, 1978), 5-10.

12. Sam Bass Warner, *Streetcar Suburbs* (Cambridge, Mass.: Harvard University Press, 1962), 15-29.

13. Ibid., 52-66.

14. Troen and Holt, *St. Louis*, 124-26.

15. Henry Mayer and Richard Wade, *Chicago: Growth of a Metropolis* (Chicago: University of Chicago Press, 1969), 117-20.

16. John Borchert, David Gebhard, David Lanegran, and Judith Martin, *Legacy of Minneapolis* (Minneapolis: Voyageur Press, 1980), 70; Kansas City Chapter of the AIA, *Kansas City* (Kansas City, 1979), n.p.

17. Mayer and Wade, *Chicago*, 252-53.

18. Gwendolyn Wright, *Moralism and the Model Home* (Chicago: University of Chicago Press, 1980), 90.

19. Ibid.

20. Richard Sennett, *Families Against the City* (New York: Vintage Books, 1974), 36-43.

Hudson

1. U.S. Department of the Interior, Census Office, *Eleventh Census, 1890,* 3, Mineral Industries in the United States (Washington, D.C., 1895), 605.

2. George A. Thiel and Carl E. Dutton, *The architectural, structural, and monumental stones of Minnesota* (Minneapolis, 1935), 63; Oliver Bowles, *Structural and Ornamental Stones of Minnesota* (Washington, D.C., 1918), 212.

3. E.P. Rothrock, *A Geology of South Dakota*, pt. 3, Bull. No. 15 (South Dakota State Geological Survey, 1944), 149.

4. Raymond C. Moore and Kenneth K. Landes, *Underground Resources of Kansas*, Bull. No. 13 (Kansas State Geological Survey, 1927), 135.

5. E.R. Buckley and H.A Buehler, *The Quarrying Industry of Missouri* (Missouri: Bureau of Geology and Mines, 1904), 2:279.

6. Ibid., 121, 131, 281.

7. Charles N. Gould, L.L. Hutchinson, and Gaylord Nelson, *Preliminary Report on the Mineral Resources of Oklahoma*, Bull. No. 1 (Oklahoma Geological Survey, 1908), 55.

8. Thiel and Dutton, *The architectural, structural, and monumental stones of Minnesota*, 146.

9. Buckley and Buehler, *Quarrying Industry of Missouri*, 2:268-77.

10. U.S. Department of the Interior, *Eleventh Census, 1890*, 3:649.

11. Rothrock, *Geology of South Dakota*, 154.

12. E.H. Sellards and C.L. Baker, *The Geology of Texas*, 2, Structural and Economic Geology, Bull. No. 3401 (University of Texas, 1934), 227-39.

13. U.S. Department of the Interior, Census Office, *Eleventh Census, 1890*, Manufacturing Industries, pt. 1 (Washington, D.C., 1895).

14. John C. Hudson, "Who was 'forest man'"? *Sources of Migration to the plains*, Great Plains Quarterly 6 (1986): 69-81.

15. Edward T. Price, "The central courthouse square in the American county seat," *Geographical Review* 58 (1968): 29-60.

16. John C. Hudson, *Plains country towns* (Minneapolis: University of Minnesota Press, 1985).

Authors

Paul Clifford Larson is special curator for architecture at the University Art Museum, University of Minnesota, Minneapolis. He also maintains a private practice in architectural research and historical design and is a contributing editor for Architecture Minnesota.

Kenneth L. Breisch teaches architectural history at the Southern California Institute of Architecture in Santa Monica. He was formerly Supervisor of Surveys for the Texas Historical Commission and is presently working on a book on American public library buildings.

John C. Hudson is professor of geography at Northwestern University. His areas of specialization include early railroad development and settlement patterns on the northern plains. He has recently published *Plains Country Towns* (1985).

Richard Longstreth is associate professor of Architectural History and director of the graduate program in Historic Preservation at George Washington University. He taught for several years in the College of Architecture and Design at the University of Kansas and has written extensively on American architectural history, most recently on commercial building types.

Judith A. Martin is assistant professor and coordinator of the Urban Studies Program at the University of Minnesota, Minneapolis. She is a specialist in urban development, particularly of the Twin Cities area, and co-author of a development history of Minneapolis.

Thomas J. Schlereth is professor of American Studies and director of graduate studies in American Studies at the University of Notre Dame, where he teaches American culture, urban landscape, and architectural history as well as material culture studies. He has recently completed a full-scale study of Chicago architect S. S. Beman.

◄ 208 Messer, Sanguinet
and Messer, Citizen's
National Bank, Waxahachie,
Texas, c.1895, colonnade

Prairie Richardsonians: A List of Architects

Dates given after each main entry are those of the firm's practice (pr.) in the city mentioned. Where the precise dates are unknown, the time during which the firm's work flourished (fl.) is given. The names and dates of a firm's partners are listed in order of seniority. Dates given after an individual architect's name indicates his life span. Draftsmen listed are those known to have contributed to the design output of the firm. Draftsmen are listed chronologically by birthdate, when known.

Blanks and question marks indicate incomplete but ongoing research. Primary records have been used where possible, resulting in several changes in dates supplied by standard texts, most notably Withey's *Biographical Dictionary of American Architects (Deceased)*, 1970.

ABBOTT, FRANK B., Chicago, Illinois (pr. 1886-?)
Frank B. Abbott, 1856-?

ADLER AND SULLIVAN, Chicago, Illinois
(pr. 1881-1895)
Dankmar Adler, 1844-1900
Louis Sullivan, 1856-1924
H.C. Trost, draftsman, 1863-1933
Charles F. Whittlesey, draftsman, 1867-1941
Frank L. Wright, draftsman, 1867-1959
George Elmslie, draftsman, 1871-1952
Charles K. Ramsey, draftsman, ?-1913
W. F. Kleinpell, draftsman

AIKEN, WILLIAM MARTIN, see Office of the Supervising Architect of the Treasury

ALLEN, T. D., Minneapolis, Minnesota (pr. 1884-1893)
T. D. Allen

ANNAN AND SON, St. Louis, Missouri (pr. 1885-1904)
Thomas B. Annan, 1837-1904

BARNETT AND HAYNES, St. Louis, Missouri
(pr. 1889-1911)
George D. Barnett, 1863 - c. 1925
John Haynes
Tom P. Barnett, draftsman, 1870-1929

BASSFORD, E. P., St. Paul, Minnesota (pr. 1871-1908)
E. P. Bassford, 1837-1912

Silas Jacobsen, draftsman, ?-1902
Edward Donahue, draftsman

BEAUMONT, GEORGE, Chicago, Illinois (pr. 1886-?)
George Beaumont, 1854-1922

BELL, MIFFLIN E., Des Moines, Iowa (pr. 1876-1881)
and Chicago, Illinois (pr. 1887-1904)
Mifflin E. Bell, 1847-1904
See also Office of the Supervising Architect of the Treasury

BEMAN, S. S., Chicago, Illinois (pr. 1878-1914)
S. S. Beman, 1853-1914
Irving K. Pond, draftsman, 1857-1929

BERLINGHOF, GEORGE A., Omaha (pr. 1891-1896) and
Beatrice, Nebraska (pr. 1897-1904)
George A. Berlinghof, 1862-1944

BEUCHNER AND JACOBSEN, St. Paul, Minnesota
(pr. 1892-1901)
Charles Buechner, 1859-?
Silas Jacobsen, ?-1902

BROWN, CHARLES P., Sioux City, Iowa (pr. 1886-1893)
Charles P. Brown, 1855-?

BUFFINGTON, L. S., Minneapolis, Minnesota
(pr. 1882-c. 1928)
L. S. Buffington, 1848-1931
Harvey Ellis, draftsman, 1852-1904
E. E. Joralemon, draftsman, 1859-1937
F. W. Fitzpatrick, draftsman, c. 1862-?
John A. Moller, draftsman

BURKEHEAD, GEORGE W., Sioux City, Iowa
(pr. 1890-c. 1925)
George W. Burkehead, 1858-1931

BURLING AND WHITEHOUSE, Chicago, Illinois
(pr. 1883-1892) and Kansas City, Missouri (pr. 1886-1888)
Edward Burling, 1819-1892
F. M. Whitehouse, 1848-1938
Arthur Heun, draftsman, 1866-1946

BURNHAM AND ROOT, Chicago, Illinois (pr. 1873-1891) and Kansas City, Missouri (pr. 1886-1888)
D. H. Burnham, 1846-1912
John W. Root, 1850-1891
J. K. Cady, draftsman, 1855-1925
George C. Nimmons, draftsman, 1865-1947
Harry Lawrie, draftsman, ?-c. 1935

CAMERON, EDWARD, see Link and Cameron

CHATTEN, HARVEY B., Quincy, Illinois
(pr. c.1883-c. 1918)
Harvey B. Chatten, 1853-1930
Ernest M. Wood, draftsman, 1863-1956

CLAY, W. W., Chicago, Illinois (pr. c. 1880-1890)
W. W. Clay, 1849-1926
Harry Lawrie, draftsman, ?-c. 1935
Frank Kruker, draftsman
Phillip Wilson, draftsman

CLAYTON, NICHOLAS J., Galveston, Texas
(pr. 1873-c. 1905)
Nicholas J. Clayton, 1840-1916

COBB, HENRY IVES, Chicago, Illinois (pr. 1889-1901)
Henry Ives Cobb, 1859-1931
E. F. Guilbert, draftsman
see also Cobb and Frost

COBB AND FROST, Chicago, Illinois (pr. 1883-1888)
Henry Ives Cobb, 1859-1931
C. S. Frost, 1856-1931
T. O. Fraenkel, draftsman, 1857-1924

COXHEAD, JOHN H., St. Paul, Minnesota
(pr. 1886-1892)
John H. Coxhead, 1863-1943

DAVIS, SEYMOUR, Topeka, Kansas (fl. 1880-1895)
Seymour Davis, c. 1869-1923

DAWSON, A. N., Fort Worth, Texas
A. N. Dawson

DENNIS, W. H., and Co., Minneapolis, Minnesota
(pr. 1884-1888)
W. H. Dennis, 1845-1929
Oliver P. Dennis, draftsman, 1858-?

DIXON, L. B., Chicago, Illinois (pr. 1866-1896)
L. B. Dixon, 1834-?
W. J. Brookes, draftsman

DOW, WALLACE, Sioux Falls, South Dakota
(pr. 1884-c. 1900)
Wallace Dow, 1844-1911

DUNHAM, C. A., Burlington, Iowa (pr. 1856-1907)
C. A. Dunham, 1830-1909

DUNNELL, W. B., Minneapolis, Minnesota
(pr. 1881-1910)
W. B. Dunnell, 1851-1931
C. A. Boehme, draftsman, 1865-1916

EAMES AND YOUNG, St. Louis, Missouri
(pr. 1885-1915)
William S. Eames, 1857-1915
Thomas Crane Young, 1858-1934
M. P. McArdle, draftsman, 1868-?

ECKEL, E. J., St. Louis, Missouri (pr. 1893-1908)
E. J. Eckel, 1845-1934
Ben Frank, draftsman
see also Eckel and Mann

ECKEL AND MANN, St. Joseph and St. Louis,
Missouri (pr. 1880-1892)
E. J. Eckel, 1845-1934
George R. Mann, 1856-1939
Harvey Ellis, draftsman, 1852-1904
John Richmond, draftsman
George Siemens, draftsman

EDBROOKE AND BURNHAM, Chicago, Illinois
(pr. 1879-1891)
W. J. Edbrooke, 1843-1896
D. H. Burnham, 1846-1912

ELLIS, F. M., and Co., Omaha, Nebraska (pr. 1886-?)
F. M. Ellis

ENDERS, OSCAR, 1865-1926, free-lance designer/
renderer, Chicago, Illinois (1885-1888), and St. Louis,
Missouri (1890-1926)

FISHER AND LAWRIE, Omaha, Nebraska
(pr. 1891-1912)
George L. Fisher, 1856-1931
Harry Lawrie, ?-c. 1935
Geroge A. Berlinghof, draftsman, 1862-1944
See also Mendelssohn, Fisher and Lawrie

FITZPATRICK, F. W., c. 1862-?, free-lance designer/
renderer, Minneapolis and St. Paul, Minnesota (fl. 1880s)
see also Buffington, L. S.; Orff, G. W. and F. D.; Joy
and Fitzpatrick; and Traphagen and Fitzpatrick

FLANDERS AND ZIMMERMAN, Chicago, Illinois
(pr. 1885-?)
John J. Flanders, 1847-1914
Carbys Zimmerman, 1856 (or 1859)-1932

FOSTER AND LIEBE, Des Moines, Iowa
(pr. 1884-1895)
William Foster, 1842-1909
H. F. Liebe, 1851-1927

FOUCART, JOSEPH, Guthrie, Oklahoma
(pr. c. 1889-1909)
Joseph Foucart

FRANK, BAILEY AND FARMER, Kearney, Nebraska
(pr. 1889-1891)
George W. Frank

FROST, C. S., Chicago, Illinois (pr. 1893-c. 1926)
C. S. Frost, 1856-1931
see also Cobb and Frost

GALBREATH, I. J., Yankton, South Dakota
(pr. 1892-1895)
I. J. Galbreath

GILBERT, CASS, St. Paul, Minnesota (pr. 1892-c. 1900)
Cass Gilbert, 1858-1934
see also Gilbert and Taylor

GILBERT AND TAYLOR, St. Paul, Minnesota
(pr. 1882-1891)
Cass Gilbert, 1858-1934
James Knox Taylor, 1857-c. 1921
Thomas Holyoke, draftsman, 1866-?

GILES, ALFRED, AND GUINDON, San Antonio,
Texas (pr. 1893-1896)
Alfred Giles, 1853-?
Henri E. M. Guindon

GORDON, J. RIELY, San Antonio, Texas
(pr. 1887-1890)
J. Riely Gordon, 1863-1937
Carl B. Staats, draftsman, 1871-1928
see also Gordon and Laub

GORDON AND LAUB, San Antonio, Texas
(pr. 1891-1892)
J. Riely Gordon, 1863-1937
D. Ernest Laub

GRAY, WILLIAM L., Lincoln, Nebraska
(pr. 1886-1895)
William L. Gray, 1851-1927

GUNN AND CURTIS, Kansas City, Missouri
(pr. 1890-c. 1900)
Frederick C. Gunn, 1865-1959
Louis S. Curtis, 1865-1924

HACKNEY AND SMITH, Kansas City, Missouri
(pr. 1892-1898)
W. F. Hackney, 1854-1899
Charles A. Smith, 1866-1948

HALLBERG, L. G., Chicago, Illinois (pr. 1877-1901)
L. G. Hallberg, 1844-1915

HAMMATT, EDWARD, Davenport, Iowa
(pr. 1883-1907)
Edward Hammatt, 1856-1907

HASKELL, JOHN G., Topeka, Kansas
(pr. 1857-1893)
John G. Haskell, 1832-1907
see also Haskell and Gunn and Haskell and Stanton

HASKELL AND GUNN, Topeka, Kansas (pr. 1903-?)
John G. Haskell, 1832-1907
Frederick C. Gunn, 1865-1959

HASKELL AND STANTON, Topeka, Kansas
(pr. 1893-?)
John G. Haskell, 1832-1907
J. F. Stanton, ?-1916

HAWKINS, J. H. W., Lincoln (pr. c. 1885-1890) and
Omaha, Nebraska (pr. c. 1890-?)
J. H. W. Hawkins, 1856-?

HEER, FRIDOLIN, AND SON, Dubuque, Iowa
(pr. 1888-1899)
Fridolin Heer, 1834-1910
Fridolin Heer, Jr., 1864-1940

HEINER, EUGENE T., Houston, Texas (pr. 1886-1901)
Eugene T. Heiner, 1852-1901

HODGSON, ISAAC, AND SON, Minneapolis, Minnesota;
Omaha, Nebraska; and Kansas City (pr. 1886-1889)
Isaac Hodgson, 1826-1909
Isaac Hodgson, Jr.

HODGSON, ISAAC, JR., Omaha, Nebraska
(pr. 1889-1892)
Isaac Hodgson, Jr.

HODGSON AND STEM, St. Paul, Minnesota
(pr. 1886-1889)
E. J. Hodgson
A. H. Stem, 1856-1931

HOLLAND, J. C., Topeka, Kansas (pr. 1889-1902)
J. C. Holland, 1853-1919
Frank C. Squires, draftsman, 1877-1934
see also Holland and Squires

HOLLAND AND SQUIRES, Topeka, Kansas
(pr. 1903-1910)
J. C. Holland, 1853-1919
Frank C. Squires, 1877-1934

HUSSEY, A. E., St. Cloud, Minnesota (pr. c. 1861-1900)
A. E. Hussey, 1829-1900

ISAACS, HENRY G., St. Louis, Missouri (pr. 1884-1895)
Henry G. Isaacs, 1840-1895

JAMES AND JAMES, Kansas City, Missouri
(pr. 1886-1891)
Arthur H. James, 1851-1904
John King James

JENNEY AND OTIS, Chicago, Illinois (pr. 1886-1889)
W. L. B. Jenney, 1832-1907
W. A. Otis, 1855-1929
W. B. Mundie, draftsman, 1863-1939

JENNEY AND MUNDIE, Chicago, Illinois
(pr. 1891-1903)
W. L. B. Jenney, 1832-1907
W. B. Mundie, 1863-1939

JOHNSTON, CLARENCE H., St. Paul, Minnesota
(pr. 1883, 1890-1924)
Clarence H. Johnston, 1859-1936
see also Willcox and Johnston

JONES, HARRY W., Minneapolis, Minnesota
(pr. 1884-1932)
Harry W. Jones, 1884-1935

E. E. JORALEMON, Minneapolis, Minnesota
(pr. 1885-1892)
E. E. Joralemon, 1859-1937
see also Long, F. B. and Co.; Buffington, L. S.; Orff,
G. W. and F. D.; and Orff and Joralemon

JOY AND FITZPATRICK, St. Paul, Minnesota
(pr. 1887-1888)
C. E. Joy, c. 1850-?
F. W. Fitzpatrick, c. 1862-?
see also Traphagen and Fitzpatrick

KOCH, H. C., AND CO., Milwaukee, Wisconsin
(pr. 1870-1910)
H. C. Koch, 1841-?

LINK, T. C., St. Louis, Missouri (pr. 1886-90,
1894-c. 1920)
T. C. Link, 1850-?
M. P. McArdle, draftsman, 1868-?
see also Link and Cameron

LINK AND CAMERON, St. Louis, Missouri
(pr. 1891-1893)
T. C. Link, 1850-?
Edward A. Cameron, 1861-1899
J. Willard Adams, draftsman

LONG, F. B., AND CO., Minneapolis, Minnesota
(pr. 1882-1884)
F. B. Long, 1841-1912
E. E. Joralemon, 1859-1937

LONG AND KEES, Minneapolis, Minnesota
(pr. 1884-1897)

F. B. Long, 1841-1912
Frederick B. Kees, 1852-1927
A. C. Chamberlin, draftsman, 1854-?
Harry T. Downs, draftsman, 1868-?
L. L. Long, draftsman, ?-1925
E. F. Guilbert, draftsman

OLIVER W. MARBLE, Chicago, Illinois (pr. 1889-?)
Oliver W. Marble

MANN, GEORGE R., St. Louis, Missouri (pr. 1893-?)
George R. Mann, 1856-1939
Harvey Ellis, draftsman, 1852-1904
see also Eckel and Mann

MAYBURY, C. G., AND SON, Winona, Minnesota
(pr. 1881-1905)
C. G. Maybury, 1830-1905
J. N. Maybury

MENDELSSOHN, FISHER, AND LAWRIE, Omaha,
Nebraska (pr. 1887-1891)
Louis Mendelssohn, ?-1894
George L. Fisher, 1856-1931
Harry Lawrie, ?-c. 1935
George A. Berlinghof, draftsman, 1862-1944
see also Fisher and Lawrie

MIX, E. TOWNSEND, Milwaukee, Wisconsin (pr. 1856-
1890) and Minneapolis, Minnesota (pr. 1888-1890)
E. Townsend Mix, 1831-1890

OFFICE OF THE SUPERVISING ARCHITECT
OF THE TREASURY
Supervising architects who worked in a Richardsonian
Romanesque idiom:
Mifflin E. Bell (tenure 1881-1886), 1847-1904
W. A. Freret (tenure 1886-1889), 1833-?
James Windrim (tenure 1889-1891), 1840-1919
W. J. Edbrooke (tenure 1891-1893), 1843-1896
Jeremiah O'Rourke (tenure 1893-1894), 1833-1915
William Martin Aiken (tenure 1895-1896), 1835-1908

OMEYER AND THORI, St. Paul, Minnesota
(pr. 1887-1904)
Diedrich A. Omeyer, ?-1904
Martin P. Thori

ORFF, G. W. AND F. D., Minneapolis, Minnesota
(pr. 1881-1892)
G. W. Orff, 1836-1908
F. D. Orff, ?-1912
Harvey Ellis, draftsman, 1852-1904
E. E. Joralemon, draftsman, 1859-1937
F. W. Fitzpatrick, draftsman, c. 1862-?

ORFF AND JORALEMON, Minneapolis, Minnesota
(pr. 1893-1896)

▲ **209 James Riely Gordon, Jay Adams House, San Antonio, Texas, 1890, side elevation detail**

F. D. Orff, ?-1912
E. E. Joralemon, 1859-1937
Albert Levering, draftsman, 1869-1929

PALMER AND HALL, Duluth, Minnesota
(pr. 1890-1893)
Emmet S. Palmer
Lucien P. Hall
William A. Hunt, draftsman, 1859-?

PATTON AND FISHER, Chicago, Illinois (pr. 1885-1899)
and Wichita, Kansas (pr. 1884-?)
Normand C. Patton, 1852-1915
Reynolds Fisher
E. M. Camp, draftsman

PERKINS, FREDERICK W., Chicago, Illinois
(pr. 1888-1928)
Frederick W. Perkins, 1866-1928

PERKINS AND ADAMS, Topeka, Kansas
(pr. c. 1888-1891)
J. H. Perkins
J. Willard Adams

PROUDFOOT AND BIRD, Wichita, Kansas
(pr. 1880-1896)
Willis Proudfoot, 1860-1928
George Washington Bird, c. 1857-1956

RICKER, N. CLIFFORD, (also known as Nathan C.)
Urbana, Illinois (fl. 1880s-1890s)
N. Clifford Ricker
James M. White

ROOT, JOHN W., see Burnham and Root

ROSENHEIM, A. P., St. Louis, Missouri (pr. 1885-1902)
A. P. Rosenheim, 1859-1943

SCHOCK, F. R., Chicago, Illinois (fl. 1880s-1890s)
F. R. Schock, 1854-?
H. F. Swanson, draftsman

SCHWARTZ, JOSEPH, Sioux Falls, South Dakota
(pr. 1884-c. 1927)
Joseph Schwartz, 1858-1927

SEDGWICK, C. S., Minneapolis, Minnesota
(pr. 1884-1922)
C. S. Sedgwick, 1856-1922

SILSBEE, J. L., Chicago, Illinois (pr. 1883-1913)
J. L. Silsbee, 1848-1913
George W. Maher, draftsman, 1864-1926
Frank L(loyd) Wright, draftsman, 1867-1959
George Elmslie, draftsman, 1871-1952

SMITH, SIDNEY, Omaha, Nebraska (pr. 1881-1893)
Sidney Smith, 1836-?

STEVENS, J. WALTER, St. Paul, Minnesota
(pr. 1880-1935)
J. Walter Stevens, 1857-1937
Harvey Ellis, draftsman, 1852-1904
William D. McLaughlin, draftsman

STRUCK, CARL F., Minneapolis, Minnesota (pr. 1881-?)
Carl F. Struck, 1842-1912

SULLIVAN, LOUIS, see Adler and Sullivan

TAYLOR, ISAAC, St. Louis, Missouri (pr. 1889-1917)
Isaac Taylor, 1850-1917
Oscar Enders, draftsman, 1865-1926

TRAPHAGEN AND FITZPATRICK, Duluth,
Minnesota (pr. 1890-1896)
Oliver G. Traphagen, 1854-1932
F. W. Fitzpatrick, c. 1862-?

TREAT AND FOLTZ, Chicago, Illinois (pr. 1872-1897)
Samuel A. Treat, 1839-1910
Frederick Foltz, 1843-1916

VAN BRUNT, ADRIANCE, Kansas City, Missouri
(pr. 1878-1913)
Adriance van Brunt, 1836-1913
John van Brunt, 1855-1925

VAN BRUNT AND HOWE, Kansas City, Missouri
(pr. 1886-1901)
Henry van Brunt, 1832-1903
Frank M. Howe, 1850-1909
Arthur H. James, draftsman, 1851-1904
George Mathews, draftsman, 1860-1903
William M. Kenyon, draftsman, 1863-1940

VOSS, HENRY, Omaha, Nebraska (pr. 1873-?)
Henry Voss, 1843-?

WASHBURN, GEORGE P., Ottawa, Kansas
(pr. 1882-1900)
George P. Washburn, 1846-1922

WASHBURN, GEORGE P., AND SON, Ottawa,
Kansas (pr. 1901-1922)
George P. Washburn, 1846-1922

WATSON, A. O., Houston, Texas
A. O. Watson, 1864-1935

WILLCOX AND JOHNSTON, St. Paul, Minnesota
(pr. 1884-1889)
William A. Willcox
Clarence H. Johnston, 1859-1936
See also Clarence H. Johnston

WILSON, H. R., Chicago, Illinois (pr. 1890-1909)
H. R. Wilson, 1858-1917
Phillip Wilson, draftsman

ZSCHOCKE, ALBERT, St. Paul, Minnesota
(pr. 1888-1891)
Albert Zschocke, 1859-1892

Photo Credits

All references are to figure numbers.

The archival photographs and drawings are published courtesy of:

Amon Carter Museum, Fort Worth, Texas 134, 135

Architecture and Planning Library, Architectural Drawings Collection, General Libraries at the University of Texas at Austin 141, 145, 153, 168; 148, 157, 158 (photo: Dana Norman)

Austin History Center, Austin (Texas) Public Library 133

Brunner and Brunner, Architects and Engineers, St. Joseph, Missouri 181

Chicago Architecture Foundation 70

Chicago Historical Society 18, 84, 92

Dallas Public Library, Texas/Dallas History and Archives Division 144

DRT Memorial Library, San Antonio, Texas, 136, 139

Hennepin County Historical Society, Minneapolis, Minnesota 173

Jocelyn Art Museum, Omaha, Nebraska 3

Kansas City (Missouri) Public Library 25, 26

Kansas State Historical Society, Topeka 100, 101, 105, 109, 112, 113, 115, 116, 117, 124, 128, 129

Leavenworth (Kansas) Public Library 6

Minneapolis (Minnesota) Public Library 23, 31, 39, 40, 41, 47, 48, 51, 71, 73, 83, 94, 111, 152, 154, 155, 156, 174, 179, 180, 200

Minnesota Historical Society, St. Paul 2, 13, 17, 28, 50, 53, 72, 137, 182, 185, 193, 197

Missouri Historical Society, St. Louis 55

Preston L. Moss 49

Nebraska State Historical Society, Lincoln 45

Northwest Architectural Archives, University of Minnesota, Minneapolis 11, 14, 16, 35, 42, 177

Ryerson and Burnham Libraries, The Art Institute of Chicago 10, 12, 34, 36, 37, 38, 59, 63, 66, 78, 81, 82, 87, 89, 90, 95, 96, 187

Thomas J. Schlereth 91, 97

Spencer Research Library, University Archives, University of Kansas, Lawrence 106

Siouxland Heritage Museums, Sioux Falls, South Dakota 192

State Agricultural Heritage Museum, South Dakota State University, Brookings 33

Stearns County Historical Society, St. Cloud, Minnesota 189

Western Heritage Museum, Bostwick-Frohardt Collection, Omaha, Nebraska 61, 93, 175, 199

Wilson Library, University of Minnesota, Minneapolis 75

Wichita-Sedgwick County Historical Museum, Wichita, Kansas 125

Private Collection 15, 24, 27, 55, 67, 74, 80, 85, 98, 138, 140, 172, 186, 203

Modern photographs are by:

Paul Clifford Larson 1, 4, 5, 7, 8, 9, 19, 21, 22, 29, 30, 32, 43, 44, 46, 52, 54, 56, 57, 58, 60, 62, 69, 76, 77, 86, 88, 99, 102, 103, 104, 107, 114, 118, 119, 127, 142, 143, 146, 147, 149, 150, 151, 163, 164, 166, 167, 169, 170, 171, 176, 178, 183, 184, 190, 191, 198, 201, 202, 205, 206, 207, 208, 209, 210, 211, 212

Philip Larson 132, 159, 160, 161, 162, 165, 196

Richard Longstreth 108, 110, 120, 121, 122, 123, 126, 130, 131

The maps in the final essay are by John Hudson.

◄ 210 Treat and Foltz,
Martin A. Ryerson House,
Chicago, Illinois, 1888,
entry gate

164

Lenders to the Exhibition

Anonymous lender

The John A. Adair Estate and Grace S. Adair

Architectural Drawings Collection, Architecture and Planning Library, General Libraries, The University of Texas at Austin

Stephen Barbosa, St. Joseph, Missouri

Charles and Jan Bumgardner, St. Joseph, Missouri

Chicago Theological Seminary

Dubuque Historical Improvement Company, Stout House, Dubuque, Iowa

Faribault County Board of Commissioners, Faribault, Minnesota

First Bank of South Dakota, Vermillion

Gardner Museum of Architecture and Design, Quincy, Illinois

The Glessner House, Chicago Architecture Foundation

Hennepin County Historical Society, Minneapolis, Minnesota

George M. Irwin

James J. Hill House, Minnesota Historical Society, St. Paul

Paul Clifford Larson

Missouri Historical Society, St. Louis

Northwest Architectural Archives, University of Minnesota, Minneapolis

Omaha History Museum, Omaha, Nebraska

Joan C. Pomeranc

Dr. Joseph A. Rammel

Riverview Cemetery, Wabasha, Minnesota

Timothy Samuelson

Siouxland Heritage Museums, Sioux Falls, South Dakota

Temple Israel, Minneapolis, Minnesota

Henry Valiukas

Watson Collection, Austin History Center, Austin Public Library, Austin, Texas

Yorkshire Manor Health Care Facility, Minneapolis, Minnesota

U.S. Postal Service, Wichita Division, Wichita, Kansas

◄ **211** J.H.W. Hawkins, R.O.
Phillips House, Lincoln,
Nebraska, 1888, chimney
detail

Index

◄ 212 Eckel and Mann,
(Harvey Ellis, probable
designer), C.D. Smith Wholesale Drug Company Building,
St. Joseph, Missouri, 1888,
corner detail

Design: Frink Chin Casey, Inc.
Printing: Arcata Graphics
Type: Century Oldstyle
      ITC Franklin Gothic Demibold
Paper: Warren Lustro Dull